Social Impact Analysis

Social Impact Analysis

An Applied Anthropology Manual

Edited by
Laurence R. Goldman

Oxford • New York

First published in 2000 by
Berg
Editorial offices:
150 Cowley Road, Oxford, OX4 1JJ, UK
838 Broadway, Third Floor, New York, NY 10003-4812, USA

Berg is an imprint of Oxford International Publishers Ltd.

Library of Congress Cataloging-in-Publication Data
A catalogue record for this book is available from the Library of Congress.

British Library Cataloguing-in-Publication Data
A catalogue record for this book is available from the British Library.

ISBN 1 85973 387 5 (Cloth)
1 85973 392 1 (Paper)

Typeset by JS Typesetting, Wellingborough, Northants.
Printed in the United Kingdom by Biddles Ltd, Guildford and King's Lynn.

Contents

–1–

Introduction

Laurence Goldman and *Scott Baum*

Introduction

This book is concerned with an area of applied anthropology broadly defined as social impact assessment (SIA). Such studies are driven by a requirement, most usually of a legal nature, to prospectively evaluate types of social and cultural change likely to follow some interventionist programme, project or scheme. Importantly, the findings of such inquiries are harnessed to policy and planning decision-making in a manner that attempts therefore to anticipate and minimize adverse impacts. We are alerted here to the fact that SIAs are generally forward-looking in nature, highly evaluative, and seek to manage change responsibly by articulating how the findings and recommendations of any study can be translated into preferred and sustainable projects.

The contributors to this volume have at least two things in common. First, they are all variously practitioners, professionals or pedagogues in the field of SIA. Second, they all share the opinion that there is a need for a unified resource text on this genre of study that prioritizes the pragmatic tasks of doing SIA, and does so from the perspective of first-time students, indigenous and government personnel, developers, consultants and social scientists. While some two decades ago it may have been appropriate for Finsterbusch to pass comment that 'ethnographic studies . . . should definitely have a larger role in SIAs' (1981:9), today such advice merely expresses what is conventional wisdom. Why should this be the case?

In the intervening period global exploration and exploitation of natural resources in the world have continued at an inexorable pace. This process has unsurprisingly been conterminous with increased public and political sensitivities to issues of native title, cultural heritage, environmental damage, and the general place and role of ethnicity as an important world resource. At the same time, anthropology has itself emerged from the reflexivity of the post-modern era with a renewed understanding and focus on what it means to study anthropology, to be an anthropologist, and to practise anthropology in a way relevant to the demands of the 21st century. Succinctly stated, the anthropologist/sociologist of tomorrow will work and study in a profoundly transformed set of institutional relationships from that of their founding predecessors. Two trajectories in particular can usefully be isolated:

1 Academic institutions that are compelled to implement rationalist economic policies in the face of dwindling financial support will require the social sciences to increasingly pursue mutually beneficial partnerships with external agencies such as industry and government. This is both in the interest of 'becoming relevant', and as a perceived means of attracting outside funding. Attached consulting wings will become the norm to maintain independent financial viability and competitiveness. Increasingly, departments will look to mount short-term courses which can train non-anthropologists, resource operators and indigenes in other countries in impact analysis. This is not to suggest that expediency should determine what anthropologists do, but merely to indicate that there will be institutional demands and pressures which shape the survival of anthropology as an academic profession within universities – 'Scholarship cannot survive in an ivory tower' (Adams, 1971:335).
2 There will be related pressures for increased interdisciplinary research, teaching and publication as reorganization in academic institutions – at the university, school, faculty or departmental level – amalgamates anthropology with other behavioural or social-science disciplines. More so than in the past, degree programmes will incorporate both and stress the importance of acquiring cross-disciplinary skills.

The combined effects of the above processes of change can be briefly charted as follows. On the one hand, and most especially in countries such as Australia and the US, anthropologists are now experiencing a rapid rise in demand for their expertise as consultants to resource developers, governments, local land councils, indigenous bodies, and various national and international aid, fiscal and legal agencies. The private-enterprise sector of anthropology has witnessed unprecedented growth in the last decade. On the other hand, those who trained during the 1970–80s generally attended universities at which curriculums in applied anthropology were either non-existent or newly emerging. These professionals who sought to engage in applied or SIA-type work would undoubtedly have encountered steep self-learning curves. By contrast, and for all of the reasons alluded to above, it is clear that the anthropology graduate of the new millennium will be, and will demand to be, equipped with applied research skills.

In many ways, then, a focus on social impact analysis is timely. While it clearly looks to the past in terms of acknowledging the importance a conventional ethnographic study has for the task of evaluating change, of importing and remaining sensitive to what we conveniently gloss as 'culture', it also looks to the future by stressing the compelling case for inter-disciplinary teamwork. 'The task of any serious assessment is almost surely beyond the ken of any single individual practitioner or profession' (Porter & Rossini, 1983:6). As a multi-task endeavour, an SIA may well team the anthropologist/sociologist with human or political geographers, geographical scientists, policy analysts, educationists, environmentalists, medical and public health specialists, engineers, economists, demographers or human resource analysts to name but a few.

For the initiate anthropologist, a paradigmatic shift occurs in work practices as a response to these new sets of demands and constraints:

1 He/she must adapt to working in a multi-skilled team where the parametric indices to be quantitatively or qualitatively measured by others will in part be critically determined by what the anthropologist reveals about the socio-cultural organization of the community.
2 The analyst will no longer be primarily driven by critical theory concerns in the discipline but by the requirement to adapt his/her knowledge of a social milieu to the practical and problem-solving tasks of forecasting or predicting change, of evaluating risk and mitigation strategies, of formulating impact monitoring systems, and of providing a voice for the impacted community in the evaluation process.
3 There will be a premium on writing in a clear, non-technical, non-jargon-infested prose so that the findings are both readable and widely accessible. That is, for example, the science of kinship/descent has to be rendered comprehensible to the non-specialist with only the amount of detail given that is absolutely relevant to the task at hand. A substituted vernacular of 'bottom-lines, cost-benefits and sustainability' is henceforth segued to the report format of executive summaries, dot-points and sub-section recommendations as the conventional style of report production.
4 While nevertheless conscious that one's report will itself become part of the literary resource for a given area, it will often remain a non-refereed item considered of lesser significance in any publication

profile. Indeed, few opportunities for publication of SIA reports as documents in their own right may exist.

5 Where the work is undertaken on a paid basis by a sponsoring organization that is also a stakeholder in the project, the risks of compromising one's position of neutrality in the community is increased with all the attendant consequences this can have for future research there.

These implications begin to beg questions about the role of SIA as critical practice, about the relationships of patrons and clients in the SIA context, and about the ethical dimensions to practising this kind of anthropology that can compromise the integrity of the researcher and breaches conventional codes of disciplinary practice.

While more than a decade ago some might have viewed SIA work as somewhat tangential to the theory-building inquiries of anthropology, the processes of social and institutional change alluded to above have effected a narrowing of the chasm between what is now peripheral and what is core in the discipline. In this regard, it is not an exaggeration to suggest that developing programme courses in environmental and social impact work is for most anthropology departments in the world an inexorable (if not mandatory) trajectory.

This volume was conceived in part as an attempt to address the need for a manual which would discuss and present in a 'how to' format the framework of tasks – for example, screening, scoping and assessing – associated with undertaking social impact assessment research. That is, it seeks to explain what is meant by impact mitigation and risk management; why the ramifications of alternative 'with-and-without' project scenarios have to be considered; what makes up a baseline study and how this can constitute an impact monitoring and management system for post-intervention analysis; and how social mapping helps identify the cross-cutting variables used to index social impact and feeds into the sectoral evaluation studies of, say, health, education, governance and communication. In tackling these issues, the contributors frequently illuminate how rational problem-solving can be achieved and, further, what kinds of resources the analyst(s) will require to complete the job. This volume is distinguished from other environmental and social impact assessment resources (cf. Bowles, 1981; Branch, Hooper, Thompson & Creighton, 1984; Burdge, 1998; Carley & Bustelo, 1984; Erickson, 1994; Finsterbusch, 1980; Finsterbusch & Wolf, 1981; Leistritz & Ekstrom, 1981; Leistritz & Murdock, 1981; Rossini & Porter, 1983; Soderstrom, 1981) in respect to both focus and priorities. These can summarily be stated as follows:

The papers in this volume exclusively engage the human rather than the biophysical/natural environment. While accepting that these are intertwined and co-dependent fields of assessment in any SIA or environmental impact study (EIS) – most especially where developments affect an environment that constitutes a residential and subsistence base for communities – the authors restrict themselves to discussing what are manifestly *social* indices of impact.

There is very little enmeshment *per se* with the profound ethical, theoretic or methodological conundrums that are part of the ongoing discourse and development in SIA research. Readers will therefore not find detailed discussion of multivariate or risk analysis, model building or forms of statistical or computational packages that could serve to tabulate or organize data. This is not, however, to suggest that the issue of methodology has been inappropriately ignored. Rather, the authors have prioritized the twin tasks of providing: (a) relevant SIA case synopses as illustrations of how problem-solving occurred in specific instances, or how research designs were adapted to given situations; and (b) examples of research tools such as questionnaires, logframe matrices and monitoring forms which can be adapted or customized by prospective practitioners. Research techniques as discussed by the authors here augment the step-by-step demonstrations of those tasks constituting each component phase of an SIA.

The contributions in this volume collectively reflect various sequential tasks depicted in the generic model (see Figure 1.1) of the SIA phases. The intention was to provide, within the limitations of a single volume, an overview of the practical requirements of doing an SIA.

Aside from the issue of having to become acquainted with the specific cant or *terms of art* in which SIA reports have to be fashioned, for the first-time student entering this field of inquiry the experience can prove daunting.

Firstly, the majority of reference papers are inevitably marked by a proliferation of tree/flow diagrams, models, route-maps, steps, pathways and signposts. Often these can appear both overwhelming in detail and simply variations on a theme. They are not, however, gratuitous. Because the social scientist effectively addresses the total realm of socio-cultural phenomena – the physical, aesthetic, recreational, psychological and institutional – subsuming unlimited types of indices within umbrella categories is no easy task. Moreover, as Simpson indicates, each of the selected social factors may require assessment or evaluation along the parameters, for example, of reversibility, probability, duration, magnitude, distribution or scope.

Secondly, the novice will be confronted by a plethora of acronyms, country-specific regulations and assessment process terminologies that are not always explicitly clarified for the beginner. In addition to the generally used terms such as SIA (social impact assessment), SEIS (social and economic impact study), EIA (environmental impact assessment), EIS (environmental impact statement), ERMP (environmental review and management programme), EMP (environmental management plan), EPA (environmental planning acts), and SEA (strategic environmental assessment), a welter of alternative impact-related acronyms have been generated in the literature such as CIA (community impact assessment) or IIA (integrated impact assessment, cf. Rossini & Porter, 1983).

Thirdly, there is the now proliferating World Wide Web (WWW), which includes sites that provide downloadable teaching and resource guides – e.g. United Nations Program EIA Training Resource Manual (http://www.erin.gov.au/portfolio/epg/eianet/manual/) – or which have registered Impact Associations defining or providing 'best practice procedures/protocols', updated information on current projects, conferences etc., list of members, associated journal publications and links (http://www.soc.titech.ac.jp/uem/eia/impactassess.html) to other international agencies – e.g. International Association for Impact Assessment (IAIA: http://www.iaia/org/), Manchester University (*http://www.art.man.ac.uk/EIA/*) or in Australia the EIA network (*http://www.erin.gov.au*). In addition to the professional organizations and codes of ethics which may by consent govern the researcher's work, these resources often function to co-ordinate the disparate SIA work that goes on around the globe.

Fourthly, there will be the perennial problems of how to identify and isolate from the complex skein of connections, and endlessly dynamic interrelationships, variables of social behaviour which might constitute beginning and end points in causal chains. On the one hand, SIAs rarely retrospectively test initial hypotheses or forecasts. Moreover, the variables one commenced research with are themselves changed once an intervention and its impacts occur. On the other hand, these impact reactions may trigger primary, secondary or even tertiary waves of changes rendering the task of crystal-ball gazing precarious. Even here, the unpractised researcher will be bemused by advice to delineate potential futures or scenarios in terms of such finely discriminated categories as the 'probable, possible, plausible, preferable and practicable' (Vlachos, 1981:212–13).

This volume responds to such minefields of complexity by providing the student with a practical guide to SIA illustrated by real-world SIA scenarios. In the same way that social phenomena can never really be presented as frozen landscapes of certitude, so too, despite sincere attempts to scaffold all possible decision-making options, 'it is recognized that research may never achieve these purist objectives' (Bowles, 1981:10). What is found in these chapters is thus more appropriately viewed as indicative suggestions for applying anthropological knowledge rather than stipulations about SIA best-practice guidelines.

What is Social Impact Assessment?

What comes to mind when we think about social impact assessment? To the average person, a social impact assessment usually involves reports made for governments that set out the impacts of large infrastructure projects such as roads and dams. These are about identifying the consequences or impacts of projects on a particular risk population. The 'at risk' population may include individuals, small communities or larger subgroups of society. Most usually, SIAs occur within a crucible of dynamic stakeholder relations – e.g. between communities, governments and developers – representing a type of policy-orientated social research. That is, they attempt to 'scientize' public policy by providing information about project outcomes, by establishing trajectories for beneficial social change, and by indicating how project success or failure can be monitored through the application of social science methodology (Bowles, 1981).

The best way to define social impact assessment is to consider a sample of definitions drawn from different sources.

A social impact assessment is defined to be the identification, analysis and evaluation of the social impacts resulting from a particular event. A social impact is a significant improvement or deterioration in people's well-being or a significant improvement change in an aspect of community concern (Dietz, 1987:54).

Social Impact Assessment (SIA) is a method of analysing what impacts actions may have on the social aspects of the environment. SIA involves characterizing the existing state of such aspects of the environment, forecasting how they may change if a given action or alternative is implemented, and developing means of mitigating changes that are likely to be adverse from the point of view of the affected population (US General Services Administration, 1998).

These definitions highlight the key points that social impact assessments are clearly related to wider processes of social change, and are an important part of the planning and political/bureaucratic framework. The argument is often made that SIAs are a sub-branch of impact assessment research (along with environmental impact assessments and economic impact assessments) which are subsumed within the more encompassing field of evaluation research. However, social impact assessments tend to concentrate on both public and private projects, while the focus of evaluation research tends to be firmly in the public domain only. In addition, the role of evaluation research is to identify the extent to which a project has achieved its stated goals. By contrast, social impact assessments are generally charged with discovering the impacts or consequences of embarking on a particular project. Finally, social impact assessments aim to anticipate the likely future outcomes before a project is implemented, while evaluation research gauges the impacts of ongoing or past projects (Burningham, 1995; Meidinger & Schnaiberg, 1980).

In applied terms, social impact assessment could be utilized to assess any potential government or non-government project. However, practical experience suggests that analysis has been limited to five sets of actions that come under the umbrella of social impact assessment. These can be identified as:

1 The assessment of new technologies to predict potential outcomes.
2 The assessment of constructed facilities such as roads, dams or power stations.
3 Environment use plans, including plans for managing public lands.
4 The assessment of environmental design, focusing on the relationship between the built form (i.e. buildings) and human behaviour.
5 Infrastructure/social projects in developing countries (Finsterbusch, 1985).

The Theoretic Context of Social Impact Analysis

Although the declared intention of this volume is not to enter into critical theory debate, it is important to briefly place the academic and policy concern with assessment processes within a broader historical and theoretical context.

A concern with social consequences was at the foundation of many of the social sciences, including the work by sociologists such as Emile Durkheim (1964) and Ferdinand Tõnnies (1963; see Freudenburg 1986). For these scholars the important questions confronting sociologists were to explain and interpret the social changes that were under way during the nineteenth and twentieth centuries. These changes have been referred to as the 'great transformation' (Polanyi, 1944) but are generally considered under the umbrella of the industrial revolution. The changes included a shift away from a largely rural, less complex, self-sufficient and traditional way of life to an increasingly complex, urban-based, rationalized and bureaucratic way of life. In essence therefore there were fundamental concerns about the social effects of industrialization and the emergence of a largely rational bureaucratic society. Social scientists were interested in explaining the changes that impacted on community life as a result of a shift from a 'pre-modern society' to a 'modern' or 'modern industrialized society'.

Whilst then scholarly concerns with social impact assessment can be traced to the development of early social science, the political genealogy is traced firstly to the seventeenth century – with the introduction of scientific analysis of demographic and health impacts in France and the UK – and more recently to the passing of the National Environmental Policy Act (NEPA 1969) in the United States (Becker, 1997). NEPA reflected an emerging concern with broader environmental issues that surfaced in the United States during the late 1960s. At the time it was passed, the Act required that any action by a federal government agency likely to have some impact on the human environment had first to be subjected to a balanced, interdisciplinary and publicly available assessment of these outcomes (Freudenburg, 1986). What followed was an expansion of the biophysical aspects of development with the inclusion of socio-economic aspects. This assessment is now what we refer to as a social impact assessment (Becker, 1997).

Similar legislation and guidelines have since been passed in other countries and within international organizations with the result that social impact assessment is increasingly being used by government agencies and commercial and non-profit-making bodies as part of a set of formal requirements both in developed and increasingly in developing countries. Within developed countries, social impact assessment has become a compulsory part of government actions so as to reduce the possibility of wastage of taxpayer money on failed projects. In developing countries, social impact assessment has increasingly been applied to large projects such as infrastructure provision, generally at the request of the funding body (Becker, 1997).

As Branch and Ross argue on pp.100–101, addressing 'the impact causing concerns of the day' with broad social science theories such as Marxism or structuralism can prove problematic. At the macro level, SIA assessors are increasingly having to grapple with, on the one hand, the question of the emergence of a set of social relations increasingly defined by risk (risk society), and on the other hand, the question of the linkages between scientific analysis, policy and participation in a democracy.

Risk and Society

In the context of shifts from the condition of 'modernity' to 'post-modernity', Giddens has commented that 'in the late twentieth century . . . we stand at the opening of a new era, to which the social sciences must respond and which is taking us beyond modernity itself (1990:1). One interesting strand of these discussions has dealt with concerns about the emerging risk society (Beck, 1992; Giddens, 1990; Luhmann, 1989). Whilst the issue of risk has been a part of the discourse in natural sciences since the 1970s, in recent years the concept has taken on new meaning by becoming part of the discourse of general social theory and decision-making. What then do we understand by a risk society?

Luhmann's (1989) – see also Reddy (1996) – concept of a risk society revolves around the distinction between natural danger, which Luhmann sees as a characteristic of pre-modern society, and risk as an engineered or manufactured characteristic of post-modern society. Dangers in the pre-modern context included floods, famine and storms and were fundamentally beyond the control of members of society. Within the modern period, technological and scientific breakthroughs have meant that these dangers have, to a certain extent, been brought under control. At the same time, however, modern societies have constructed a technological and institutional order in which risk is built into social life. Giddens has drawn much the same point:

> In all traditional cultures, one could say, and in industrial society right to the threshold of the present day, human beings worry about the risks coming from external nature – from bad harvests, floods, plagues and famines. At a certain point, however – very recently in historical times – we started to worry less about what nature can do to us, and more about what we can do to nature. (1999:3)

Despite precautions, certain minimal levels of accident are inevitable. Risk in a risk society has therefore become socially constructed.

The work of the German sociologist Urlick Beck (1992) is perhaps the most well known in respect to risk society theories. Beck's concern with risk society can be summed up thus: 'The driving force in the class society can be summarized in the phrase: *I am hungry*. The movement set in motion by the risk society, on the other hand, is expressed in the statement: *I am afraid*' (Beck, 1992:49). For Beck, western nations have undergone transitions from an industrial society whereby the central issue was how produced wealth can be distributed in a socially unequal way, to a paradigm focused on a risk society in which risks and uncertainty are produced by the very act of modernization. One paradox of these processes is the realization that although science becomes more and more necessary, it becomes less and less significant for socially binding definitions of the truth. That is, 'techno-scientific development becomes contradictory' (Beck, 1992:155). While, on the one hand, scientific analysis is important in identifying and finding solutions to risk, it is, on the other hand, seen as increasingly losing legitimacy. Concerned communities (Hannigan, 1995) exert pressure for change with the result that new forms of alternative and advocacy sciences have to be engendered. In other words, there is a much-needed caution and corrective to any claims that SIA experts are somehow the last word on 'impact' evaluation. Again, Giddens has eloquently commented on the 'limitations of expertise'.

> Widespread lay knowledge of modern risk environments leads to awareness of the limits of expertise and forms one of the 'public relations' problems that has to be faced by those who seek to sustain lay trust in expert systems. The faith that supports lay trust in expert systems involves blocking off the ignorance of the lay person when faced with the claims of expertise; but realization of the areas of ignorance which confront the experts themselves, as individual practitioners and in terms of overall fields of knowledge, may weaken or undermine that faith on the part of the individuals. Experts often take risks 'on behalf' of lay clients while concealing, or fudging over, the true nature of those risks or even the fact that there are risks at all. More damaging than the lay discovery of this kind of concealment is the circumstance where the full extent of a particular set of dangers and risks associated with them is not realized by the experts. For in this case what is in question is not only the limits of, or gaps in, expert knowledge, but an inadequacy which compromises the very idea of expertise. (1990:130)

Succinctly stated, for these theorists, the conditions that surround the risk society are the root of the increasing inefficacy of experts and expertise.

The questions raised by our understanding of global change as risk are:

1 How do we deal with the increase in risk associated with this new period of social life? – 'how can the risks and hazards systematically produced as part of modernization be prevented, minimized, dramatized and channelled . . . how can they be limited and distributed away so that they neither hamper the modernization process nor exceed the limits of that which is tolerable – ecologically, medically, psychologically and socially?' (Beck, 1992:19).

2 Where does this leave our appreciation of the nature, role and function of social impact assessments?

The theorists' (e.g. Giddens, 1990; Luhmann, 1989) answer to the first question is that what is needed to address these problems is a more public means of engaging with science and technology and allowing society to reduce some of the more damaging consequences of manufactured risk. The key concepts here are those of participation and dialogue. In answer to the second question, social impact assessments are uniquely equipped to facilitate dialogue between public and professional both because they deal with risk management as a policy tool, and because (as contributors to this volume reiterate) the risk community constitutes a fundamental resource input into every facet of the SIA process (Figure 1.1).

Science, Policy and Participation

As indicated above, social impact assessors are also grappling with issues about the linkages between scientific analysis, policy and participation. This embraces concerns not just about the emerging risk society, but the more general political science discussions about legitimacy and political participation. In respect to the former, we have already noted the limitations of scientific analysis which seek to de-voice the participatory input of impacted communities. Beck has suggested that debates about the subject matter of risk have remained at heart technocratic and naturalistic: 'There exists accordingly a danger that an environmental discussion conducted exclusively in chemical, biological and technological terms will inadvertently include human beings in the picture only as organic material' (1992:24). With specific regard to the process of social impact assessment the dilemma faced by policy analysts is just how one integrates the values of competing individuals and interest groups with information derived from scientific analysis. Where is the middle ground between expert and impacted citizen?

Members of the general public are often at a disadvantage in terms of their understanding of technical procedures, specifications, risk analysis or cost–benefit ratios in resource projects. Equally, not all experts are capable of assessing work done by analysts in a different field. The end result is that policy/project analysis can become unintelligible to interested parties, especially those not well versed in scientific procedures or language. Moreover, because of the status granted to scientific technical analysis within a modern society, such analysis is afforded a great deal of legitimacy and becomes a source of power for those whose political positions are aligned to the technical outcomes (Dietz, 1987). The problem as articulated by Habermas (see also Ritzer, 1992) is 'one of the relation of technology and democracy: how can the power of technological control be brought within the range of consensus of acting and transacting citizens?' (1971:57).

Habermas (1971) considers three possible models to deal with this problem – the decisionistic model, the technocratic model and the pragmatistic model. Each places different emphasis on the role of science and values. In the decisionistic model, science is subordinated to politics in such a way that decisions reached are in response to the lobbying of pressure groups. The key ingredient in the policy process becomes the values of interest groups. Scientific analysis enters decision-making in terms of clarifying implications of policy to key stakeholders and in terms of providing legitimation for decisions made on a political basis. In terms of the broader goal of unconstrained communication, this model is problematic as it places too little emphasis on the rational overview of outcomes and relies instead on reconciling the desires to promote public interest with the interests of well-informed pressure groups.

The second model Habermas discusses is the technocratic model in which the role of the scientist and the politician appear to be reversed: 'The later becomes the mere agent of a scientific intelligentsia, which, in concrete circumstances, elaborate the objective implications and requirements of available techniques and resources as well as of optimal strategies and rules of control' (1971:63–4). In this case the initiative has passed to scientific analysis and the planner as the technical expert (Howe, 1980; Vasu, 1979). The social system, rather than being determined by the free flow of ideas, is determined by the logic of scientific-technological progress. The role of values and political processes in this case are to legitimate decisions to the public. As such this model follows arguments that policy prescriptions that are dominated by special interest groups have resulted in irrational and counter-productive outputs and that the only resolution is to leave key decisions to rational-scientific decision processes.

The third model, and the one that Habermas sees as most useful in terms of meeting the goal of unconstrained communication, is the pragmatistic. In this model the separation between the function of the expert and the politician gives way to interaction. Habermas argues that:

> On the one hand the development of new techniques is governed by a horizon of needs and historically determined interpretation of those needs in other words, of value systems . . . On the other hand, these social interests, as

> reflected in the value systems, are regulated by being tested with regard to the technical possibilities and strategic means for their gratification. (1971:67)

In this case, discussion by an informed public integrates values and scientific information (Dietz, 1987) and the repressive nature of communication that is dominated and legitimized by technology and science is removed or at least mitigated.

What lessons can be learnt from the above discussions in respect to SIA? Clearly social impact assessment has the capacity to open up the policy decision-making process by encouraging strong lines of participation by affected communities. That is, social impact assessment has the potential to address some of the concerns about the linkages between scientific analysis, policy and participation. In short, 'social impact assessment can be designed to make the mode by which science and values are integrated into policy closer to Habermas' pragmatistic ideal' (Dietz, 1987:60).

Ethical Dimensions to Social Impact Assessment

There is little doubt that social impact analyses are never scientifically or politically neutral endeavours. They are by definition orientated towards providing a critical platform from which to engage development processes. As such they invoke for the investigator profound ethical issues concerning their commission, their conduct, their communication, and judgements about their efficacy for the community about which, if not for which, they speak. While we cannot hope here to satisfactorily disentangle all issues germane to SIA from those more widely associated with the discipline in which the researcher works, we can outline some key issues likely to confront all SIA practitioners.

Stuart Kirsch (private communication), when pondering the power milieu in which SIAs are conducted, has posed a number of pertinent questions, which we have paraphrased as follows: Who really benefits from SIAs and the information they contain? Does the multi-national corporation that is often charged with the responsibility of commissioning and paying for SIAs seek to use them for corporate objectives? If so, is the scientific authority of the anthropologist here co-opted to endorse these agendas? How can the anthropologist or social scientist address this concern, guard against a 'use and abuse' attitude, and on what basis should the anthropologist's recommendations in any event be privileged over those of the resource developer, national government, community or local operator?

Finding answers to these questions is important precisely because all the contributors to this volume have highlighted the importance of community participation in SIA. Adherence to this principle implies for most anthropologists a professional responsibility to give something back to the host populace in return for their input or assistance. Their agency or voice in the eventual SIA cannot be a quiescent one. At the same time, while we may not be able to tolerate, either intentionally or unintentionally, the disempowerment of our clients, defining what an acceptable level of community involvement looks like in each instance is equally no simple matter. That is, while we acknowledge the need for SIAs to become a critical practice for anthropology, searching for guidelines inevitably enmeshes one in the philosophical and ethical dilemmas of anthropology itself (cf. Jorgensen, 1971) about which there are as many views as there are anthropologists. Recourse can be made to the professional organizations but many recoil at the idea that such institutions and their codes of ethical conduct can effectively and appropriately regulate all SIA activity. While these codes continue to be refined they are often couched in such generalities as to leave many questions unanswered. A good example of this is the following code taken from the International Association of Impact Analysis website (*http://www.iaia.org*):

Code of Ethics for IAIA Members

1 The member shall carry out his or her professional activities, as far as possible, in accordance with emerging principles of sustainable development and the highest standards of environmental protection.
2 The member shall at all times place the integrity of the natural environment and the health, safety and welfare of the human community above any commitment to sectoral or private interests.
3 The member shall ensure the incorporation of environmental protection and social or socioeconomic impact considerations from the earliest stages of project design or policy development.
4 The member shall not conduct professional activities in a manner involving dishonesty, fraud, deceit, misrepresentation or bias.
5 The member shall not advertise or present the member's services in a manner that may bring discredit to the profession.

While few practitioners would disagree that these 'best practice' protocols deserve to be promulgated, they clearly cannot be automatically applied like some calculus for good disciplinary behaviour, nor do they in and of themselves suffice to answer either the kind of questions posed above by Kirsch, or those which will inevitably arise during the course of any SIA fieldwork.

In inception, an SIA engenders a series of ethical relationships that arise out of the association of the investigator with the commissioning agent, with the people he or she studies, with the institution to which they belong or which gives support, with the various governments of the nation in which research is conducted, and ultimately with the profession and discipline under whose rubric they claim identity. Each of these associations will have attached layers of legal, economic and political constraints. It may seem a somewhat trite point to make but the fledgling SIA analyst always confronts choices concerning the advisability of conducting an SIA in this kind of moral milieu. Clearly, a risk assessment and management overview should be undertaken which (a) attempts where possible to anticipate and therefore minimize the possible and foreseeable harms that can eventuate from information getting into the wrong hands; (b) puts in place checks and constraints on organisations attempting to distort findings through opportunistic editing or blatant misrepresentation; and (c) which always remains sensitive to issues of consent, confidentiality and privacy. We cannot hope here to legislate for every scenario, nor adumbrate a definitive list of harms or avoidable circumstances. The SIA contractee can exercise a degree of control through the SIA terms of reference, and clearly can instigate strategies to remove politically dangerous and confidential information – e.g. genealogies, sacred sites, or oral history accounts – from the final report.

Exercising self-control is of course much easier than limiting the capacity of a commissioning agent or anyone else to exploit the SIA for their own agendas. Limiting privileged information and distributing copies back amongst the host community may appear sensible but not efficacious where there are low levels of literacy among the people. While on the one hand there may be little the SIA analyst can do to effect an attitudinal change within the corporate culture which perceives the report as a milestone tick on the road to project fruition – as merely a matter of compliance with government regulations – on the other hand the relevant government agencies to whom the report is submitted have a gate-keeping function to enforce compliance with recommendations made in the report. How effective this will prove will depend on the infrastructure capacity and willingness of those agencies to police statutory processes. The problem is not whether the investigator can be reasonably held responsible for any inadequacies of the host nation government but whether, with foreknowledge of this, it is reckless or irresponsible to continue or commence an SIA in such a climate. Is there an ethical obligation to withhold one's research services – even where one is an acknowledged expert on an area or people – until a satisfactory outcome appears likely or achievable?

While then the questions posed by Kirsch are at the very heart of an ethically responsible SIA endeavour, we are not of the opinion that appealing to a professional community for such decision making is a viable, judicious or even desirable course of action. The factors to be weighed are multiple and require a 'situation sensitive' judgement that in part reposes on professional conduct criteria and in part on the value frameworks which etch the researcher as a human being. Not every situation will present itself as clear-cut or resolvable. Pierce comes closest to the views held by many of the present contributors when he noted:

> there is only one solution to the ethics problem, and that is for each of us to do the very best that he can to assure that his materials are not misused, that his informants are not hurt, and that his data is not distorted. However the only man who can make a decision in the field as to what is and is not ethical is the anthropologist on the spot, because in every situation there will be hundreds of variables, many of which have never been encountered before, and all of which will bear on the decision of what to do. The proper evaluation of that situation should be the responsibility of the anthropologist who is there and faced with the problem . . . anthropologists, of all people, should stop attempting to legislate morality (1971:346)

However sensitive and concerned the multi-national corporation may be about community development their expectations may equally be hampered by government laws concerning the provision of infrastructure, personnel and support in sectoral fields such as health and education. The passageway from SIA recommendations to project implementation is, as Simpson indicates in his chapter, fraught with problems. What can usefully be indicated here is the need for the researcher to ensure there is a post-SIA forum process which is attended by all stakeholders and which has as its explicit agenda the objective of discussing, dismissing or prioritizing the SIA findings. That is, a committee has to be established which is given the task of reading the SIA, and making principled choices in discussion with community representatives about what is and what is not achievable, and what should and should not be implemented. If the analyst has any doubt about the intentions of the commissioning agent in this regard it is always an option to include this item as a contractual term of reference.

Just as the decisions in Family Law Courts concerning custody are loosely based on the canon of 'what is in the best interests of the child' so in many senses the SIA analyst has continually to orientate to the overarching concern with 'what is in the best interest of the community'. Playing god or social engineer inevitably opens a can of ethical worms;

this anxiety is all the more heightened for the fact that so much of what is included in an SIA incorporates elements of crystal-ball gazing. Responsible SIA research is no guarantee of perfect results or sustained community benefit. Because SIAs are not conducted in a political vacuum, their intervention within a development situation will inevitably carry risks no matter what cautions are issued or checks exercised. Lessons learnt, as disseminated through the collective experience of practitioners, can prove illuminating, but equally the negative corporate management or government department of today can be quite different to their successive incumbents of tomorrow. Those hoping that by importing critical theory – whatever that may look like – we can establish SIAs as a platform or practice governed by some professionally encoded absolutist rules are likely premature in their aspirations. Such is the variability and differing nature of circumstances which may intrude on the analyst's decision-making that accentuating particular elements over others – the analyst as advocate, activist or advisor – can appear arbitrary. While we do not here suggest that one should recoil from broaching these complex theoretic or ethical issues, we rather express the opinion that progress in SIA work is likely to evolve through inductive, if pedestrian, attempts to demonstrate the validity of applying culture concepts. The perennial question that will be asked of the SIA is how can this type of work 'make a difference.'? This book is a partial attempt to explore some answers.

Social Impact Assessment Phases

Figure 1.1 presents an overview of the component phases and tasks which are conventionally associated with the conduct of an SIA. Also shown are some of the standard consultative resources and regulatory inputs which contribute to each of the principal SIA steps.

Figure 1.2 depicts how the various contributing chapters refer, explain and cross-reference the delineated SIA phases. There is some degree of overlap between the various discussions which mirrors precisely the interconnected nature of the tasks within and across the phases isolated below.

Phase 1: Screening

Following the submission of a proposal by a proponent the initial phase is constituted by what is commonly referred to as screening. This process will be informed by statutory legal requirements, and policy and planning objectives. Whimp provides a succinct introduction to the kinds of issues

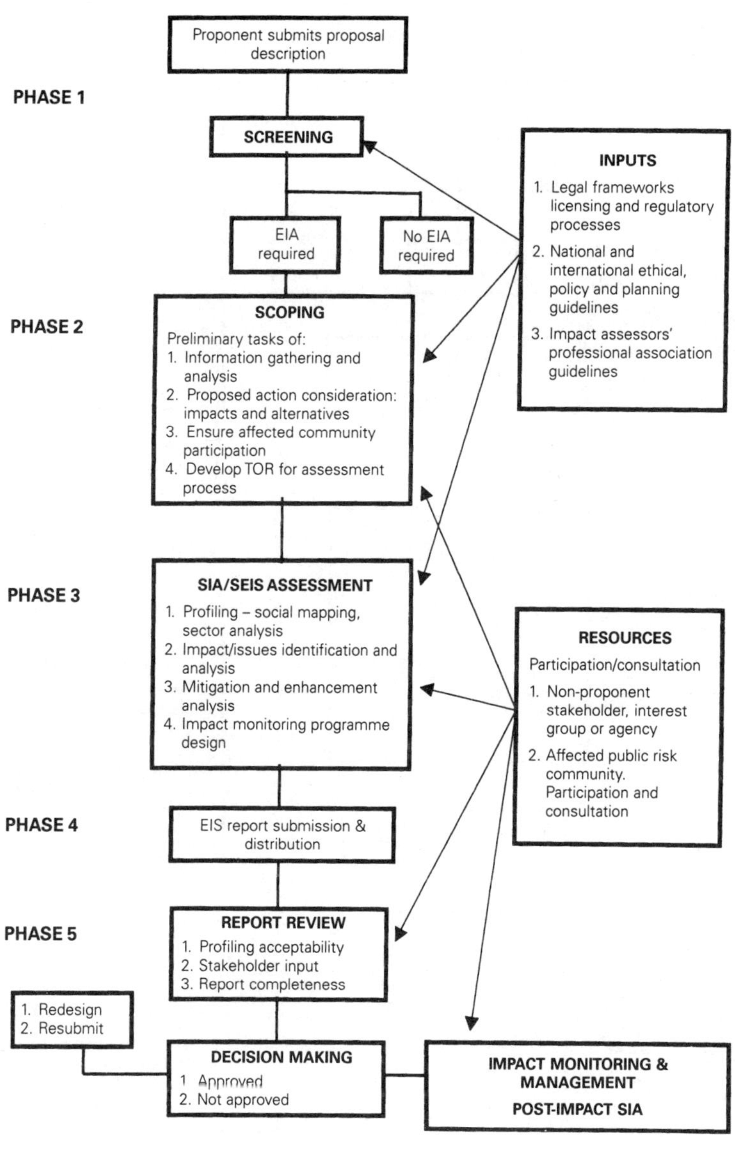

EIS: Environmental impact statement
EIA: Environmental impact assessment
SIA/SEIS: Social impact assessment/social and economic impact study
TOR: Terms of reference

Figure 1.1 SIA Phase Delineation

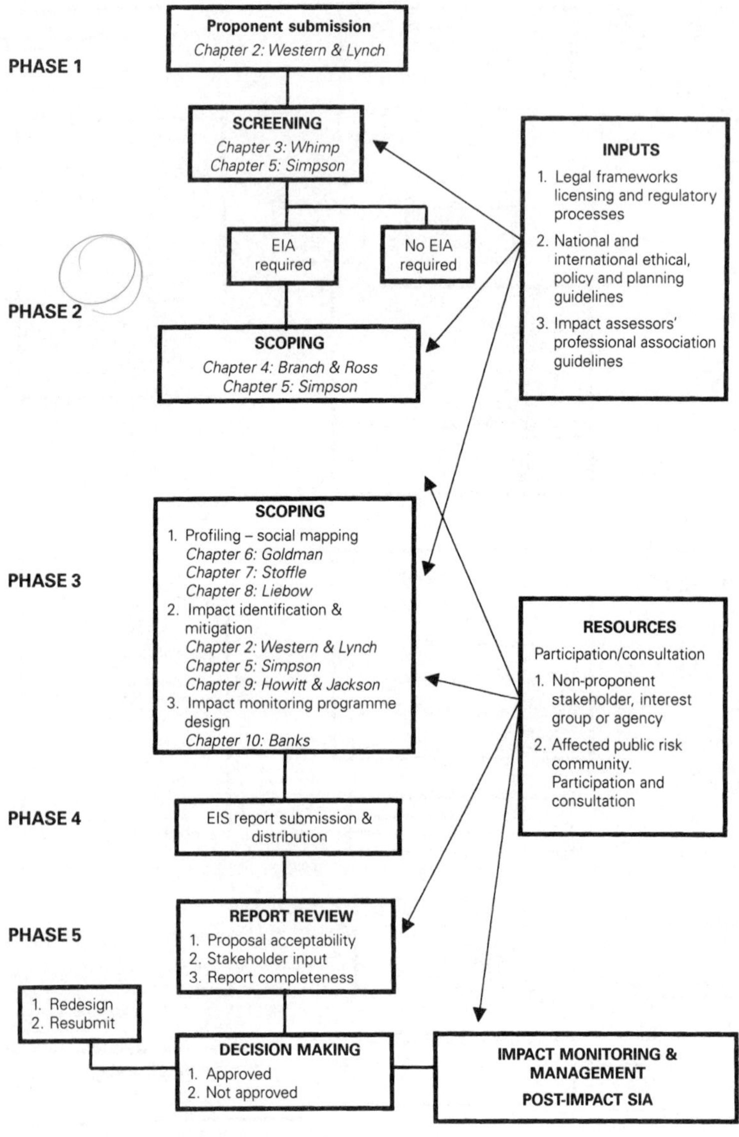

EIS: Environmental impact statement
EIA: Environmental impact assessment
SIA: Social impact assessment

Figure 1.2 Phase Schema of Chapter Contributions

likely to be governed by laws at various supervening levels within a country. These include national resource ownership, customary land registration, native title legislation, the fiscal regimes governing benefits and royalties, and the complicated overlay of politico-legal definitions of 'boundaries'. Whilst then these concerns manifest the importance of understanding SIAs as policy and planning tools, they equally argue for a natural role of the law expert on SIA teams.

As Simpson makes clear, the screening process will effectively determine whether an EIA is required or not. The EIA is a process which leads to the submission of a report known as the EIS. The SIA/SEIS is thus a sub-component of, or task encompassed by, the EIS. The simplest explanation of what is entailed by an EIA, much of which is illustrated above in Figure 1.1, is given on the web page (*http://www.ext.nodak.edu./IAIA/* principles) of the IAIA: 'The process of identifying, predicting, evaluating and mitigating the biophysical, social, and other relevant effects of development proposals prior to major decisions being taken and commitments made'.

Operating Principles The EIA process should be applied:

- as early as possible in decision making and throughout the life cycle of the proposed activity;
- to all development proposals that may cause potentially significant effects;
- to biophysical impacts and relevant socio-economic factors, including health, culture, gender, lifestyle, age, and cumulative effects consistent with the concept and principles of sustainable development;
- to provide for the involvement and input of communities and industries affected by a proposal, as well as the interested public, in accordance with internationally agreed measures and activities.

Specifically the EIA process should provide for:

Screening. To determine whether or not a proposal should be subject to EIA and, if so, at what level of detail.

Scoping. To identify the issues and impacts that are likely to be important and to establish terms of reference for EIA.

Examination of alternatives. To establish the preferred or most environmentally sound and benign option for achieving proposal objectives.

Impact analysis. To identify and predict the likely environmental, social and other related effects of the proposal.

Mitigation and impact management. To establish the measures that are necessary to avoid, minimize or offset predicted adverse impacts and, where appropriate, to incorporate these into an environmental management plan or system.
Evaluation of significance. To determine the relative importance and acceptability of residual impacts (i.e. impacts that cannot be mitigated).
Preparation of environmental impact statement (EIS) or report. To document clearly and impartially impacts of the proposal, the proposed measures for mitigation, the significance of effects, and the concerns of the interested public and the communities affected by the proposal.
Review of the EIS. To determine whether the report meets its terms of reference, provides a satisfactory assessment of the proposal(s) and contains the information required for decision making.
Decision making. To approve or reject the proposal and to establish the terms and conditions for its implementation.
Follow up. To ensure that the terms and condition of approval are met; to monitor the impacts of development and the effectiveness of mitigation measures; to strengthen future EIA applications and mitigation measures; and, where required, to undertake environmental audit and process evaluation to optimize environmental management.[1]

The research processes which pursue these objectives were succinctly stated by Wolf to be those of 'SIA profilings – assessment, evaluation, mitigation and monitoring' (1981:ix). Research is undertaken to establish what the social situation is, the provision of baseline data, what is proposed by way of intervention, what processes affect what kinds of social phenomena, and how change comes about through non-project factors as part of the state-of-society assumptions. This is followed by forecasting and projecting work as to the likely type, scope and sequential timing of change in both a with- and without-project/scheme scenario. The investigator then attempts to identify strategies which might minimize or mitigate negative impacts and those which might maximize or enhance the positive benefits.

Ultimately, all of these findings provide informed input into decision-making forums with respect to alternatives, cost–benefit ratios, plans or projects that can sustain acceptable development. International as well as national considerations may come into play here. For example, there has been a quantum shift in policy priorities to aid in the Pacific rim area in the last few years. Supporting infrastructure is now regarded as a less efficacious, less productive use of financial assistance than initiating and managing 'projects'. As Simpson reminds us, the EIS submission may further be augmented by the need to also provide ERMP/EMP, which is precisely the avenue for recommendation of 'project' required finance. In this kind of work, there is a requirement for assessors to lay out costings, timings, service requirements, etc., which Simpson graphically illustrates for some health-related projects.

Phase 2: Scoping

As Branch & Ross indicate in their synoptic overview, the legal requirements for a scoping phase differ from country to country. Where it is not legally mandatory, it may equally be driven by acceptance of 'best practice' protocols or common-sense reasoning that for cost estimations a forward projection of the work to be done in the assessment phase needs to be completed. In essence, scoping is all about setting the terms of reference for the assessment phase. 'Scoping serves disclosure, problem definition, and planning functions' (Branch & Ross, p.95). However, for this to happen a preliminary assessment is conducted, as outlined in Branch & Ross's five-step scoping framework. All the contributors variously touch on some foundation principles generic to any scoping exercise.

Because, in scoping, one is concerned to insightfully grasp the 'big picture', phases and tasks are never wholly discrete operations in time. Identifying who the stakeholders are, where the risk constituency geographically and socially stops and starts, and who functions as community representatives, all requires a preliminary social mapping. What appear then as independent time-managed tasks in a flow diagram are, in practice, overlapping research jobs.

To mitigate the kinds of alienation between risk public and professional expert alluded to in the above discussions, scoping should always seek the participation of the potentially affected community and other interested stakeholders. Getting community relations right from the outset by precisely this kind of consultative empowerment is both cost-effective for operators and defines what is meant by an 'open' scoping process. Excluding communities from this part of an SIA risks their non-cooperation during the remainder of the research and may serve to engender an antipathy towards the proponent's scheme

As touched upon by both Western & Lynch and Simpson, scoping provides the opportunity to assess the costs, timing schedules, and the requisite human and technical resources necessary to complete the task within the given constraints. Simpson provides an example matrix worksheet pertinent to a health-assessment programme that would form part of a scoping exercise (p.135).

Phase 3: Assessment

The assessment phase proper gets down to the core business of examining alternatives, of indicating impacts, and of identifying how these can be managed across space and time. Irrespective of how one defines the component tasks here (see for example, the generic assessment paradigm in Branch & Ross, p.102), the commencement point is always the conduct of what is more frequently referred to nowadays as 'social mapping'. That is, a description of the initial conditions of an impact situation which provides both baseline social data and constitutes a before-measure of social conditions. This is very much the conventional theatre of anthropological operations.

The dilemma for most analysts writing SIAs is circumscribing or delimiting fields of relevance when one is dealing with possible change of a tangible and intangible nature, and change that has the potential to ramify throughout just about every sphere of social behaviour.

More often than not, separate sectoral analyses are conducted usually under the umbrella rubrics of :

- governance;
- education;
- health;
- subsistence;
- business/employment;
- transport/communications;
- management;
- benefit streams;
- socio-cultural organization.

These sectors are indicative rather than exhaustive, and each may present phenomena more amenable to qualitative than quantitative analysis. For example, under socio-cultural organization it may be relevant to consider psychological impacts on values and beliefs (Enk & Hornvick, 1983:59); equally, as Western & Lynch detail (p.39), mining activities or urban renewal programmes frequently have aesthetic impacts pertinent to community values about their ecological landscapes. Attempting any definitive list of topic areas or indices then is redundant because no SIA textbook is capable of covering the variety of circumstances or social systems likely to be encountered by assessors throughout the world. Notwithstanding this caveat, some general principles are adhered to and include:

1 Complementing the expert analysis with a balanced presentation of affected public views about the impending intervention, about the scope and timing of benefit streams, and about their social priorities and problems.
2 Accounting for endogenous and exogenous factors in an ongoing dynamic of change into which the proposed scheme may enter. The intervention is never presented as a totally isolated catalyst for change since the social environment is never in a quiescent state.

The first three contributions, which address the assessment phase, descend in generality from a discussion by Goldman of the conventional ethnographic task of social mapping in a small-scale indigenous context of Papua New Guinea, to a sub-sector consideration of cultural heritage by Liebow among North American Indians, followed by a sectoral analysis of environmental health by Liebow. Common to all three studies is the attempt to portray the problems involved in actually doing the tasks described; that is, how to present and apply knowledge being extracted by the tools of one discipline for a readership conventionally outside that discipline. Descent principles can be complex things to convey in a non-technical language and in a manner capable of being accessed by the non-specialist. Goldman talks us through some of the ways of presenting the importance of understanding kinship systems in terms of their nomenclatures as codes which can crucially affect decisions about landowner representation and landowner status. Equally of interest will be the types of compromises he illuminates for researchers who are required to cover large numbers of clans spread over equally large and inhospitable terrain.

Stoffle develops on the social-mapping sector of cultural heritage with an in-depth demonstration of how to gauge impacts on archaeological sites, flora, fauna and mineral resources. Stressing the input of public consultation, Stoffle shares with the reader the interview and inventory questionnaires he has used in his own SIA work. Much as anthropologists have always argued, physical landscapes have cosmological and sacred properties which need to be taken account of in EMPs and which form part of the 'common knowledge base' constituting the partnership between assessment team and risk community.

In many ways Liebow's consideration of the environmental health sector should be read in conjunction with Simpson's human health-focused examples. Like all other contributors Liebow stresses the singular importance of engaging and collaborating with the potentially affected community in order to strengthen their 'capacity-building' endeavours. What he presents is the other side of the structured interview form: the graded series of questions each researcher must ask in the assessment of hazards and risks, and in the formulation of risk reduction measures. In the field of environmental health, baseline indices will include impacts not only on risk factors, but perceptions of risk – that is, the differences between a 'hazard' and a 'stigma' – and changes in the delivery of health-care services. In these regards the scientific status of the investigator and the conduct of the research are themselves factors which can exacerbate impacts. For example, restricting access to data may increase misinformation, or relying on technical language risks alienating a community. These processes fall within what Liebow refers to as the 'social amplification of risk' and ultimately harks back to the problems discussed above of minimizing the distances between public and professional in SIA work.

The final contribution in this section of the book reflects an important point, 'the characteristics of the resource development project and the characteristics of the site area interact to influence virtually all impact dimensions and all phases of the impact process' (Leistritz & Murdock, 1981:6). Howitt and Jackson contrast 'linear' projects – those which traverse more than one cultural, political or geographic boundary – with 'site-specific' projects such as dams or mines. They take the example of a rail-link in Australia's Northern Territory, Goldman's discussion of the proposed Papua New Guinea–Queensland Gas pipeline is similarly linear in nature – to flesh out the specific methodological issues such projects engender. The detailed history of this scheme presented by the authors is a graphic demonstration of the lessons learnt when the resource of Aboriginal views and interests are inadequately addressed in an EIS. Critical issues were noise, sacred sites, tourism, land boundaries, and benefit streams.

Howitt & Jackson highlight: (a) the political machinations involved in simply doing the study with conflicting interests, priorities and perceptions between local representatives and government bodies; (b) the final recommendations made in the SIA to the particular problems which emerged from consultation with the community. There are no universal panaceas one can reach for and apply in each individual SIA as a ready option for one's recommendation section. Indeed, what emerges from this detailed case example is that any wholesale reliance on statistical or technical formulae to solve problems can be doomed to failure. The surest route to continued satisfaction of all stakeholders is ongoing consultation and ongoing impact monitoring and mitigation.

How does one do this? Banks provides some answers by explaining the evaluation tool of Household Surveys still much favoured amongst analysts working in Papua New Guinea. As part of the task of providing baseline profiles other standard social research tools include rapid rural appraisals (RRA), random sample surveys (RSS) or participatory rural appraisals (PRA). He looks at the issues of survey design, the problems of sampling, the perils of question language, responses and the problems of survey implementation. In the task of extrapolating trends, deviations, etc, Banks argues for supplementing findings with other primary and secondary data sources. In an ideal world, ongoing post-intervention monitoring should occur by follow-up surveys which aim to track a selected number of variables from the larger pool gathered by the initial pre-project baseline survey.

Conclusion

No pretence has been made here that this manual will answer every query or address every topic related to SIAs or doing SIA research. There remain, for example, a host of questions concerning the final product which we have not dealt with: What are my professional responsibilities as an anthropologist/sociologist to ensuring the community receives a copy of my work? What copyright does the researcher have on the data and its utilization for other purposes such as publication? How can I ensure that politically sensitive information, or 'sacred' knowledge given in confidence, is not misused advertently or inadvertently by others? Figure 1 has indicated that the ethics codes of professional bodies – e.g. Association of Social Anthropologists, American Association of Anthropologists, Australian Anthropological Society – will be an input factor into the formulation of SIA foci. Equally, they may stipulate what is regarded as a 'duty of care' in specific consultancy contexts as aids to decision making in the above contexts. Very little has also been said about the actual process or format of report writing itself. Like many other SIA monographs, a presumption is made that readers will seek out relevant resource manuals in this or consult actual SIAs for comparative enlightenment. Notwithstanding this, however, it will be evident that many of the chapters are in fact written and formatted in precisely the same style the authors have used in their applied work.

No apologia is necessary then for reiterating that our intention in this volume was to provide a starting pack in SIA for first-time students, indigenous and government personnel, developers, consultants and social scientists. The catch-cry of our contributors might be succinctly stated as 'there is no such thing as too much community consultation and empowerment'. Any SIA has to aim at improving the quality of communication and minimizing the risk of conflict between the developer/proponent and other stakeholders. This belief is predicated on the need for mutual trust and clarified communication especially between community and consultant team. To achieve these objectives, risk publics have to be aware of what goes into the complex task of SIA through mediums such as this volume. While then we have attempted to provide a set of tools, methods and apt examples, readers looking for a trouble-shooting guide (in the mould of an 'SIA for Dummies' guidebook) will be sorely disappointed. The sheer scope of phenomena addressed, the almost infinite range of possible social milieu, in addition to context specific factors associated with the proposed intervention, would defeat any such attempt. In this regard, the book is better appreciated as an opening rather than a closing on a vector of applied anthropology now very much at the centre of disciplinary attention.

References

Adams, R. (1971), 'Responsibilities of the Foreign Scholar to the Local Scholarly Community', *Current Anthropology* 12 (3):335–9.

Beck, U. (1992), *Risk Society: Towards a New Modernity*, translated by M. Ritter, London: Sage Publications.

Becker, H. (1997), *Social Impact Assessment*, London: UCL Press.

Bowles, R.T. (1981), *Social Impact Assessment in Small Communities: An Integrative Review of Selected Literature*, Toronto: Butterworths.

Branch, K., Hooper, D., Thompson, J. and Creighton, J. (1984), *Guide to Social Assessment: A Framework for Assessing Social Change*, Social impact assessment series no 11, Boulder, CO: Westview Press.

Burdge, R. (1998), *A Conceptual Approach to Social Impact Assessment*, Middleton, WI: Social Ecology Press.

Burningham, K. (1995), 'Attitudes, accounts and impact assessment', *The Sociological Review*, 43(1):100–22.

Carley, M. and Bustelo, E. (1984), *Social Impact Assessment and Monitoring: A Guide to the Literature*, Boulder, CO: Westview Press.

Dietz, D. (1987), 'Theory and method in social impact assessment', *Sociological Inquiry*, 57(1):54–69.

Durkheim, E. (1964), *The Division of Labour in Society*, New York: Free Press.

Enk, G.A. and Hornvik, W.F. (1983), 'Human values and impact assessment', in F.A. Rossini and A.L. Porter (eds), *Integrated Impact Assessment*, Boulder, CO: Westview Press, pp.56–71.

Erickson, P.A. (1994), *A Practical Guide to Environmental Impact Assessment*, San Diego, CA: Academic Press.

Finsterbusch, K. (1980), *Understanding Social Impacts*, Beverly Hills: Sage.

Finsterbusch, K. (1981), 'The potential role of SIA in instituting public policies', in K. Finsterbusch and C. Wolf (eds) *Methodology of Social Impact Assessment*, Strousburg, PA: Dowden, Hutchinson & Ross Inc., pp.2–12.

Finsterbusch, K. (1985), 'State of the art in social impact assessment', *Environment and Behaviour*, 17(2):193–221.

Finsterbusch, K. and Wolf, C. (1981) (eds) *Methodology of Social Impact Assessment*, Stroudsburg, PA: Dowden, Hutchinson & Ross Inc.

Freudenburg, W. (1986), 'Social impact assessment', *Annual Review of Sociology*, 12:451–78.

Giddens, A. (1990), *The Consequences of Modernity*, Stanford, CA: Stanford University Press.

Giddens, A. (1999), *Risk: 1999 BBC Reith Lectures*, *http://news.bbc.co.uk/hi/english/static//events/reith 99/week2/htm* [date accessed: 4th September 1999]

Habermas, J. (1971), *Towards a Rational Society*, Boston: Beacon Press.

Hannigan, J. (1995), *Environmental Sociology: a Social Constructionist Perspective*, New York: Routledge.

Howe, E. (1980), 'Role choices of urban planners', *Journal of the American Institute of Planners*, 46(4):398–435.

Jorgensen, J. (1971), 'On Ethics and Anthropology'. *Current Anthropology,* 12 (3):321–34.

Leistritz, F. and Ekstrom, B. (1981), *Social Impact Assessment and Management: An Annotated Bibliography*, New York: Garland.

Leistritz, F. & Murdock, S. (1977), 'The use of scenarios for social impact assessment', in K. Finsterbusch and C. Wolf (eds) *Methodology of Social Impact Assessment*, Strousburg, PA: Dowden, Hutchinson & Ross Inc., pp. 211–23.

Leistritz, F. and Murdock, S. (1981), *The Socioeconomic Impact of Resource Development: Methods for Assessment*, Boulder, CO: Westview Press.

Luhmann, N. (1989), *Ecological Communication*, translated by J. Bednarz, Cambridge: Polity Press.

Meidinger, E. and Schnaiberg, A. (1980), 'Social impact assessment as evaluation research: Claimants and claims', *Evaluation Research*, 4(4):507–35.

Pierce, J. (1971) 'Comments', *Current Anthropology* 12(3):346.

Polanyi, K. (1944), *The Great Transformation*, New York: Farrer and Rinehart.

Porter, A.L. and Rossini, F.A. (1983), 'Why integrated impact assessment', in F.A. Rossini and A.L. Porter (eds), *Integrated Impact Assessment*, Boulder, CO: Westview Press, pp. 3–16.

Reddy, S. (1996), 'Claims to expert knowledge and subversion of democracy: the triumph of risk over uncertainty', *Economy and Society*, 25 (2):222–54.

Ritzer, G. (1992), *Sociological Theory*, New York: McGraw Hill.

Rossini, F.A. and Porter, A.L. (eds) (1983), *Integrated Impact Assessment*, Boulder, CO: Westview Press.

Soderstrom, E.J. (1981), *Social Impact Assessment: Experimental Methods and Approaches*, New York: Praeger.

Tönnies, F. (1963), *Community and Society*, New York: Harper and Row.

US General Services Administration (1998), *Social Impact Assessment Fact Sheet*, *http://www.gsa.gov/pbs/pt/call-in/factshet/1098b/1098bfact.htm* [accessed: 10th October 99].

Vasu, M. (1979), *Politics and Planning: a National Study of American Planners*, Chapel Hill: University of North Carolina Press.

Vlachos, E. (1981), 'The use of Scenarios for Social Impact Assessment', in K. Finsterbusch and C. Wolf (eds) *Methodology of Social Impact Assessment*, Strousburg, PA: Dowden, Hutchinson & Ross. Inc., pp.162–74.

Wolf, C. (1981), Preface to the second edition, in K. Finsterbusch and C. Wolf (eds), *Methodology of Social Impact Assessment*, Strousburg, PA: Dowden, Hutchinson & Ross Inc., pp.ix–xi.

Note

1 It is desirable, whenever possible, if monitoring, evaluation and management plan indicators are designed so they also contribute to local, national and global monitoring of the state of the environment and sustainable development.

Part I
Social Impact Assessment

–2–

Overview of the Social Impact Assessment Process

John Western and *Mark Lynch*

Introduction

Social impact assessment is one of four elements in the planning process and, because planning is an aspect of broader political processes, social impact assessment has important political components. The acknowledgement of the need for social impact assessment derives from a recognition of the extent to which the unanticipated consequences of development strategies can seriously diminish the benefits of the development.

For example, the introduction of a shopping centre frequently increases traffic densities in communities not well equipped to cope. Bringing in a construction workforce to a mine site or to the site of a new power station may produce significant pressures on local communities. Constructing a hydro-electric scheme which would involve the flooding of significant areas of land might require the relocation of a number of communities, again with a set of problematic consequences.

Recognition of the occurrence of unanticipated consequences has prompted governments in both developed and developing countries to require those concerned with new industries to try to identify what are essentially negative impacts ahead of time with a view to controlling them. Social impact assessments (SIAs) are part of a parcel of strategies which could also include feasibility studies and evaluation studies. Briefly, feasibility studies, as the name implies, involve assessing the appropriateness of particular development strategies and the likelihood of achieving successful outcomes. Evaluation studies are characterized by a focus on the evaluation of an intervention programme to determine whether the outcomes were designed and intended or alternatively were unanticipated and unintended.

More formally perhaps we can define a social impact assessment as an evaluation of policy alternatives in terms of their estimated consequences.

The complete policy process involves four stages: (a) the formulation of policy alternatives; (b) the selection of an alternative for implementation; (c) implementation; (d) evaluation and modification. Social impact assessment is a decision tool typically for the second stage in which the alternative for implementation is selected (Finsterbusch, 1980) although it may also be a critical component of the fourth stage.

Areas of Impact

Finsterbusch (1980) suggests that there are at least twelve areas in which social impact assessments can be made. These refer to:

1 Population changes.
2 Employment changes.
3 Displacement and relocation.
4 Neighbourhood disruption.
5 Noise impacts.
6 Aesthetic impacts.
7 Accessibility changes.
8 Leisure and recreation impacts.
9 Health and safety.
10 Citizens' reactions.
11 Community impact.
12 Land use changes.

At a minimum, SIAs should include a consideration of the full range of significant social impacts which are likely to occur following the implementation of a particular social or economic programme. More comprehensively, an SIA might report on the activities and possible reactions of all interested partners to the policy alternatives and might perhaps recommend modification to the alternatives which could minimize dysfunctional consequences of the programme and maximize benefits.

We now turn to a quick consideration of the twelve areas listed above in the context of the assessment of social impacts.

Population Changes Social impact assessment almost always begins with an analysis of the demographic characteristics of the population likely to be affected by the project or policy that is to be implemented. As well, estimates of population changes, either growth or decline, need to be made. For example, the decision to site a new open-cut mine or a power station adjacent to a rural community is likely to have a sizeable impact on that community. The introduction of construction workforces could see a substantial, rapid but temporary, population growth which could place considerable pressure on existing social infrastructure. The decision to cease logging in rural areas, together with the closure of timber mills which might result, followed by a significant reduction in the workforce, is likely to impact on the population of the local community. Impacts on population size and structure following the introduction of a project or policy will always need to be determined in the context of an SIA.

Employment Changes Large-scale construction projects typically make high demands for labour at least in the construction phase of the project. The construction workforce for the two to three years construction phase for a power station, for example, may be of the order of 200–300 persons. Once the power station has been built, the operational workforce may be no more than thirty or forty workers. It is often believed that development projects provide a range of employment opportunities for persons in the area in which the development project is located. On many occasions this is far from the truth. Developers frequently bring in their own construction workforce. There is often very little demand for workers from the neighbouring area, and when the project is operational, the level of skill required of the operational workforce may again mean that few opportunities are available for local people. The increasingly common practice of flying in workforces to remote and not-so-remote sites and then flying them out on the completion of a twelve- to fourteen-day shift again means that opportunities for employment of local inhabitants are at a minimum.

Employment changes may at times be in terms of rising unemployment, particularly if the concern is in winding back particular economic activity. The example we talk about later in this chapter focusing on the cessation of logging in an area of northern Queensland had, as one of its significant impacts, a marked increase in unemployment. A significant component of any SIA is to assess the likely employment changes that may take place and to suggest strategies for minimizing any negative effects.

Displacement and Relocation The impact of major urban renewal programmes can involve major displacement and relocation of total communities. The new town policies of Great Britain some forty years ago involved massive urban relocation of inner-city dwellers to outer suburban areas (Orlans, 1952; Morris & Mogey, 1965). The urban renewal programme of Singapore in the 1960s, 1970s and 1980s involved massive rehousing of almost half the island's population (Weldon, Western & Tan, 1974; Western, Weldon & Tan, 1974). The social impacts of these programmes have been the subject of a variety of studies over the years, the results of which have suggested that their unidentified consequences have frequently been considerable and, in important ways, militated against programme success. Simply changing the physical conditions of life seldom results in improved social living. Planners and others have learned this lesson on numerous occasions. To improve the quality of life of urban dwellers, it is not sufficient simply to modify the physical environment.

Neighbourhood Disruption Development projects may affect people's residential habitat in a variety of ways. Expanding highways and introducing new runways to airports can increase background noise in residential areas to levels that interfere with conversations and sleep. Homes and neighbourhoods typically provide not only shelter and physical services but also social and psychological functions for their residents. The latter are more difficult to understand, assess and compensate. Studies undertaken in a variety of locations subject to urban renewal and relocation consistently find that the elderly and the less well-educated find the social adjustment to movement from well-known neighbourhoods to be far more difficult to cope with than the younger and better-educated.

An interesting variation on this theme emerged from a study carried out in Darwin, Australia following Cyclone Tracy in 1974. A major initiative of the authorities set up to cope with the disaster was to evacuate large numbers of the families most badly affected by the cyclone to other centres. Some were sent to Melbourne, some to Adelaide and some to Sydney. A study of the impact of this movement on these families suggested that the effects on their psychological well-being were greater than the effects of the cyclone. Those who stayed behind, although they had suffered as much physical damage to their houses, were better able to cope with the situation than those who had been removed (Western & Milne, 1979). Neighbourhood disruption in the wake of development programmes can be significant in its psychological and social effects.

Noise Impacts Finsterbusch comments that 'noise is unwanted sound and has become an important social problem affecting the quality of life of many Americans' (1980:195). Noise is a major consideration in airport development. The introduction of a third runway at Sydney Airport in

1997 was accompanied by considerable public unrest and demonstrations protesting the increased noise that would be generated by aircraft landing and departing. Noise is also a consideration in major development projects where the impact on local communities may be considerable. Finsterbusch claims that 'noise is a negative social impact because it affects sleep, the performance of some kinds of tasks and communication' (1980:195). Generally, in urban areas, noise sources are increasing rapidly and noise levels in cities are rising substantially. Noise is a major complaint of those living in cities.

Aesthetic Impacts Very little attention is paid to the aesthetic impacts of development programmes. Concern is often expressed about environmental degradation following major construction activities and land restoration is frequently a requirement of mining activity, but the aesthetic implications of urban renewal programmes or major city developments are seldom considered.

Accessibility Changes Forced relocation following the acquisition of property for some development programme may result in changes in accessibility to employment, service and activities. Commuting distances to jobs and services may change as a consequence of relocation.

Leisure and Recreation Impacts New recreational resources are often created by development projects. For example, the impact of dam projects relates to the recreational resources which they create. The impact of the cessation of logging in north Queensland and on Fraser Island had, as one of the consequences, an increase in environmental tourism. Leisure and recreational impacts can be significant consequences of particular development activities although they are frequently not adequately assessed. It is often important in undertaking an impact assessment to understand the role of leisure and recreation in the life of people. Increasingly, both leisure and recreation are occupying more of the time of particular groups in the community. To take advantage of the demand for an increasing range of leisure and recreational activities while implementing development programs can impact positively on develop ment strategies.

Health and Safety While it is frequently said that there are health and safety consequences of development programmes, little of a systematic nature has been reported. In the planning of new communities and suburbs, attempts are often made to shield pedestrians from motor vehicle traffic. Housing estates are sometimes planned with roads for vehicle traffic at the rear rather than in front of houses. The objective here is to increase safety, particularly as it impacts on children.

Health is another consideration. On occasion, the impact will be on the psychological health of individuals who are forced to relocate and, in the process, disrupt valued patterns of social relationships, but as already noted, little systematic evidence is available on the health and safety impacts of development activity.

Citizens' Reactions Citizens are increasingly becoming active in the context of development activity. Demonstrations are not uncommon, the formation of lobby groups to influence policy-makers in one direction or another are frequently seen and, at election time, politicians have felt the ire of their constituents. In a recent state election in Queensland, the Labour government lost office because it persisted in ignoring the opposition of significant groups to a proposed freeway development. Its inactivity resulted in the loss of four seats and consequently government.

Citizens have come to realize the power they possess and development projects, particularly in developed countries, are no longer the *fait accompli* they once might have been.

Community Impact Development projects may result in community growth but they may also result in community decline. Community growth may follow from the introduction of a construction workforce into an area. This may have stressful consequences. The social infrastructure of a small community may be quite inadequate to cope with the demands that are placed upon it by a sudden increase in population.

The withdrawal of economic activity following decisions to return particular areas to wilderness or the decision to restrict economic activity for environmental reasons may result in substantial community decline. Once viable small communities dependent upon a single industry may cease to exist if the industry is closed down. A small town in the Queensland wet tropics, Ravenshoe, was a case in point. The issue will be briefly dealt with in the section which follows (see pp.50–56).

Land Use Changes Development projects will typically impact on land use. Farming areas may cease to exist when a dam is constructed, green space may be replaced by freeways, and native animal habitat may disappear with the movement of suburbs to the outer reaches of cities.

Not all social impact assessments will need to canvass the impact of development programmes on each of the areas briefly discussed. Some projects will impact more heavily on particular areas, while different projects will have different impacts. The task of the social impact analyst is to identify the critical areas and subject these to systematic assessment.

Major Sources of SIA Information

There are three major sources of information that can be used in the development of social impact assessments. These are:

1 The literature.
2 Experts.
   (a) project data
   (b) documents and other published information
   (c) field observations
   (d) interviews with affected persons
   (e) questionnaire surveys (Finsterbusch, 1980).
3 Direct experience.

The Literature

The literature includes basic research on the social impact areas noted in the previous section, case studies of similar projects and theories and empirical material which can be applied to the SIA situation.

Experts

Experts can be used as a source to supplement published material, and can also be useful to fill in gaps in knowledge or understanding. Finsterbusch (1980), however, suggests they should be used with caution as they may have preconceived ideas or vested interests in particular project outcomes. Their views should always be tested against other sources.

Project Data Documents and published material, sometimes from government sources and sometimes from the private sector, are important in providing an overview of the project, the rationale for the project, what is known about the area, and the likely outcome of programme implementation.

Direct Experience

This documentary material can be supplemented by observations in the field and interviews with affected persons. This information helps to round out the investigator's understanding of the area and likely impact of the project on the residents. Finally, systematic surveys of strategic groups of individuals may be carried out.

In undertaking the SIA, careful synthesis of data from the different sources will strengthen the reliability and validity of the findings. Sometimes the approach known as 'rapid appraisal' may be valuable. This technique is based on in-depth interviews with critical informants known to be knowledgeable about the issues to be explored. In-depth interviewing is supplemented by analysis of secondary data and group interviews with representatives of relevant groups in the community. The key to rapid appraisal techniques is to compress the research process so that data are collected, analysed and put together in a useable form in the shortest possible time span.

In the sections which follow, the steps to be taken in any assessment process will be briefly identified and an example of social impact assessment will be provided.

Social Impact Assessment in Practice

Once the decision has been made to undertake an SIA, the next step is to determine what form the SIA should take. There are two points at which an SIA can be undertaken: preceding the intervention or change (the impact of which we want to determine) or, alternatively, following the intervention or change to determine the nature and extent of any associated impacts. In an ideal world, both pre- and post-SIA research should be conducted, however this occurs rarely in practice. In reality, pre-intervention SIAs are often conducted only in order to fulfil some legislative requirement that it be undertaken, and post-intervention SIAs are undertaken only because unanticipated negative impacts have occurred.

Whilst the issues that an SIA may address can be quite diverse (see the previous section), the procedure for undertaking any SIA essentially involves answering three questions. These are:

1 What was planned to be done/what is planned to be done?
2 What was actually done/what is likely to be done?

3 What needs to be done (to maximize positive impacts and minimize negative impacts)?

Undertaking the SIA, and so answering these three questions, involves a five-step process. These five steps are:

1 Clarify the issue at the heart of the SIA in terms of the three fundamental questions characterizing all SIAs.
2 Preliminary scoping of the SIA.
3 Structuring the SIA/definitive scoping.
4 Undertaking the SIA.
5 Drawing the SIA together. That is, the final documenting and interpreting of the SIA research data in terms of the three questions underpinning all SIA exercises.

Each of these five steps will now be described in more detail. This is then followed by a brief account of a major SIA undertaken in the Australian context in order to illustrate how successful completion of each of the five SIA steps results in empirically sound and policy-relevant research data.

Step One: Clarifying the Issue

Irrespective of whether the SIA is pre- or post-intervention, there are three stages to be completed. These three stages essentially involve applying the three general questions which characterize any SIA to the specific issue being examined. The first stage of Step One is thus clarifying in general terms what happened, or is planned to happen. Usually the brief defining the terms of the SIA will provide the basis for this stage. For example, a pipeline is to be built linking Community A with Community B.

The second stage of Step One involves clarifying in more detail what is likely to happen (or actually happened). A certain amount of information bearing on this question will usually be provided in the research brief. For example, linking Community A with Community B entails the destruction of natural resources important to some community members, who are to be compensated for this loss by an external agency (the government or a private company, for example). It is at this point however that the SIA researcher must begin to move beyond the material contained in any preliminary information/briefing papers.

Given that this is only stage two of the first step in the SIA process, we are not seeking any definitive answers at this point. We are simply seeking to clarify the general issues involved, and obtain a more complete picture of the way in which competing agendas may be at work. We need to begin to think in terms of the way in which there may be positive impacts for some individuals but negative consequences for others. In addition, and crucially, we need to begin to develop a sense of the extent to which the potential for negative impacts has been recognized by those responsible for implementing the intervention or change we are examining.

Stage three of Step One draws upon our third question characterizing all SIA research and involves a focus upon the issue of what needs to happen if positive impacts are to be maximized and negative impacts minimized. That is, we are interested in obtaining a preliminary sense of the extent to which the potential for negative impacts has been recognized and mitigating strategies built into the intervention or change.

It is important to understand that in each of these three stages of Step One we are not attempting to pre-empt the result of the SIA. What we are attempting to do is more comprehensively specify the range of issues our study will need to examine if it is to constitute a rigorous and useful research exercise. The three stages of Step One can be illustrated diagrammatically as in Figure 2.1.

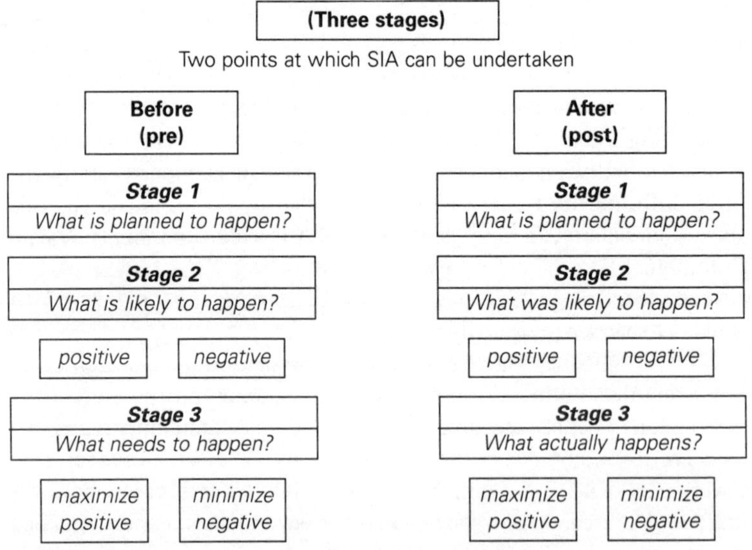

Figure 2.1 Step One of Social Impact Assessment: Clarifying Issues

Step Two: Preliminary Scoping

The second step in the SIA process involves answering four questions:

1 What is the general nature of the issue to be addressed?
2 How much time is available?
3 What resources are available?
4 What data are available?

The answer to the first of these questions should have been provided in the course of undertaking Step One of the SIA process. The second question is usually defined by the brief for the study, although in some situations time frames may be flexible or open-ended. The third question relating to the issue of resources is crucial and requires detailed attention by the SIA researcher. The availability of three types of resources needs to be determined. These three types are: (a) personnel; (b) material; (c) financial. The next question to be answered in terms of the preliminary scoping of the SIA is that of the extent to which relevant data are available. On the basis of the preceding Steps/stages, the researcher should be in a position to identify the extent to which it will be necessary to draw upon qualitative and/or quantitative data.

In considering the issue of data, we need to determine the extent to which relevant data already exist and the extent to which we may need to acquire relevant data through fieldwork or by some other means.

The final question to be answered in terms of the preliminary scoping of the SIA concerns the level of access to necessary resources. Undertaking any SIA needs to take account of the way in which the available resources may most effectively be utilized. Developing a research methodology at odds with the available resources is obviously of little use. It is at this point of the SIA process that the researcher may become aware of the necessity to very quickly organize access to resources of a different type to those initially anticipated. In some circumstances this may even involve re-negotiating the SIA brief.

The four questions which characterize Step Two of the SIA can be illustrated as in Figure 2.2.

Step Three: Structuring the SIA/Definitive Scoping

On the basis of the preceding two steps, the next phase in the SIA process is to define very precisely the research methodology to be employed. Essentially this involves the detailed specification of Impactors (cause)

Four questions to be asked
(irrespective of whether SIA pre or post)

1 What is the general nature of the issue to be addressed?
2 How much time is available?
3 What data are available?
4 What resources are available?

Personnel	**Material**	**Financial**

Figure 2.2 Step Two of Social Impact Assessment: Preliminary Scoping

and Impacts (effects). For both Impactors and Impacts there are three levels of analysis we need to consider. These are:

Impactors (Causes) (a) micro level; (b) meso level; (c) macro level.

Impacts (Effects) (a) individual-level focus; (b) local-level focus; (c) wider focus.

What is meant by these different levels of analysis can be seen by briefly returning to our example of a pipeline linking Communities A and B. Taking impacts first, by individual focus we are literally indicating impacts upon individuals: for example, individuals whose land is resumed to make way for the pipeline. By local focus, we are indicating local-community level: for example, the impact on the communities of being linked by the pipeline coupled with a pool of individuals from both communities who no longer have access to the land which had previously provided them with a livelihood.

In taking into account a wider-level focus, we are recognizing that there are important issues that may need to be considered, which go beyond any impacts possibly being experienced by either Community A or Community B. For example, any disadvantages for the local communities may be substantially outweighed by advantages for a much larger Community C.

Turning now to impactors (causes), we need to very carefully distinguish between our three levels of analysis. In understanding the differences between these three levels of impactors it is easiest to move from macro to micro. Macro-level impactors are those operating at the broadest or most general level. For example, if our reason for the pipeline between communities A and B was to prevent a reliance upon bore water which was raising the water table and so increasing the salinity levels of the larger and more populous Community C, our macro-level impactors is the mechanism being employed by Community C to impose the pipeline on Community A. This might be a government or a private body, but either way it is necessary for us to understand the bureaucratic/administrative structure underpinning the intervention, and the policy objective to which this bureaucratic/administrative structure is intended to give substance.

Our next level of analysis is the meso level. The focus here is upon those aspects of the macro level which are actually involved in the intervention we are examining. For example, in our pipeline scenario, the meso level would refer to the actual administrative structures and processes imposed upon Communities A and B by the agents of Community C.

Our final level of analysis is the micro level. What we are referring to here are the 'on the ground' manifestations of the meso level articulation of the macro level. That is, what is it that individuals are actually doing when they attempt to achieve macro-level goals in terms of meso-level structures/processes?

These three levels of causes and effects can be presented as a three-by-three matrix. The nine cells resulting from this three-by-three matrix exhaustively define all the areas our SIA needs to address. The methodology we develop on the basis of the preceding steps must address each of these nine cells if the SIA is to be capable of withstanding external scrutiny and prove policy relevant.

Step Three of the SIA process can be illustrated diagrammatically as in Figure 2.3.

Step Four: Undertaking the SIA

Step Four in the SIA process is the actual undertaking of the research. If the preceding three steps have been properly completed, an appropriate research methodology should have been developed which provides a transparent basis for all aspects of the research endeavour. Importantly, the appropriate data allowing for a focus upon each of the cells in our three-by-three matrix should have been defined (bearing in mind the issues and constraints addressed in Steps One and Two). Step Four can be illustrated as in Figure 2.4

Definitive scoping

- Clarify Impactors and Impacts (cause and effect)

- Develop SIA methodology – on the basis of results of Step Two – develop research plan which addresses each of the cells identified below.

IMPACTORS (causes)	**IMPACTS (effects)**		
	Individual focus	Local focus	Wider focus
Micro	**A1**	**B1**	**C1**
Meso	**A2**	**B2**	**C2**
Macro	**A3**	**B3**	**C3**

Figure 2.3 Step Three of Social Impact Assessment: Structuring the SIA

- Taking Step Two and Step Three into account
- determining what can be said about A1–C3
- paying particular attention to appropriateness of data used to address A1–C3 issues.

Figure 2.4 Step Four of Social Impact Assessment: Undertaking the SIA

Step Five: Drawing the SIA Together (Returning to Step One)

The final stage in the SIA process involves addressing the overall issues identified in a preliminary fashion in Step One. This final stage in the SIA process involves four discrete exercises:

1 Summarizing what has/will happen given the 'spread' of impacts across the nine cells in our three-by-three matrix).
2 Making a judgement as to whether stage one in Step One was (will be) realized. For example, in our pipeline scenario, did/will salinity levels in Community C decline?
3 Making a judgement with respect to stage two in Step One. For example, what were the consequences, both anticipated and (especially) unanticipated, associated with changing salinity levels.
4 The identification of issues for stage three in Step One. For example, assuming our pipeline successfully reduces salinity levels but provokes political unrest as a result of dramatically increased unemployment in Community A, what strategies are necessary to address this development?

Step Five can be illustrated as in Figure 2.5:

Returning to STEP 1

Now positioned to address overall issues identified in Step One:

- identified what will/has happened (A1 to C3)
- can now make judgement as to whether stage 1 in Step One realized
- can now make judgements as to stage 2 in Step One
- can now identify/determine issues for stage 3 in Step One.

Figure 2.5 Step Five of Social Impact Assessment: Drawing the SIA Together

A 'real-world' example of the five-step approach to the SIA process

In 1987 the Commonwealth Government of Australia sought and obtained World Heritage Listing (WHL) status for the Wet Tropics region of North Queensland. The listing of the Wet Tropics meant it was no longer possible for the Queensland timber industry to log the forest of North Queensland. The Commonwealth Government readily acknowledged that forcing the cessation of logging in this region would involve significant negative impacts for communities dependent upon the timber industry. However, in the view of the Commonwealth Government the preservation of the forests of the Wet Tropics represented an important 'social good', which outweighed the interests of a number of small townships which relied upon the logging of crown land.

In 1990, the Commonwealth Government commissioned an SIA in order to determine what the impacts of WHL had been, and the extent to which government policies associated with the listing had successfully maximized positive impacts and minimized negative impacts (Lynch-Blosse, Turrell & Western, 1991).

Step One

Stage One (What was Planned to Happen?) World Heritage Listing was intended to result in closure of timber mills drawing upon crown land, thereby preserving the forests for future generations of Australians. Timber workers were to be compensated for the loss of their livelihood and were to be assisted in obtaining new skills which would equip them for alternative employment trajectories.

Stage Two (What Actually Happened?) It was clear by 1990 that the timber industry in North Queensland had largely ceased to exist, and outside of North Queensland the preservation of the forests was widely supported. However, over the three-year period since WHL, a variety of community groups had continually sought to publicize the fact that local communities had suffered greatly as a result of WHL and many individuals had experienced considerable hardship. The fact that the Commonwealth Government commissioned the SIA in 1990 was perhaps an indicator in itself that the compensation mechanisms associated with WHL did not appear to have been as successful as anticipated. The brief for the SIA drew specific attention to the need to identify those aspects of the compensation package offered by the government that had not operated as originally envisaged.

Stage Three (What Needs to Happen?) Recommendations were sought as to how to improve the government's delivery of compensation packages in any future exercise of the same type as WHL. It is important to note that these recommendations were not simply of academic interest. Further areas of old forest had already been earmarked for preservation despite the fact that further 'timber towns' would be seriously affected. In particular, the government wished to know how best to assist individuals and communities to manage the transition from dependence upon a single industry to growth based upon a more diverse and sustainable set of local industries.

Step Two (Preliminary Scoping)

Question One (What is the General Nature of the Issue to be Addressed?) In order to manage any negative impacts associated with WHL the government implemented a 'Structural Adjustment Package' (SAP). The SAP comprised three major elements: business compensation, labour adjustment assistance (dislocation allowance, early retirement benefits, re-training subsidy, relocation allowance) and alternative employment creation strategies (public works projects, tree planting projects, private sector initiatives and local community initiatives). In undertaking the SIA it was important that the success or otherwise of each of these elements of the SAP was examined and evaluated.

Question Two (How Much Time is Available?) Less than six months was available for the completion of this SIA. It was not possible to negotiate a longer and more realistic timeframe given the political imperatives associated with the exercise.

Question Three (What Data were Available?) A wide range of quantitative data was available from a variety of arms of government (both State and Commonwealth). These data, when drawn together, offered the potential to provide a detailed overview of the consequences of WHL with respect to the economic health of the North Queensland communities. In addition, the arm of government responsible for the administration of the SAP could provide detailed individual-level data relating to the uptake of the various aspects of the SAP. What was not readily available were any qualitative data that addressed the experiential aspects of what WHL had actually meant for timber workers, their families and local communities.

Question Four (What Resources were Available?) The budget for the SIA did not permit more than two people to work part-time for the six months available for the research to be completed. However, ready access to all necessary official statistics was guaranteed, and the researchers on the SIA had previously established strong links with the communities affected and, accordingly, were well positioned to obtain qualitative data of a high quality.

Step Three (Structuring the SIA/Definitive Scoping) At this point in the SIA exercise we are defining the SIA methodology in terms of the nine cells (A1 to C3) defined by the three-by-three matrix of impactors (causes) and impacts (effects); see Figure 2.3. Central to the methodology is the necessity to take into account the various components of the SAP and the way in which they collectively served to maximize positive impacts and minimize negative impacts.

At this point it is necessary to describe the nature of the Impactors (causes) as they apply to this particular SIA.

Impactors (Causes) – Macro Level In this instance, the most significant macro-level impactor was the Commonwealth Government seeking to harness the 'green' vote by preserving the North Queensland Wet Tropics. In developing and implementing the SAP, the government had sought to retain its traditional working-class constituency who were to be negatively affected in the interests of a more distant and urbanized community.

It is at the macro level that the elements of the SAP are defined, both in overall terms and in terms of specific legislative/regulatory provisions.

Impactors (Causes) – Meso Level The implementation of the SAP was made the responsibility of the 'Rain Forest Unit' (RFU). The RFU was located in Cairns (a major city on the North Queensland Coast) and it was from here that the SAP was administered by a small office of six persons, four of whom were administrative support staff and two of whom were environmental biologists.

It is at the meso level that the legislative/regulatory provisions of the SAP are delivered by the arm of government given carriage of the SAP.

Impactors (Causes) – Micro Level In this instance the micro-level impactor was the RFU staff and their attempts to reconcile the concerns of individual displaced workers with the options provided for by the SAP.

It is at the micro level that carriage of the SAP is realized in terms of the actions and behaviours of individuals attempting to give substance to the macro-level objectives of government.

Definitively Scoping the SIA Methodology

Given the issues addressed in the preceding steps, it was determined that detailed qualitative data would be required to address the issues signalled by cells A1, A2, B1 and B2. In particular, qualitative data were seen as central to A1. Quantitative data would be required for all cells and in particular C3. A wide variety of quantitative data was identified as desirable if the concerns of each cell were to be appropriately addressed. For example, timber industry data would be required together with data held by the Department of Primary Industries, the Commonwealth Employment Service, the Australian Bureau of Statistics, the Department of Arts, Sport, the Environment, Tourism and Territories, and the Department of Employment, Education and Training.

Given the time and resource constraints associated with the SIA it was decided to subcontract the production of detailed economic profiles of all regions affected by WHL to the Institute of Applied Environmental Research (Griffith University, Brisbane). Whilst the Institute was compiling these profiles two field workers would travel through the affected regions undertaking one-to-one interviews, and hosting focus group sessions. These two exercises would be undertaken simultaneously during the first three months of the study and then the two sources of data would be brought together for the final three months of the SIA.

In addition, at the same time the interviews were being undertaken and the economic profiles developed, detailed data requests would be made of the relevant arms of government for data pertaining to cells A1 to C3 (for example, numbers of persons taking advantage of the various SAP components, number of persons receiving unemployment benefits, number of persons forced out of business but not compensated by the SAP).

Step Four – Undertaking the SIA

The primary aim at this point in the SIA is to address as comprehensively and effectively as possible each of the sets of issues defined by the three-by-three matrix of cells A1 to C3. In the case of the WHL-related SIA, use of this matrix yielded pertinent and informative data for each of the nine cells.

A1 – Micro Level (Cause) by Individual Level (Impact) In both the economically robust and economically fragile communities, the qualitative data revealed that the closure of the timber mills had adversely affected timber workers and their families. Displaced timber workers consistently reported the difficulty they were experiencing in relinquishing a sense of self inextricably linked with working in the timber industry. Displaced workers were united in the view that their dealings with individuals responsible for managing the SAP were less effective than desirable. There was a common perception that the Rain Forest Unit (RFU) officers did not fully appreciate their situation, were tardy in their dealings with them, and unsympathetic in the management of their plight.

Some elements of the SAP were almost universally accepted as an effective response to the short-term needs of individuals forced to give up their livelihood (for example, the dislocation allowance and the public sector projects). Other aspects of the package were less widely appreciated (for example, the early retirement assistance) and some aspects were the cause of wide spread irritation (for example, the private initiatives scheme).

A2 – Meso Level (Cause) by Individual Level (Impact) The RFU was the target of considerable criticism. Not only was the office not located in the most affected region but it was not adequately staffed and delays with processing compensation related issues were continual reported.

A3 – Macro Level (Cause) by Individual Level (Impact) The SAP developed by the government to minimize WHL-related negative impacts entailed a novel approach to compensation that reflected a genuine concern to ensure timber workers were not unnecessarily disadvantaged by WHL. However, the quantitative data clearly indicated that a substantial number of timber workers had been disadvantaged and the qualitative data indicated that resentment of the government because of WHL was widespread and deep-seated. Even in communities where timber workers had apparently adjusted well to the forced cessation of logging, there was a surprising degree of hostility towards the government.

B1 – Micro Level (Cause) by Local Level (Impact) Communities dependent on the timber industry had experienced a dramatic fracturing of the social bonds that had previously characterized their townships.

Friendships had suffered as individuals sought to obtain for themselves the best possible result of their changed circumstances. Differences of opinion as to how best to deal with RFU staff and Commonwealth Government officials had produced a politically charged atmosphere, which had fundamentally changed the general tenor of life in these small towns.

B2 – Meso Level (Cause) by Local Level (Impact) It was widely believed in the smaller and more forest-industry-dependent townships that the RFU demonstrated a lack of commitment on the part of government to the concerns of a relatively small number of displaced timber workers. The size of the RFU and its inability to do more than (very slowly) address the concerns of individual workers was interpreted as a lack of interest in community-wide concerns. Issues such as the potential closure of schools or secondary industries, as a result of timber workers leaving the area, could not be addressed by the RFU.

B3 – Macro Level (Cause) by Local Level (Impact) Perhaps not surprisingly, both the qualitative and quantitative data revealed that negative impacts were most pronounced where communities were most heavily dependent upon the timber industry. The quantitative data clearly documented the extent to which economically diverse communities had proved capable of absorbing the work-force displaced by the closure of the timber industry. Conversely, the quantitative data also documented the extent to which communities more dependent on the timber industry had not been able to absorb displaced workers.

The macro level concern of government to close the timber mills across the Wet Tropics of North Queensland had been achieved as intended. However, the SAP devised by the government had proved more effective in some communities than in others. The package had proved least effective in the region least well equipped to cope with the impact of WHL.

C1 – Micro Level (Cause) by Wider Level (Impact) In terms of the wider Australian community, negative WHL-related individual-level impacts were a matter of almost no consequence. In terms of absolute numbers, the tourist industry was associated with fluctuations in employment levels substantially greater than anything associated with the timber industry or WHL.

C2 – Meso Level (Cause) by Wider Level (Impact) The RFU successfully administered more than A$40 million dollars' worth of compensation payments via the different elements of the SAP. Despite the widespread dissatisfaction with some SAP components, the RFU was able to assist almost all displaced timber workers take advantage of at least one element of the SAP. In some instances, the RFU was able to assist timber workers with public sector projects that resulted in the creation of public assets of long-term value to the wider community.

C3 – Macro Level (Cause) by Wider Level (Impact) The Wet Tropics of North Queensland were preserved for the benefit of all Australians. There is almost no likelihood that any government would seek to overturn WHL. In those communities that were economically robust prior to WHL, the forced closure of the timber industry resulted in no long-term negative impacts. In those more economically fragile communities, more heavily dependent upon the timber industry, negative impacts were restricted to the local and individual level. From the point of view of the Commonwealth Government, this containment of negative impacts and diffusion of positive impacts signals the successful management of a potentially divisive intervention into local economies.

Step Five – Drawing the SIA Together (Returning to Step One)

Summarizing what happened given the 'spread' of impacts across the nine cells in the three-by-three matrix, the SIA of WHL concluded that:

> The SAP was reasonably successful in meeting its objective. The level of success achieved by the package is noteworthy because it was an innovative and untried form of assistance . . . However . . . the rationale, structure and implementation of the SAP was limited in a number of important respects. These limitations are as follows:
>
> ***Rationale***
>
> The rationale underpinning the SAP was the mitigation of short-term financial and employment difficulties caused by WHL . . . the focus of the SAP upon objective economic factors overlooks the fact that many WHL related impacts were social and psychological in origin and therefore, by definition, were unlikely to be adequately addressed by interventions whose orientation was almost exclusively economic.
>
> ***Structure***
>
> The formal structure of the SAP, as embodied in its administrative guidelines, was not always well suited to the effective delivery of the SAP programs . . .

Implementation

> The extent to which the SAP could effectively mitigate negative impacts was significantly undermined by under-resourcing and administrative guidelines that were not always well suited to the delivery of a large, complex and innovative adjustment package. (Lynch-Blosse et al., 1991:86–7)

Determining if the Stage One/Step One Objectives were Realized Clearly, the stage one/Step One objectives were realized. The Commonwealth Government achieved its objective of preserving the forests without undue disruption to an unnecessarily large numbers of individuals.

Determining what Actually Happened with Respect to Stage Two/Step One At an individual level, the SAP was seriously flawed in terms of its rationale, its structure and its implementation.

Determining what Needs to be Done in Order to Minimize Negative Impacts and Maximize Positive Impacts In this particular instance, the recommendations that derived from the SIA focused upon two issues. Firstly, the necessity to broaden the conception of any future SAP beyond the economic. Secondly, the necessity of more effective (better-resourced) methods of delivering the measures intended to minimize negative impacts and maximize positive impacts. On the basis of the research across all nine evaluation levels, the SIA report was able to provide a detailed alternative conception of how any future SAP might be constructed and delivered. The Queensland State Government subsequently adopted this alternative model when it decided to force the closure of the Fraser Island/ Maryborough timber industry.

Conclusion

We have argued in this chapter that social impact assessment is part of the planning process. It can be undertaken before the implementation of a (usually) planned intervention to anticipate, and therefore perhaps to control for, certain impacts or it may follow the intervention in order to determine the nature and extent of any associated impacts.

No matter when an SIA is undertaken, it involves answering three questions: (a) What was planned to be done/what is planned to be done? (b) What was done/what is likely to be done? (c) What needs to be done to maximize positive impacts and minimize negative ones?

Answering these questions requires a five-step process:

1 Clarifying the issues at the heart of the SIA.
2 Preliminary scoping of the SIA.
3 Structuring the SIA.
4 Undertaking the SIA.
5 Drawing the SIA together.

Four strategies are available to provide the necessary information:

1 Analysis of secondary data.
2 Field observations.
3 Interviews and surveys.
4 Direct experience.

In undertaking an SIA, the careful synthesis of data from the different sources will strengthen the reliability and validity of the findings.

Finally, it must be recognized that, as part of the planning process, social impact assessment is importantly a political act which will accord advantages to some and disadvantages to others. The logging and clearing of rain forests will benefit loggers and millers. The cessation of logging is likely to impact negatively on the same millers and loggers but with arguably longer-term benefits for the society more generally. The calculation of costs and benefits is a task with unenviable political overtones.

References

Finsterbusch, K. (1980), *Understanding Social Impacts*, Beverly Hills, CA: Sage Publications.

Lynch-Blosse, M., Turrell, G. and Western, J. (1991), *Impact Assessment: World Heritage Listing*, A Consultancy Report to the Australian Commonwealth Department of the Arts, Sport, Environment, Territories and Tourism, Canberra: Australian Capital Territory.

Morris, R.N. and Mogey, J. (1965), *The Sociology of Housing*, London: Routledge and Kegan Paul.

Orlans, H. (1952), *Stevenage – A Sociological Study of a New Town*, London: Routledge and Kegan Paul.

Weldon, P.D., Western, J.S. and Tan Tsu Hang (1974), 'Housing and satisfaction with environment in Singapore', *Journal of the American Institute of Planning*, 40(3):201–8.

Western, J.S. and Milne, G. (1979), 'Some Social Effects of a Natural Hazard: Darwin Residents and Cyclone Tracy', in Heathcote, R.L. and Thom, B.G. (eds), *Natural Hazards in Australia*, Canberra: Australian Academy of Science.

Western, J.S., Weldon, P.D. and Tan Tsu Hang (1974), 'Poverty, urban renewal and public housing in Singapore', *Environment and Planning*, 5:584–600.

Part II
Scoping

–3–

Legal Framework Studies

Kathy Whimp

The legal framework within which resource development occurs is critical to the manner in which the social impacts of development are understood, and responses to them evolved. Within the context of a specific project, this framework provides an understanding of:

- the legal and administrative conditions which set the scene for project developers' interactions with host communities;
- the statutory and other legal constraints and opportunities that affect how those relationships are shaped;
- how indigenous people who are affected by projects intersect with the national legal system and others who have rights flowing from it.

Framework studies can also serve a wider purpose in policy development, by providing a contextual background for the development of sector-specific policy about how project impact and benefit distribution issues ought to be approached in future.

Legal research relevant to social impact analysis concentrates on answering four questions:

1 What system of government and what arrangements for inter-governmental relations are in place, and which levels of government are responsible for what aspects of regulation and service delivery?
2 What laws, policies and practices determine and regulate ownership, management and use of natural resources?
3 What systems of land tenure apply, and how are the owners of land formally represented, organized and involved in development activity?
4 How are the benefits of the development activity shared with the local community, what benefits are they entitled to (or entitled to expect to receive) and how are these paid?

At the heart of these four questions lies the interconnecting and central issue of indigenous peoples and their relationships to land. In undertaking a legal framework study, the analyst seeks to understand how that connection between people and land sits within the wider political, administrative and legal environment.

The purpose of this chapter is to outline the legal and policy considerations that should inform a legal framework study, and to give a brief overview of the kinds of issues that are likely to be relevant. In making observations about how these issues might be investigated and analysed, the chapter uses the example of a study of policy responses to issues of customary land ownership in the hydrocarbon sector in Papua New Guinea (Taylor & Whimp, 1997). This broad study provides a useful illustration of how a systematic analysis can be approached. Some other examples from different jurisdictions are also provided to highlight particular issues.

Systems of Government and Inter-governmental Relations

An understanding of a country's system of government should underpin any investigation into its legal framework. This should begin with an overview of the organs (institutions) of government and their relationship to each other. Most countries in the world now are governed according to democratic principles enshrined in a written constitution. This means that they have some form of legislature that is responsible for making laws, an executive that carries the laws into effect and a judicial system which adjudicates disputes between citizens, and between the state and its citizens. Key differences to identify include:

1 The constitutional framework for government, and the system of government (including the role of political parties, the structure of the national law-making body and the relationship of public servants to elected leaders.
2 The kind of legal system which is in place (most countries operate broadly in either the Westminster model or have a 'code' system of laws, although in some developing countries laws are still made or vetoed by a hereditary monarchy), and whether customary law is recognized and enforced as part of the mainstream legal system.
3 Whether there is a system of sub-national government and the nature of its relationship to the centre.

While it is an important starting point, the extent to which a framework study needs to focus on these broader issues will often vary depending on the context and the audience. In the Papua New Guinea (PNG) hydrocarbon sector study, the report sketched out only briefly the constitutional framework and then focused on decentralization issues. Virtually all of the report's readers were familiar with the Papua New Guinean system of government. However, the legal arrangements for provincial government had changed dramatically during the two years before the report was written. These changes had an important impact on the capacity of the national government to deliver services in rural areas, and affected the role that provincial governments play in resource development, so they were a critical focus of the study.

Decentralized Government

Unlike Australia, which has a federal system, PNG became independent in 1975 under the governance of a single-tier national government. Over the two years that followed independence, and prompted in part by unrest on the island of Bougainville (which hosted what was at the time PNG's only significant mining development), a system of provincial government was developed and enshrined through constitutional amendments. The system of provincial government has always been important in the context of resource development in Papua New Guinea. It was provincial governments who initiated changes that gave rise to much greater landowner involvement in resource development during the late 1980s, and the constant political tension between provincial and national politicians often manifests itself in competition to secure access to the benefits of mining and petroleum development.

The structure of the decentralization arrangements will often be a significant factor in the political and legal setting for resource development. Developments occur typically in remote areas where the reach of central government is weaker and parochial interests are strong. The constitutional, legal, financial and administrative arrangements between different tiers of government determine how the balance of power between them is struck. Federal systems are characterized by a structure in which the composite units (states or provinces) have ceded defined powers to the centre and retain the balance of legal power at the sub-national level. Papua New Guinea's present system of government is an interesting and relatively unusual arrangement. The decentralized system has three tiers: in the middle level provincial governments are composed of members elected to either local or national government, with one of the national members of Parliament occupying the office of provincial Governor.

The structure of decentralized government will usually be set out either in the constitution, or in some other law. Papua New Guinea, for example, has a system of constitutional laws called organic laws, which set out important structural components of the government system, including the system of decentralization. However, things are not always what they seem. The new system of decentralization is far from fully implemented, and the lack of subsidiary laws to carry into effect some elements of the new system means that some of the provisions in the Organic Law are virtually meaningless.

The impact of the new law is also apparently not what its framers had intended. Although heralded as returning power to the centre (the proper locus of power in the opinion of national politicians), in fact the effect of the law has been to give provincial governments a guaranteed share of the national budget, and considerably more discretion to determine how grant funds are used. This came about because the earlier law establishing provincial government in 1976 had itself not been fully implemented, in particular in relation to the payment of unconditional grants to provinces. The effect of the new law was to set aside previous administrative arrangements that had ensured a high degree of national control over provincial budget allocation.

The hydrocarbon sector study examined the nature of the changes brought about by the new law in some detail. A proper picture of the way the new system of operates could only be gained from a wide range of sources, including public service arrangements, budget implementation information and policy documents.

A number of critical issues affect the relationship between national and sub-national government. First, how is law-making power distributed between the different levels of government, and how do their laws intersect? In general, national laws will usually override sub-national ones, but it may be that in some areas provincial laws are superior. How is a conflict between the laws of two different levels of government defined, and what happens in that event? In Australia, for example, the powers of the central government are specified and limited in the Constitution. Although the states hold the balance of power, federal laws override state ones to the extent of any inconsistency. It is important to appreciate the extent to which these formal arrangements are affected by interpretation in the courts. 'Inconsistency' between federal and state laws has been defined increasingly narrowly in High-Court decisions, with the effect that the scope of federal law-making power has become wider over the period since federation.

Case Study 1 Solomon Islands' System of Provincial Government

The Solomon Islands is a nation of around 450,000 people, located in the eastern Pacific to the west of Papua New Guinea. It was ruled as a British territory until independence in 1978. In 1982 a system of provincial government was introduced through an ordinary act of Parliament. It sets out the way that the nine provincial assemblies are formed, and provides for them to be modelled along Westminster lines – executive powers are exercised by an executive headed by a Premier, who is elected on the floor of the provincial assembly. The provincial assembly can pass laws called ordinances, provided they are within the 'legislative competence' of the assembly. Schedule 4 of the Act sets out eleven areas in which provincial governments have power to make laws, including local government, control and use of river waters (including pollution), codification of customary rights to land, management of agricultural land and business licences.

At the time the system of provincial government was established, all services in what became the provinces were delivered by the national government. The Provincial Government Act allows the Minister for Provincial Government to make 'devolution orders' which operate to transfer statutory functions and assets to the provincial government. A list of statutory powers under national legislation is set out in Schedule 5 of the Act. The Minister is permitted to transfer any of these functions to the provincial government.

Funding for provincial governments is provided in a variety of ways. A number of purpose-specific grants are provided through the national budget, for the provision of services such as health promotion and education, wages of less senior staff of health centres, and the operation of primary schools. Some grants are provided through the Department of Provincial Affairs, while others are provided through the Departments of Health and Medical Services, and Education and Human Services. This means that a number of national departments have responsibility for supervising the carrying out of provincial government functions. Although these grants are in theory tied to particular purposes, in practice the Department of Finance is unable to monitor their use effectively, since Provincial Governments operate their own financial management systems, and it rarely receives reports from them.

Second, what powers of supervision does the national government have over the lower level of government? The Australian system is at one end of the spectrum, with states being largely independent of the federal government. Other systems incorporate varying levels of supervision and control. In PNG, the national government can suspend the powers of a provincial government. The National Executive Council (cabinet) exercises the lower-level government's powers during the period of suspension.

National governments can also exercise effective control over sub-national governments through constraints on funding. The scheme of funding provided for in legislation, especially when contrasted with that which operates in practice, provide important indicators about how this relationship works. Some schemes of decentralization provide for guaranteed transfers of untied funding. In these circumstances, the opportunity for the national government to exercise informal control over provincial governments is limited. Other systems rely on national government to determine how much will be allocated to lover levels of government and for what purpose.

The Australian federal system, for example, now operates very differently from the way it did at federation in 1901. The removal of income tax powers from state governments earlier this century meant that they lost their financial independence. Funding for a range of activities, in particular social services, is provided by the Commonwealth under complex memoranda of agreement dealing with services such as health, education and housing. This mechanism allows the Commonwealth Government to retain substantial policy control even though virtually all service delivery is by state agencies.

Indigenous Rights

A key issue in setting the stage for examining how relationships between people and land are regulated is the formal recognition of indigenous rights. In some jurisdictions, specific constitutional recognition and protection of indigenous rights provide an overarching umbrella within which specific recognition of land tenure, rights to resources and other inherent rights may be the subject of more specific provisions. This is more significant in some countries than in others. In developing and newly industrializing countries an umbrella recognition of indigenous rights may be more important because it signals a benchmark that other laws will be expected to meet. Canada is one of the few developed countries with a constitution formally recognizing indigenous ownership and enshrining basic rights.

Laws and Policies Relating to Land and Natural Resources

The management of land and natural resources is one of the main functions of government. In most countries the greatest impacts of colonization on indigenous people were felt when colonizers used their superior firepower to secure land for economic development from its previous owners.

Although land use was largely unregulated in many countries (particularly colonial territories) until this century, the allocation of land was always a central function of government. With expanding populations and intensifying land uses, the need to regulate the competing interests of different land users grew. Land and resource management is now a critical feature of virtually every modern government system. It is through their intersection with these regulatory systems that indigenous people experience in a practical way the extent to which their interests are, or are not, recognized and protected.

A wide range of laws are likely to be relevant to a legal framework study undertaken in a resource development context. They include:

1 Laws regulating the extraction of natural resources, which usually emphasize the efficient allocation and utilization of the resource, capture of economic rent and safe work sites.
2 Land use laws providing a basis for regulating development activities, often through a system of land use planning, and usually operating at least within urban areas.
3 Environmental laws dealing with environmentally relevant activities generally, or with particular sectors of the environment such as water; these usually provide for regulation of site-specific activities and possibly for prohibition of certain kinds of activities.
4 Laws dealing with conservation, for example providing for the protection and/or management of certain species, and the designation and management of protected areas, sometimes under joint or community representative management.
5 Customs or other export or import control legislation, which may have wider purposes than just revenue generation and may trigger the requirement for other processes to be undertaken before export permission will be granted (for example, the export of uranium from Australia requires a licence issued by the Federal Government).

Not all these laws will be of relevance in a particular study. The PNG hydrocarbon sector study concentrated on those laws which impacted directly on the business of petroleum explorers and developers. A particular issue of importance in the PNG context is the ownership of sub-surface reserves of minerals and petroleum.

Ownership of Natural Resources

There are significant differences in the way different jurisdictions deal with ownership of natural resources. In some countries, the government owns sub-surface mineral rights, whereas in other countries they attach to the surface title to the land. In most countries, the right to harvest things growing on the land, like timber, belongs to the landowner.

The right of government to alienate sub-surface rights from surface ownership illustrates a fundamental point of conflict between indigenous and Anglo-European systems of land tenure. Most indigenous people will argue that rights associated with land can only be divested by its owners (and then not permanently), but they cannot be taken by government. In a country such as PNG, state ownership of sub-surface deposits represents the legacy of a colonial past, rather than an expression of modern government policy. It would be difficult to find any politicians in PNG today who openly advocate state alienation of minerals. Despite this, the situation remains as it was prior to independence, and this legal and political dichotomy has created a state of 'policy schizophrenia', in which sub-surface deposits remain in state ownership, but the benefit distribution regime reflects a recognition of *de facto* landowner control over access to the resources.

The legacy of British law prevails in many of its former colonies in the Pacific, North America and Africa. In Australia, most sub-surface mineral rights were alienated from the surface title rights. The state (called the 'Crown') retained the right to control the disposition of mineral deposits, subject to the payment of compensation for disturbance to the rights of surface owners. This alienation was not always absolute – in Queensland, for example, many titles until around the beginning of the twentieth century included sub-surface rights to some minerals. In some places only gold and silver were alienated to the Crown. In South Australia pressure from free settlers led to prerogative rights to gold and silver being included in land titles allocated by the colonial administration well into the nineteenth century. By the twentieth century, however, public ownership of sub-surface rights was well entrenched.

The assertion of state ownership over minerals will normally be explicitly stated in legislation, most commonly in a Mining Act (similar provision is usually made for hydrocarbon resources). In some cases it may be found in the constitution. However, it is also important to understand the extent to which government does or is expected to exercise control over the use of private resources. In PNG, for example, while mineral resources are legally the property of the state, their location in remote rural areas where the government has little or no presence means that landowners exercise *de facto* powers of veto over access. In reality, mineral development in these areas today can only occur with the consent of the landowners.

Resource Allocation and Management

Control over access to minerals can amount to *de facto* ownership. In the United States, for example, Indian lands do not usually include sub-surface mineral rights, but they do carry a right to veto access. This means that prospective miners must deal with the surface owners much as if they were the owners of the sub-surface too. A similar situation prevails in northern Australia on land that has been claimed under the Northern Territory Land Rights Act, and more recently those with successful (or prospectively successful) native title claims have been able to negotiate similar agreements.

Where sub-surface mineral rights are owned by the state, a system of granting access will usually provide limited rights to prospect under an exploration licence or lease, followed by a tenement to extract and sell the minerals. Sometimes a bidding or auction system is used to obtain the highest price for the concession, or else a fixed-rate royalty system provides a return to government. The most common system provides for the miner to own the resources that have been extracted, but some countries retain state ownership to the point of sale.

Regimes for the management of renewable resources such as forestry and fisheries once concentrated on promoting development of these industries, and providing research and development services to the private sector. Sustainable management is now the major focus. The legal framework for resource management will usually require that the levels of extraction and the manner in which it is undertaken should be highly regulated.

Water

The laws governing rights to use and control the flow of water formed a critical focus of the PNG hydrocarbon sector study. Water is critical to most development activities, and it is particularly crucial for petroleum exploration because water is used for drilling operations. Water management laws are also important in PNG resource developments for another, somewhat unique reason. A major limitation of mining laws in PNG is that the legal entitlement to compensation for disturbance by mining only applies to those landowners living within the area of the mining lease. The Water Resources Act provides the only formal mechanism to compensate those landowners living outside the lease areas.

Although customary rights to water are given broad recognition in PNG, the full extent of what this means has not yet been entirely explored. For now, water is managed by the state using a model drawn from Australian state legislation, which is in turn based on English law. Under English common law, it has usually been the case that while riparian (riverside) landowners have rights to use water, they do not own it and cannot control its flow, although they were sometimes able to prevent others from accessing it. As the importance of water as a finite natural resource is increasingly recognized, many governments are now legislating to broaden their control over water resources to include the right to control overland flows that are not confined to permanent riverbeds (for example, flooding), and systems are now established to balance the rights of upstream users with those downstream. This is probably in conflict with custom.

Because water is such an important resource, in many jurisdictions it was the first component of the environment to be subject to some form of environmental protection. In some countries, a water-resources or rivers law may still be the only form of environmental regulation. These laws typically deal with both the allocation of rights to the resource, and the imposition of controls on its use to prevent depletion, diversion of flows or pollution. More recently developed approaches to environmental regulation of water resources concentrate on catchment management, recognizing that many non-water-based activities have the potential to affect the quality of both ground and surface water.

Environment and Conservation Laws

Environmental regulation systems can provide an avenue for indigenous people and other local communities affected by a development to register their interests and objections. Until the late 1980s or early 1990s, most environmental protection laws were focused on specific sectors of the environment (for example, water or air). The emphasis was generally on regulating discharges or emissions to the environment, most commonly concentrating on 'end of pipe' discharges.

A number of countries have now moved toward a more holistic approach to environmental regulation. Some ambitious attempts have been made to embrace a wide range of environmental concerns within the ambit of one legislative scheme. The New Zealand Resource Management Act, for example, attempts to integrate environmental regulation with development planning, and to provide a framework for decision making by a wide range of agencies at different levels of government. Fiji has recently drafted a Sustainable Development Bill that attempts to address a wide range of environmental issues that have become more important in the last ten years of the twentieth century. These include maintenance of biodiversity (including access to genetic resources), protection of sensitive ecosystems such as coral reefs, and sustainable management of resources.

Environment legislation falls into two broad categories: legislation that regulates the impact of development and land-use activities, and legislation providing for conservation. Development impacts are usually regulated in two ways: first by requiring a process of environmental impact assessment, and second by subjecting the development activity to a regime of consents that allow conditions to be imposed on how it operates.

Environmental Impact Assessment Environmental impact assessment (EIA) is often set out in separate legislation, and is sometimes combined with a broader land-use consent system. Most social impact analysis is a sub-component of environmental impact analysis. If a legal framework study is being undertaken as part of a broader EIA process, it is important to understand how that operates. An initial assessment of impacts is usually undertaken by the proponent of the development. Mechanisms for scoping the range of issues to be covered may be provided, or there may be guidelines that specify what the assessment is to cover. This should then be subject to evaluation or review by the regulatory authority, or the public, or both. Sometimes hearings are conducted. A final EIA may form the basis of licence conditions that are later imposed.

Sometimes more than one level of government will require EIA. Until recently, the Australian Commonwealth Government required development activities to undergo a separate parallel process of impact assessment at the federal level. This requirement was triggered where some form of

Commonwealth consent (such as the approval of an export permit for uranium) was required.

Environmental Consents Environmental consents (licences or permits) are now increasingly required in most countries for a wide range of development activities. Often the legislation will include a schedule setting out which activities are subject to these requirements. Although permit conditions are usually tailored to the environmental issues specific to a particular development, standards are also used as a basis for bench-marking acceptable performance. Environment legislation may provide a framework for a raft of subsidiary legislation. In Australia and other countries, the use of statutory environment policies (a form of descriptive regulation) is becoming common. This subsidiary legislation can usually be found in regulations, gazette notices and similar instruments.

Whereas early environmental laws were geared toward a 'top-down' approach, modern environmental laws stress co-regulation, recognizing that government resources to police environmental laws are not boundless and the range of issues that require monitoring is expanding. The usefulness of 'process' standards such as International Standards Organisation (ISO) 14,000 as a means of independently verifying environmental performance is recognized. This allows the regulator to concentrate on identifying the environmental values that should be protected and the means by which that can best be achieved.

Conservation Conservation laws can also be important in regulating the relationship between indigenous landowners, other land users and the state. In PNG, for example, there is a strong movement toward locally controlled conservation areas over customary land. These provide both a *de facto* means to formalize traditional land titles, and a mechanism for landowners to interact with other land users and exert some control over land-use decision making.

Conservation laws are most commonly directed toward particular species or the protection of areas of high conservation value (although protected areas also serve other purposes such as recreation or protection of cultural heritage). Species protection legislation is generally focused on the protection of species considered to be endangered, although more modern legislation also provides for the sustainable management of economically and culturally important species, even though they are not endangered.

Conservation areas are important because they promote *in situ* conservation of ecosystems, rather than individual species. It is often possible to integrate development activities with conservation objectives (for example, by leaving conservation set-asides or providing wildlife corridors within development areas). Models for protected area management sometimes require state ownership of land (as, for example, national parks). Increasingly, however, conservation policy targets private land. Laws may restrict the clearing of native vegetation or impose land-use controls based on the high conservation value of a particular area (for example, the restrictions imposed under the Australian World Heritage Properties Conservation Act).

Even in those countries that have not developed significant protected-area systems, protection is usually provided for water catchments. These may be provided for in water resource management legislation, or they can be located within forestry legislation. A search of gazette notices or subsidiary instruments may be necessary to find out the precise boundaries of area that have been protected in this way. The parent legislation will usually provide for the kinds of activity restrictions that apply, which will generally be aimed at preserving vegetation cover and maintaining soil stability in order to ensure water quality.

International Treaties and Conventions

International treaties, agreements and conventions can be very significant within a national legal framework. Multilateral and bilateral agreements do not have effect within a country until they are implemented through domestic legislation. If a country is party to an international convention then there is a good possibility that it will enact laws to meet its obligations at some time in the future.

During the 1990s a number of important conventions concerning the environment were adopted. There were also some significant international developments concerning the rights of indigenous peoples. In particular, the Convention on Biological Diversity reversed the age-old assumption that biological resources are the common heritage of mankind, and reaffirmed the right of nations to control the disposition of natural resources within their boundaries, including genetic resources. Most centres of high biodiversity are located in developing countries. They are now seeking avenues to control access to genetic resources, although only a few have so far adopted laws for this purpose.

It is not always easy to identify the treaties and conventions to which a particular country is party, and whether or not they have been ratified domestically. Although officials from a responsible line department will usually be involved, this is most often the responsibility of a unit or office within the department or ministry responsible for foreign affairs.

Land Tenure and Landowner Organization and Representation

Customary land tenure issues are likely to be important in any framework analysis. Many resource developments occur in rural areas where there are more likely to be indigenous people whose relationship to their land will be very different from those of the other landowners. Customary land tenure is by its nature fluid and integrally connected with the social systems of the culture from which it originates. Resource developers typically focus on identifying with certainty which landowners they should deal with in negotiating a project, how disputes about ownership should be resolved, and how landowner groups will make the decisions that are demanded of them when they become involved with a project. By far the most significant issues canvassed in the PNG hydrocarbon sector study were those relating to land tenure and the arrangements for landowners to organize themselves to participate in decision making about hydrocarbon projects. These issues are equally significant in the context of hard-rock mining in PNG, but are addressed in quite different ways in the two sectors.

Customary Land Tenure

Generally speaking, the processes of colonization and modernization in most countries have involved a transition from feudal or customary land tenure to more formal systems of state-granted land title. A number of countries, however, continue to recognize customary tenure or common property in a variety of forms. In PNG, for example, more than 99 per cent of the land area is under customary tenure. In the Solomon Islands the figure is around 85 per cent.

Customary land tenure is a major issue in virtually all economic development in PNG, and negotiating customary land tenure issues is an important focus of attention in preparing for resource developments. The countries of the Pacific were colonized by Britain later than the former British colonies of Australia and New Zealand, and those in the African continent, at a time when there was a greater awareness of the social cost of alienating indigenous inhabitants from their land. Accordingly, the colonial administrations placed major restrictions on dealings in customary land, with the result that systems of customary land tenure are still largely intact.

In the areas where customary land still exists, it is usually subject to restrictions on its alienability (whether it can be permanently disposed of) and dealings in it are usually also limited. For a variety of legal and political reasons, inalienability is a fundamental feature of systems for the recognition of customary land. Land claimed under both the Northern Territory and New South Wales Land Rights Acts in Australia is transferred to Aboriginal groups as an inalienable title. The common law on native title in Australia as settled in 'Mabo' also prohibits transfer outside of disposal provided for in customary law.

In PNG, the Land Act provides that customary land cannot be leased for development purposes except through a process involving acquisition of the land by the state, and subsequent leasing to whomever will undertake the development. Although periodically subject to abuse, this system generally ensures that unscrupulous dealings in land do not dispossess land holders. Even where the landowners themselves wish to undertake development and require a title to secure finance, this process is required.

Customary Land Registration The fluidity and flexibility that characterize systems of customary land ownership contrast sharply with the rigidity of modern Euro-American systems, particularly the title registration systems that developed during the twentieth century. During the 1950s, as many British colonies moved toward independence, it was thought that customary land tenure should be codified in some way to facilitate the economic development of this land. A number of different systems of customary land registration were developed in Africa and the Pacific. Although many of these laws are still on the statute books, the extent to which they were carried into effect and remain relevant varies greatly.

In PNG, for example, initial efforts at systematic and even sporadic registration eventually stopped after independence. The difficulty of resolving disputes and the cost of the bureaucratic systems involved presented insurmountable barriers to effective implementation. In the 1980s and 1990s, registration of customary land in PNG was actively opposed by landowners on the basis that it might facilitate dispossession by the government. In nearby Solomon Islands, there was no formal system of customary land registration during the period of colonial administration (although there was a system for alienating customary land and registering it in the name of the customary owners). Recording of customary land is now seen as essential for economic development. In 1997 the government passed a Customary Land Records Act. It provides a framework for recording (but not registering) the ownership of all customary land in the Solomon Islands.

Dispute Settlement Disputes about ownership rarely arise in relation to land that is incorporated into modern title registration systems. Indeed, this is exactly what they were designed to avoid. Conversely, disputes about ownership and boundaries are an integral part of many customary systems. These disputes often escalate as population pressure increases, traditional systems of social control fragment and development creates new economic opportunities.

Most countries with intact customary tenure have established mechanisms for resolution of disputes about customary land. Depending on the context in which these arise, more than one mechanism might be provided. An understanding of the broader legal framework of land and resource development law is usually required to understand how the system operates in practice. In addition, customary dispute mechanisms commonly suffer resource-starvation because they are remotely located and at the periphery of government services. In some countries the systems established some time ago have all but disappeared completely. The lack of an accessible means of resolving disputes to the satisfaction of all the participants is of primary concern to resource developers. In the PNG hydrocarbon sector study the problems with existing dispute resolution systems were subject to extensive analysis, and a number of recommendations were made to improve them.

Case Study 2 An Analysis of Customary Land Dispute Resolution in Solomon Islands

The Solomon Islands Local Court Act and Land and Titles Act provides for customary land disputes to be heard by local courts, with appeals from Local Court decisions to a Customary Land Appeal Court (CLAC), which sits as a three member panel. The decision of the CLAC is intended to be final. Although a number of land disputes were heard and resolved in this way during the 1970s and early 1980s, it can now be extremely difficult to convene a local court or CLAC because of the lack of funds to pay sitting fees. It seems likely that the record-keeping system which once provided such a wealth of information about customary ownership is no longer as accurate as it was.

Today, most customary disputes arise in the context of forestry developments. Forest resources are privately owned and, once the Commissioner for Forests has given his consent, landowners can negotiate directly with logging companies to harvest their timber. Many disputes arise because the processes for determining whether landowners consent to the logging company proposal are circumvented or do not successfully inform all those who are owners of the land.

A major issue is the apparent distinction made in the Forest Resources and Timber Utilisation Act between ownership of land and ownership of the timber growing on it. According to a recent report by the Solomon Islands Law Reform Commission, this artificial distinction emerged during the 1970s. At the time it was considered too time consuming to convert customary land to state-owned land before logging it (as had previously been the case) and acquisition of customary land, as opposed to timber, by private individuals is prohibited. On the basis of this legal separation of timber from the land it grows on, the Forest Resources and Timber Utilisation Act provided for a different process of determining disputes about ownership from that which applies to resolution of land disputes. This process by-passes the local court and allows a dispute to be determined by a CLAC, but according to different procedures provided for under the Land and Titles Act.

A different process again of ownership determination is provided for in the Mining Act. Government officers are required to hold meetings in the area of a mining development and make a determination about ownership of land for the purpose of compensation agreements. While all these systems are essentially aimed at the same end – determining who are the owners of customary land – they all use different processes and potentially might yield different outcomes in relation to the same area of land.

Any development that takes place on customary land is likely to generate ownership disputes. The extent to which ownership issues can be resolved before the development begins will largely determine how intractable they are likely to become later. An understanding of how dispute resolution systems function is critical.

Native Title

Even in those countries where land has been alienated from its original owners, there is an increasing awareness of the need to recognize and respect customary tenure. Australia, New Zealand and Canada have taken significant steps in the last three decades of the twentieth century toward legal recognition that the original act of colonisation did not completely extinguish the indigenous inhabitants' 'native title'. These countries now have dual systems of land tenure. One is based on the 'radical title' of the Crown (in effect a kind of legal manifestation of the sovereignty of the state) and is formalized into different types of tenure such as freehold and leasehold. The other is based on indigenous law and custom and is enforced (but not sourced) through the modern common-law legal system.

The concept of native title has been part of English common law for a long time. The legal foundation of the concept is to be found in one of the central underpinning philosophies of the common-law system: the rule of law. Broadly speaking, the rule of law provides a basis for mediating the power of the state over its citizens by requiring that the state, too, act in accordance with the law. During the period of Britain's colonial expansion activities, a body of law developed about the way in which state power should be exercised over new territories. It required that (unless Britain had conquered the other territory during a war) the property rights of citizens in a country which had come under British rule should be respected. The legal assumption that Australia had been uninhabited (*terra nullius*) meant that native title was not recognized there until 1992, when this assumption was overturned by the Federal High Court in the Mabo decision. In other former British colonies, including Canada, the United States and a number of African States, native title has been recognized for some time.

In some countries, native title continues to be recognized and developed through the common law – in court decisions. This is the case in Canada. In Australia, and to some extent New Zealand, legislation sets out a claims procedure. Since the passage of the Commonwealth Native Title Act in 1993, there have been substantial developments in the policy and practice surrounding the making of claims for native title, and the procedures accompanying approval of development proposals on land that is the subject of a determination of native title, or is under claim.

Land Rights

Some jurisdictions provide mechanisms for claims to be made over government-owned land even if no prior right or title to it can be established. The Northern Territory Land Rights Act, for example, provides for claims to pastoral leases and Crown land based on assertion of traditional ownership. Land that is successfully claimed is registered in the name of a trust, and managed under a statutory framework that includes procedures for applications to undertake mining on the land. A network of regional land councils plays an important role in providing a conduit between mainstream legal and economic systems and the systems of customary law that still operate in these remote areas. Unlike native title, which is recognized by force of the underlying common law, land rights schemes have effect only by virtue of the statute under which they are established.

Legal Framework for Indigenous Property Rights

Perhaps the overwhelming requirement for economic development on indigenous land is certainty. Investment in a resource-based development cannot occur unless investors are able to enter into binding arrangements with other landowners and land users as to the basis on which the development is allowed to go ahead.

In a western legal context, this 'resource security' is provided in part by the law of contract. Where development on indigenous land is involved, many uncertainties inhibit such a simple solution. Who owns the land? Who has a right to represent those who own the land? With whom should a contract relating to the land be negotiated? These are among the most complex issues involved in the recognition and incorporation of customary land ownership into modern land-management legal frameworks.

Identification and Recognition of Landowners Many customary systems are typically characterized by fluidity both as to territorial boundaries and the precise identity of customary owners. Nevertheless, owners of land who have lived with this flexibility for thousands of years are likely to feel compelled to assert any claim, however tenuous, when the potential to control or benefit from a resource development is at stake. The unique circumstances created by a mining or forestry project in a previously undeveloped area generate pressures for which there is no customary precedent. These disputes over ownership are not evidence that claims are illegitimate, rather they signal a fundamental conflict between the underlying fluidity of the tenurial system and the constraints of one-off opportunities generated by modern economic development. Indeed, development often brings to the surface disputes that have fermented over thousands of years, such as those over the right to govern the former Yugoslavian states.

Landowners are identified in a variety of ways. The customary land registration systems and dispute resolution mechanisms described above are two of the ways in which landowners are identified. In Australia the claims procedures under the Native Title Act require land disputes between competing owners to be adjudicated before a claim can proceed. In PNG, the failure of land dispute settlement mechanisms (and the perception that they are not impartial) often leads to such disputes being taken to the Land Titles Commission (the body originally established to undertake customary land registration). Some customary systems have developed their own systems for recording landownership and resolving disputes (for example, those in Samoa).

Most mechanisms for landowner identification are inadequate and have the potential to generate as much dispute as they resolve. This is not least of all because they attempt to codify in writing what has always been recorded orally (and is therefore amenable to be altered depending on the circumstances). Reliance is often placed on genealogies to determine the membership of groups. Incorporation of landowner groups (such as incorporated land groups: see p.83) has also been used as a mechanism for identifying owners. This approach has the advantage that it relies less on identification of individuals, focusing instead on the social units that are the most significant in terms of social and local organization.

A variety of mechanisms can usually be accessed in order to resolve landowner identification issues. These may range from legalistic approaches such as the inquiries conducted by the Papua New Guinea Land Titles Commission, to mediation like that undertaken with the assistance of the Australian Native Title Tribunal. Some provide short-term solutions that are less likely to be long lasting, others take longer but produce more durable results. A combination of approaches is most likely to be successful, and a good legal framework analysis should examine the different mechanisms and assess their suitability for different situations.

Landowner identification mechanisms were examined extensively in the PNG hydrocarbon sector study. The study made a number of observations about the processes for identification and the potential for confusion and overlap between identification of landowners and the establishment of organizations to represent landowners in project negotiations. The confusion of these two quite separate functions not surprisingly confuses the two objectives. Organizations may come to be seen by project developers as taking the place of landowners, because they are a legally more 'visible' form than an unincorporated customary group.

Landowner Representation Mechanisms Western legal systems provide for the representation of groups through artificial legal constructs called corporations. The purpose of 'in-corporation' is to turn a group of people into a single (corporate) legal personality capable of speaking with a common voice and to place the corporate entity at arm's length from the individuals that comprise it. The rules by which companies and incorporated associations operate provide a way of generating decisions that bind all the members of the company or association, at least as far as their involvement in that body is concerned.

Corporate bodies are the main vehicle for the incorporation of indigenous people into western land and resource management regimes. An early approach was the use of 'land trust boards' in Africa and Fiji. There was no attempt to render the customary land itself into non-customary title, but rather to establish a mechanism for prospective developers to deal with its owners.

In developed countries with significant populations of indigenous people – the United States, Canada, New Zealand and Australia – a range of not dissimilar mechanisms have emerged for the representation of indigenous people within the wider legal system. Some use conventional legal structures (for example, companies and incorporated associations). Others provide corporate forms designed for a specific purpose. The Commonwealth Native Title Act, for example, requires that determinations of native title be held by Prescribed Bodies Corporate which can be established as trusts or as associations under the Aboriginal Councils and Associations Act.

It is essential to have a good understanding of the legal constraints under which these indigenous organizations operate and the practical difficulties they experience. For example, a large number of Aboriginal organizations in Australia are established under mainstream incorporated association legislation, which is intended for use by non-profit groups such as sporting clubs. The legislation under which they are established often prohibits the payment of anything like dividends to members, so these organizations cannot be used as a means of distributing compensation benefits to members of the community. Many of the purpose-specific organizations have been designed differently, and have shortcomings which may not have been identified at the time the legislation providing for them was established. The Papua New Guinea Land Groups Incorporation Act, for example, was originally intended to create bodies to hold group titles that were to be registered under another companion Act that was never passed. Accordingly, the accountability provisions are relatively limited. In particular, there is no provision for external scrutiny of financial accountability by the executive of a group to its members. Since these bodies are the vehicle for distribution of large amounts of compensation and benefit payments, it is not surprising that financial probity is the subject of a majority of complaints about them, but there is no capacity for it to be investigated or rectified by government.

One of the main reasons why landowner organizations have become so important in the Papua New Guinean and Australian contexts is that indigenous landowners in both countries are now in an unprecedented position to negotiate a share of the benefits of a resource development project. Landowner organizations are essential as a conduit for the distribution of royalties and other cash benefits. As such, the membership and control of these bodies may be highly contested. The PNG hydrocarbon sector study observed that the distribution of revenue by incorporated land groups is virtually unregulated (because of the lack of any external accountability provisions in the governing legislation), so that disenfranchised members have no avenue to pursue defaulting leaders. The potential for unresolved complaints of this kind to destablize projects, and expose developers to further claims, are of serious concern to many developers. In the future, the ability of PNG to mobilize its natural resources may well depend on how well it manages landowner involvement in developments. Structures for the identification, organization and representation of landowners are essential to developing that capacity.

Revenue Arrangements

Resource developments generate a flow of income to be captured by the developer, landowners and government. Governments normally capture 'resource rent' through taxation and royalty payments. Taxation systems are often designed to capture an increasing proportion of the income flow as the profitability of the resource extraction increases: for example, the percentage at which export duty payable for timber harvesting is payable increases as the price per cubic metre paid for the timber increases.

In many cases, the resource rent captured by government is redistributed to those in the area of the development in the form of grants and other government benefits. These redistributions can be significant in securing support for the development from local or regional government, and from those who are likely to suffer impacts but are not directly entitled to compensation. Arrangements for the distribution of benefits from a resource development can be exceedingly complex. They are unlikely to be understood just by reading legislation, and the insights and historical knowledge of those with long involvement in a particular sector are invaluable in understanding them.

Compensation for Use and Access

Where private landowners do not have rights of ownership to subsurface deposits, or the right to veto access, they will usually still enjoy some right to be compensated for the disturbance caused by mining or abstraction of water. A common model used in Australia and a number of other countries is for compensation to be negotiated or, in the absence of agreement, adjudicated. It is important to distinguish these systems of compensation from broader bases for compensation that may arise from common law (for example, claims for environmental compensation based on negligence or occupier's liability). Statutory systems of compensation for disturbance to surface rights are usually very limited. As noted above, a serious drawback of the compensation regimes in the mining sector in PNG is their failure to provide adequately for downstream landowners.

The nature of compensation regimes can affect the way relationships between developers and landowners evolve. Landowners in PNG, for example, have been commonly observed to plant 'compensation gardens' in the path of developers' planned new roads. This practice arises at least partly from the restrictions inherent in the compensation regime (in that compensation can only be paid for economically valuable vegetation that is cleared), although it is also testament to the ingenuity of landowners in maximizing the opportunities to gain from developments.

Benefit Sharing

Where landowners have the right to veto access to sub-surface minerals, even though they do not own them, agreements relating to the granting of access rights are usually negotiated as private arrangements not subject to government control. In other circumstances, there may be a scheme of statutory benefit sharing or compensation. The Northern Territory Land Rights Act, for example, sets out a requirement for 'royalty-equivalent' transfers to traditional owners of land that has been subject to mining. Where there is no formal right to veto access, but political or other circumstances require benefit sharing arrangements, these may be the subject of government policy or precedent based on prior practice (as in PNG, for example). These kinds of provisions are often not written and can be difficult to track down.

The PNG hydrocarbon sector study made an extensive analysis of the different forms of benefits landowners can receive under current policy relating to petroleum and mining projects. These benefits include:

- royalties and additional 'royalty-equivalent' payments;
- equity in the unincorporated joint venture partnership, usually paid for by the government and subject to restrictions designed to ensure proper participation in future capital injections into the project;

- access to infrastructure developments paid for by developers but subject to tax relief (known as the 'tax-credit' scheme;
- access (at least theoretically) to funding provided to the provincial government for expenditure in the project development area (known as Special Support Grant).

The scheme for distribution of benefits is complex and until the passage of the Oil and Gas Act in 1998, there was no legislative basis at all for any of the different strands likely to be contained in a benefit package.

Mechanisms for Payment of Compensation

The ways in which compensation or shared benefits are paid is as important as the amount. A range of different arrangements is used. Sometimes governments receive benefits and pay them to landowners. If this is the case, the effectiveness of the system by which payment is made can be an issue. Problems can occur around the delays involved in transferring payment and concerning who is to receive the distribution. Sometimes these arrangements do not involve a direct transfer so much as a government payment (out of consolidated revenue), which is consequent on a revenue receipt in the form of royalties or export duty.

One of the key issues addressed in the PNG hydrocarbon sector study is the question of how to balance competing interests in the distribution of benefits. First, there is the issue of safeguarding the interests of future generations. There are real concerns that the influx of cash benefits into some areas will undermine the existing capacity of host communities to be self-sustaining, but without substituting any sustainable income-generating activities. Second, there is the balance to be struck between the rights of landowners in the immediate area of a development, those of people living in the wider impact area, and the country as a whole. There are real risks that emphasis on the rights of those who are *de facto* resource owners will create an elite of 'lucky-strike' landowners at the expense of wider community interests.

Case Study 3 Changes in Compensation and Benefit Sharing in Mining and Petroleum Development in Papua New Guinea

Until ten years ago, the owners of customary land in Papua New Guinea were entitled to receive only a limited amount of compensation for mining and petroleum development. The level of compensation is determined under the mining legislation and provided compensation is available only on certain specified grounds, basically where there is disturbance to surface rights. For the most part, this compensation was confined to loss of economic trees and plants, paid at a scale fixed by the Valuer-General. This system had two major drawbacks. First, the level of compensation was very small in comparison to the level of profit generated by the resource extraction activities. Second, it was payable only to landowners within the mining tenement. Those living outside the mining lease area, even if they suffered the effects of the development, had no entitlement to compensation. The only other benefit to which landowners were entitled was a small share of royalties, as provided for under the Mining Act. This amount, too, was payable only to landowners within the area of the mining tenement.

In 1990, the eruption of civil unrest over the Panguna copper mine on the island of Bougainville raised real questions about the equity of benefit distribution arrangements. The national government introduced a policy in the same year for the new Porgera gold mine in Enga province. Under the new arrangements for distribution of revenue from mining activities, royalties were to be shared by Provincial Governments and landowners, with Provincial Governments also receiving a special government grant. The new arrangements were reflected in memoranda of agreement between the landowners and the provincial and national governments. These agreements also provided for landowners and provincial government to each receive half the national government's 10 per cent equity share in the project. However, the Organic Law on Provincial Government and the Mining Act continued to provide for a different distribution arrangement.

Benefit-sharing packages in relation to the mining and petroleum developments since 1990 have been negotiated according to the 'development forum process' pioneered during the Porgera negotiations. Notwithstanding the broad acceptance of this process, it has not been incorporated into the mining legislation (except by a single line reference), nor is there any framework limiting the level of benefits that the government will provide. Agreements about benefit sharing in relation to the four major developments since that time reflect substantial increases over the Porgera package, which initially incorporated a transfer of a total of 20 per cent of royalties. This increased to 30 per cent when the Kutubu oil project started up in 1992, 50 per cent when the Lihir negotiations concluded in early 1995, and landowners successfully negotiated a transfer of 100 per cent of royalties for the Gobe oil project, which commenced in 1998.

Research Methods

The legal and policy analysis set out in the PNG hydrocarbon sector study drew on a variety of sources extending well beyond legislation. Cabinet decisions, negotiated agreements, internal company reports, environmental assessments and a wide range of other material were used. In undertaking research in a developing country context, accuracy is a prime consideration as much of the available material may be outdated or inaccurate and require careful checking.

Sources of Legal Information

Laws can be remarkably difficult to find in some developing countries where systems for the publication and dissemination of laws may have collapsed in the face of more pressing public priorities. A good starting point is usually the department or authority that administers the area in question, but care should be taken to cross-check for any amendments. It is not uncommon for bureaucrats in developing countries to be working from copies of legislation that are out of date and do not include recently enacted amendments.

A number of countries now provide access to their laws on the internet. The Australian Legal Information Institute's website is a particularly useful source of information about Australian Commonwealth and State laws,[1] and has a number of links to other sources of worldwide legal information. The Asian Development Bank's DIAL project is gradually assembling the laws of its member countries on to a website. At the time of writing, in 2000, this project was in its infancy and many countries have posted laws passed within the last one or two years. The laws of a wide range of developing countries can also be found in some law libraries.

If up-to-date copies of laws are not available electronically, or from the government printer, the agency responsible for drafting laws is the most likely source of accurate copies. This agency is often called parliamentary or legislative counsel, or legal draftsman, and is usually located within either the justice department or ministry or the Prime Minister's office (in a Westminster system). The legislature (assembly, senate, congress or parliament) should also maintain up-to-date records.

Provincial and State Laws If national laws are difficult to find, then the task of tracking down the laws of sub-national governments in developing countries can be almost impossible. Provincial and local governments themselves may not maintain systems for printing or distributing laws and may not even hold complete collections of them. The staff that service the legislature or officials responsible for administering the law are the most likely sources. If they are not able to provide a copy of the law, the chances are they will not enforce it either!

Subsidiary Legislation As law-making has become more complex, subsidiary or delegated legislation has assumed greater importance. Most laws make provision for a body or authority other than the legislature to make laws within certain well-defined limits. In many jurisdictions the responsible minister or the Governor (acting on advice) has power to make delegated legislation in the form of regulations or gazette notices.

Regulations are usually used to flesh out the Act or to provide rules for a specific activity or purpose (under fisheries legislation, for example, regulations might provide specifications for the use of vessel-monitoring equipment). Gazette notices are most commonly used to extend the range of application of a law. For example, a conservation law might provide that certain activities are restricted within those areas that are gazetted as conservation areas. They are also used to fix levels that might need to be updated on a regular basis – for example the fee for an environment permit. In those jurisdictions that use them, gazette notices (also called by other names including 'legal' or 'statutory' notices) are published on a regular basis, usually in a circular bulletin often called the Government Gazette. Identifying all the notices that are relevant to a particular piece of legislation over a long time can be very time consuming. Comprehensive collections of relevant notices are most likely to be held by the agency responsible for administration of the legislation or by the parliamentary counsel.

Verifying Information

Most practitioners operating outside the jurisdiction with which they are most familiar have experienced having their conclusions undermined by the revelation that some important information on which they relied was incorrect, or that a vital piece of the jigsaw was missing. It is very important to check information carefully with more than one source. The more extensive the consultations that are conducted, the more likely it is that the information obtained will be accurate.

Reading and Understanding Legislation

Legislation alone does not always present a complete picture of the policy objectives it is intended to implement. It is useful to think of a law as merely the visible tip of an iceberg: beneath the surface a whole raft of written and informal policy, practice, and past experience underpin what the law makes explicit. A range of policy documents including those developed during policy formulation (discussion papers, issue papers, reviews and green papers) and those representing a formal statement of government policy (white papers) may be necessary to properly understand the 'mischief' and the remedy to which a particular law is directed.

In common-law countries, statute law is complemented by a broad range of 'unwritten' common law in the form of court decisions. An investigation into the legal framework for administration of a particular sector of government should encompass court decisions, administrative directions, guidelines and an examination of the practices by which the law is carried into effect.

Understanding how Government Functions

Budget documents and organization charts for government agencies provide invaluable sources of information about what levels of government are responsible for service delivery. Budget documents usually reveal the arrangements for funding of sub-national governments (although the real picture will not always be clear). Similarly, departmental organization charts or 'establishment registers' provide a road-map for negotiating the labyrinthine halls of bureaucracy.

Conclusion

The accuracy and usefulness of a legal framework analysis is likely to depend to a large extent on the effectiveness of information-gathering techniques. The more broad-ranging the sources from which information is drawn, the more likely it is that the resulting picture will be complete. The art of a framework study is to build a big picture from the small detail. The ability to sift what is relevant from what is not is therefore of crucial importance.

It is important to situate the formal and factual information within an understanding of the 'softer' factors which affect its relevance. A legal framework cannot be understood outside its social context. The examples outlined in this chapter have attempted to illustrate the complexity of divining a picture of reality from a mixture of policy, law and practice, both written and unwritten.

The forgoing discussion also highlights the need to look behind the formal expression of law to the administrative arrangements that are actually in place. Many developing country government systems are very weak. Administrative and financial management systems are sometimes inadequate to support the effective management of public resources or the implementation of legislation. Bureaucratic systems early in their life are often characterized by a high degree of informality. Excessive rigidity and complexity in rules, coupled with poor accountability and a lack of transparency, lead to rules being ignored or circumvented. Many former colonies that achieved independence only recently have inherited highly regulated administrative systems, which have since been abandoned in the countries from which they originally came. The inappropriateness of these systems (and their cultural unsuitability) militates against their effective functioning.

It is not uncommon in developing countries for laws to establish systems of regulation that are not implemented because of lack of funding. Some laws may be implemented only in part. For example, PNG enacted an Environmental Contaminants Act in 1979 that requires all contaminants deposited or emitted to the environment to be licensed. So far, however, the only pesticides are required to be licensed. Careful cross-checking to ascertain how regulatory systems actually operate in practice is essential.

Finally, a framework analysis should be sensitive to the purpose for which it is conducted. This chapter has outlined a broad range of the kinds of issues that will generally be relevant. A complete framework study could not ignore any of them, but the extent to which each features will vary greatly. An analysis undertaken to set the scene for national policy development will necessarily be aimed at different issues from one that is undertaken as part of a due diligence investigation for a specific development project. While both may range across similar territory, the emphasis will be different, as will the implicit questions each seeks to answer.

References

Taylor, M. and Whimp, K. (1997), *Report on Land Issues and Hydrocarbon Framework Study*. Report to the Asian Development Bank and

PNG Department of Mining and Petroleum. ADB Technical Assistance Grant No 2418-PNG. Mimeo.

Note

1 Internet: http:\\austlii.edu.au

–4–

Scoping for Social Impact Assessment

Kristi M. Branch and *Helen Ross*

Introduction

Social assessment combines research, analytic and participatory processes to identify, describe and interpret changes in the 'human environment' that result from any of a wide variety of change agents – development projects, new policies or planning activities. Scoping for social impact assessment draws upon these same three processes – research, analysis and participation – to:

1. Disclose information about the proposed action, preliminary estimates of impacts, and plans for the decision-making and assessment effort.
2. Initiate dialogue with the interested and potentially affected publics and decision makers.
3. Establish the focus and level of detail of the assessment, identify particular issues that need to be addressed, and clarify how potentially affected publics will be consulted and involved.

Quite simply, 'scoping' is a procedure for deciding the scope of a study. It is particularly valuable for ensuring that effort is devoted to exploring key issues, and not dissipated on issues which are unlikely to be pertinent to environmental or social impacts or to contribute appreciably to decision making. It ensures transparency about the issues to be investigated and – where there is public participation in the scoping process – helps to ensure widespread confidence that all key issues have been considered for study.

Although scoping has been established as a formally defined component of the environmental and social impact assessment processes required by law in many countries, and has therefore taken on specific meaning and requirements in this forum, it is also a necessary component of any social assessment, even those conducted outside of this regulatory context.

Because both scoping and social assessment deal with people and their responses, the overlap in the information and skills used by the social scientist in scoping and assessment is greater than for most other members of an interdisciplinary environmental assessment team. (Typically, major environmental assessments are conducted by a team, in which anthropologists may or may not be included among the social scientists). Since scoping comes early in the assessment process, it provides an opportunity for the social scientists to step forward to help design and conduct the scoping process and, in countries that adopt a participatory approach to scoping, to help ensure that it is accessible to all members of the affected communities. In addition, the scoping process is frequently the first formal presentation of the proposed action and assessment team to the affected publics, and may well be the first formal activity of the assessment team. Consequently, it is important to be prepared to participate effectively in this aspect of the assessment process.

This chapter describes the function and key objectives of the scoping process, explains the assessment framework and the conventions and issues that set the context for the scoping process, provides some suggestions about how to plan and conduct scoping for a social assessment, and discusses some of the key issues that must be addressed in designing an effective scoping process for social impact assessment. Our approach recognizes that anthropologists and other social scientists may be involved in assessment tasks that include disciplinary areas besides their own. This may be an Environmental Impact Assessment (EIA), Strategic Environmental Assessment (SEA, the analysis of the impacts of policies or plans, or the combination of impact assessment with planning), or a planning process.

Since the function of deciding the 'scope' of a social impact assessment is conducted quite differently in different countries and jurisdictions (see Wood, 1995 for details), we concentrate here on the USA system of scoping. This is a participatory system, in which regulations guarantee certain parties' rights to be included. We contrast with Australia, which does not have formal public participation in scoping, and Canada, which includes public participation in scoping under its panel system of assessment.

Few countries adopt a fully participatory approach to scoping. The UK has no formal requirement for scoping at all, although it is recommended (Wood 1995:135–6). Australia[1] does not emphasize the term in its procedures but embeds the scope of the study in the guidelines the regulatory body issues to the proponent and assessment team. These are decided in-house, with some discretionary consultation with other agencies and on occasions, the public. Wood (1995:140) notes that this scoping has not succeeded in focusing the studies or eliminating unimportant issues. In Canada, a special panel is convened to conduct each EIA. It may conduct hearings as part of the scoping process. The panel, after listening to and analysing this public input, issues guidelines to the proponent/assessment team concerning the scope and requirements of the assessment. The scoping for the proposed Great Whale hydro-lelectric project in northern Quebec was managed by a joint review panel of federal, provincial, Inuit and Cree representatives[2] (Mulvihill and Jacobs, 1998). In the United States, analysing and interpreting the implications of the public input for the scope of the assessment is usually the responsibility of the proponent or the lead agency responsible for the assessment, with the assistance of the assessment team and oversight by the regulator/permitting agency. However, the validity of this interpretation and appropriateness of the subsequent scope of the assessment is generally tested/challenged through the courts by public interest groups.

Scoping: Nature and Purpose

The Function of Scoping

Scoping serves disclosure, problem definition, and planning functions for the social assessment and overall impact assessment process. The US Council on Environmental Quality (CEQ) views the principal goal of scoping to be 'an adequately and efficiently prepared' environmental impact statement (CEQ, 1981:2). Brown (1998), however, points out that scoping should be used to design an assessment process that is integrated with the series of decisions that are involved in programme planning and design.

Although scoping is typically identified as the first step in an environmental assessment process, effective scoping requires preparation and a preliminary formulation of the key components of the assessment itself: a description of the proposed action (project, policy, programme, planning process), an outline of anticipated impacts, a description of the assessment team and the assessment approach, and an explanation of the planned decision-making process and schedule, including how interested and affected parties will be involved. (Some countries cover some of these functions in the 'screening' process used to decide whether a proposal requires an EIA – see Wood, 1995.) The requirement to conduct an open scoping process enables those outside the group of proponents, assessment team and regulators to participate in the definition of the problems and issues to be addressed. This requirement for openness is considered one of the most important and influential aspects of the US National Environmental Policy Act (NEPA) and the Council for Environmental Quality regulations for its implementation (CEQ, 1978, 1981; Swartz and Reinke, 1999).

The open scoping process has been crucial in providing a forum for potentially affected publics to clarify links between the biophysical and social environments, raise issues about social impacts, articulate their different world views and values, and differing definitions of the environment, and insist that the assessment and decision process pay attention to them. This has been particularly important for assessments that deal with indigenous peoples, where the greatest differences and least mutual understanding are likely to occur and where scoping is especially challenging because of the diversity of stakeholders and perspectives and the challenges of incorporating different value sets, knowledge systems, and ways of describing environmental components and impacts (Craig & Ehrlich *et al.*, 1996; Mulvihill and Jacobs, 1998; Ross, 1990, 1992). Participatory scoping also provides the opportunity to engage those with concerns and interests in the assessment in the process of identifying and working through their own assessment of the trade-offs associated with alternative courses of action (Wynne, 1996; Yankelovich, 1991). Since scoping requires information about the people who are likely to be affected by and interested in the assessment and an ability to design the public forums (if any) of the scoping process, it has tended to clarify (for others) the importance of having anthropologists and other social scientists on the environmental assessment team.

It is particularly important to be familiar with the regulatory framework for environmental and social impact assessment, and with the conventions about the impact assessment process, because the social assessment is often combined with an environmental assessment or planning process. A number of helpful reference manuals and guidelines are available (Erickson, 1994; Interorganizational Committee on Guidelines and Principles, 1994; Jain, Urban & Stacey, 1977; Shirley, Hickey, Strong & Sander, 1985; Swartz & Reinke, 1999;).

Regulatory Requirements

Over the last three decades of the twentieth century, a variety of laws and regulations have been implemented that require governmental agencies and those making policies or utilizing public resources to clearly identify economic, environmental and social impacts before making a decision or taking action, and to make this information known to the potentially affected publics. The US National Environmental Policy Act (NEPA) of 1969 and the Council of Environmental Quality (CEQ) Regulations and Policy Guidance are key documents that were influential in setting the stage for formal environmental impact assessment processes worldwide. A number of countries, including Australia, modelled their EIS Acts on NEPA, albeit with some key differences.

Section 1501.7 of the CEQ regulations (40 *Code of Federal Regulations*) states:

> There shall be an early and open process for determining the scope of issues to be addressed and for identifying the significant issues related to a proposed action. As soon as practicable after its decision to prepare an environmental impact statement and before the scoping process the lead agency shall publish a notice of intent (Section 1508.22) in the *Federal Register*. . . As part of the scoping process the lead agency [responsible for the assessment] shall:
>
> - Invite the participation of affected federal, state and local agencies, any affected Indian tribe, the proponent of the action, and other interested persons (including those who might not be in accord with the action on environmental grounds – with some limited exceptions).
> - Determine the scope . . . and the significant issues to be analysed in depth in the environmental impact statement.
> - Identify and eliminate from detailed study the issues which are not significant or which have been covered by prior environmental review . . . narrowing the discussion of these issues in the statement to a brief presentation of why they will not have a significant effect on the human environment or providing a reference to their coverage elsewhere.
> - Allocate assignments for preparation of the environmental impact statement among the lead and cooperating agencies, with the lead agency retaining responsibility for the statement.
> - Indicate any public environmental assessments and other environmental impact statements which are being or will be prepared that are related to but are not part of the scope of the impact statement under consideration.
> - Identify other environmental review and consultation requirements so the lead and cooperating agencies may prepare other required analyses and studies concurrently with, and integrated with, the environmental impact statement.
> - Indicate the relationship between the timing of the preparation of environmental analyses and the agency's tentative planning and decision-making schedule.

Section 1508.25, on the Scope of the assessment states:

> Scope consists of the range of actions, alternatives and impacts to be considered in an environmental impact statement. The scope of an individual statement may depend on its relationships to other statements . . . To determine the scope of environmental impact statements, agencies shall consider 3 types of actions, 3 types of alternatives, and 3 types of impacts. They include:
>
> - Actions (other than unconnected single actions) which may be:
>   - Connected actions . . .
>   - Cumulative actions, which when viewed with other proposed actions have cumulatively significant impacts and should therefore be discussed in the same impact statement.
>   - Similar actions, which when viewed with other reasonably foreseeable or proposed agency actions, have similarities that provide a basis for evaluating their environmental consequences together, such as common timing or geography.
> - Alternatives, which include:
>   - No action alternative.
>   - Other reasonable courses of actions.
>   - Mitigation measures (not in the proposed action).
> - Impacts, which may be:
>   - Direct.
>   - Indirect.
>   - Cumulative.

It is important to note the systematic basis for including representatives of stakeholder groups, especially indigenous peoples, the focus on identifying where study effort is best expended, and the opportunity to consider interactive effects with other change-actions which are not within the brief of your study.

The Environmental Assessment Process

In order to plan and conduct an effective scoping process, it is vital to understand some of the core concepts, conventions, and methods of the environmental assessment paradigm and process under which the social assessment will be conducted. These vary from country to country (Wood, 1995) and it is quite possible for accepted practice to be far in advance of that prescribed – sometimes decades before – in legislation.

The typical environmental assessment process involves stages of :

1. Problem identification and scoping
2. Formulation of alternatives to the proposed action
3. Evaluation of the alternatives

4 Formulation and evaluation of mitigation and enhancement measures
5 Design and implementation of a monitoring program.

Theoretical Foundations

Both environmental and social assessments are based on the premise that change, and hence impacts, can be predicted or forecast well enough to inform planning and management decisions. By and large, these predictions are based on cause and effect change analyses of greater or less complexity, theoretical grounding, and rigour. At one extreme, predictions are derived through the logic of analogy, at the other they are based on theoretically sophisticated and empirically grounded computerized models that work through first-, second- and third-order interactions and feedback linkages.

These assumptions about causality and the ability to forecast the future are long overdue for reconsideration (Branch & Ross, 1998). Analysis of social change is complicated by the emergent nature of human response and social organization, and by the important role played by people's values and interpretations in forming their responses to anticipated and actual change. Indeed, individuals' and communities' responses to actions with the potential to cause social change are so variable that one cannot be definitive about eventual impacts. The art is more akin to forecasting or assessment of risks: one can highlight an impact as probable or highly damaging (even if not highly probable), and hence deserving of care. Not all individuals or communities will be affected in the same ways, however, and a myriad of intervention opportunities exist for the outcomes to differ from expectations.

There is an on-going effort to buttress the theoretical and empirical bases for social impact assessment. In impact assessment, social scientists expect, and are expected, to use the theories of their disciplines. A frustrating aspect of this for social assessors is that social theories tend to be either too broad (the Marxist and sociological theories presenting conflict as an essential process generating social change; anthropological theories such as structural/functionalism[3]), or too specific (the myriad of micro-level psychological theories such as relative deprivation) to afford adequate guidance in the assessment of particular projects and issues. Like applied researchers in other fields, many social assessors have adopted variants of grounded theory (Glaser & Strauss, 1967), in effect an approach rather than a theory, which advocates building up theory from observation of a situation. (Ethnography often works in a similar way to grounded theory, by building up a 'picture' of how a society works through an iterative process of cumulation and critical analysis of observations.) Effective *meso-theories* that combine insights from across the social sciences are needed to guide social assessment and scoping.

Over the three decades since the passage of the US National Environmental Policy Act in 1969, social impact assessment has progressively extended its scope and become more differentiated as it adapted to address the *impact-causing concerns of the day* – the introduction or shut-down of large projects in small isolated communities; exposure to the risks and damage of hazardous materials and toxic wastes; restrictions on the use of natural resources. Whereas *social* impacts were initially defined as and limited to economic consequences, public clamour and professional effort gradually extended the concept to include demographic, then fiscal and facilities/services, then social structure, and finally psychological, cultural, and health impacts.[4] Social impact assessment has participated in the continuing transition toward *systems thinking* that has occurred during the three decades of its formal existence, and social impact assessors are now concerned (or should be) with incorporating social concerns and planning approaches into Strategic Environmental Assessment (SEA). Policy issues and public concerns associated with global systemic changes such as the globalization of the world's economies, the introduction of genetically engineered crops and livestock, and climate change are emerging and are likely to be subject to impact assessment in the relatively near future (Branch & Ross, 1998; Rayner & Malone, 1998; Ross 1994). So, one cannot rely only on what has been found important in previous impact assessments, but must design a process that responds to changing types of proposed actions/alternatives and changing public perceptions about what is acceptable and what is of concern.

Several theoretical frameworks have been published to help social impact assessors identify key aspects of vulnerability or resilience to impacts (e.g. Branch, Hooper, Thompson & Creighton, 1984; Bowles, 1981, Blishen, Lockhart, Craig & Lockhart, 1979; Deitz, 1987; Little & Krannich, 1988). The choice of an appropriate model depends upon the types of impacts that might occur: the frameworks cited above are appropriate for large projects affecting small communities, where there is a potential for changes in occupational and population characteristics to affect the overall social organization of the community (levels of diversity/complexity; outside linkages; distribution of resources/power; co-ordination and co-operation/conflict; personal interactions). Edelstein (1988) describes common patterns of response to contamination from land and water, and also provides a useful model to illustrate how individual and various scales of social impact can be considered. The existing frameworks have yet to be widely tested for their adaptability to new sets of impacts (McGee & Ross, forthcoming).

The Generic Assessment Paradigm

The fundamental purpose of an assessment is to determine what difference a particular 'proposed action' (project, policy, or planning process) will make while also identifying situations where the changes caused by the proposed action will combine with those caused by other, unrelated actions to produce 'cumulative impacts' (Buckley, 1998; Carley & Bustelo, 1984). Assessments are usually conducted on actions that themselves extend over a substantial period of time (months or years) and that have significant effects on the natural and human environment that persist at least this long or longer. Indeed, one of the major responsibilities of an assessment is to determine whether the effects will be transitory or long-lasting and to determine how they will be distributed across geographic space and social groups.

The need to analyse effects over time introduces difficult analytic complications that are often compounded by the presence of other change agents. Neither the natural nor the human environment is static over time – both undergo continual change. The assessment paradigm therefore calls for the construction and comparison of two forecasts. The first, usually called the 'baseline projection' or the 'future without', describes future conditions as they would be without the proposed action; the second, often called the 'with-project forecast', describes future conditions as they would be with the proposed action (Branch *et al.*, 1984; Leistritz & Murdock, 1981). Unless current conditions would continue unchanged into the future in the absence of the proposed action, differences between current and future conditions cannot be attributed to the proposed action. Figure 4.1 illustrates the generic environmental assessment paradigm used in a number of countries.

Because impacts develop and occur over time, a significant aspect of impact assessment is to identify and take into account second- and third-order consequences that occur as initial changes affect other elements of the biophysical and social environment, and as the receiving systems respond to the initial changes. For example, an increase in jobs can increase population, which can create a demand for additional housing, change land use (Leistritz & Murdock, 1981), and marginalize Aboriginal people within their region (Howitt, 1993). Burning a forest can create a meadow that increases deer population, which can lead to an increase in the number of hunters, and so on (Taylor, Bryan & Goodrich, 1995:80).

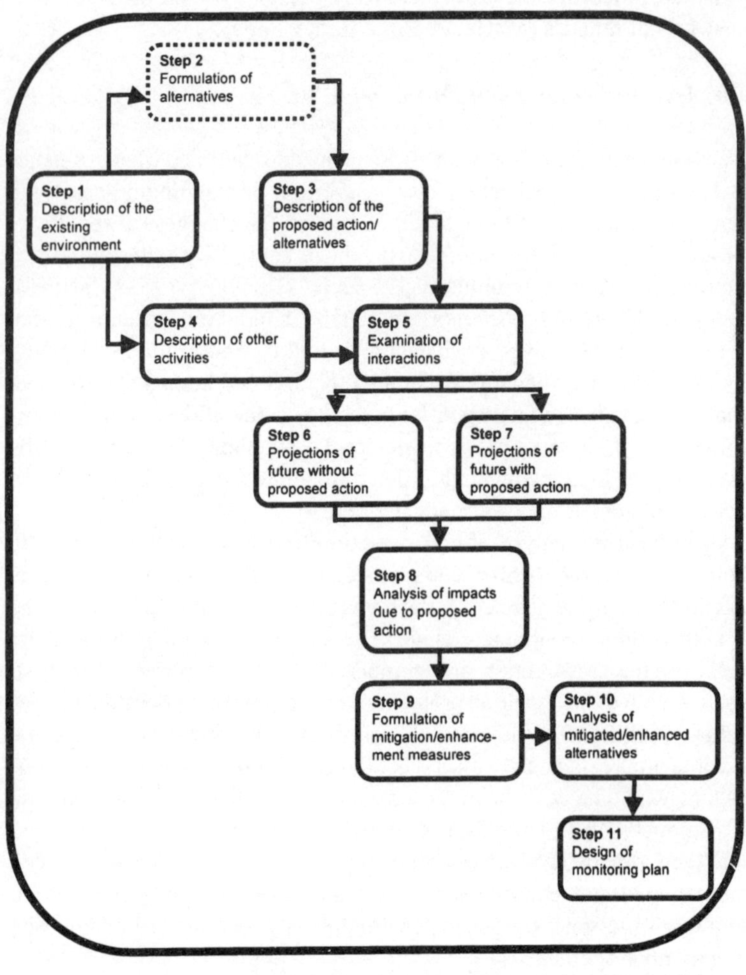

Figure 4.1 The Impact Assessment Process

Although there has been much discussion about the limited ability to develop a single prediction of social impacts, given the complexity and reflexivity of social change, and the potential value of alternative paradigms (e.g. scenario building) in formal assessments, the single forecast has generally persisted (Burdge, 1998:13–39).

The Participatory Framework

An increasingly important premise of impact assessment worldwide is that the potentially affected publics have a right to know about a proposed action and the assessment process, to participate in defining the scope and focus of the assessment, and to have their views taken into account in the assessment and decision making process (Branch & Ross, 1998; Cernea & Kudar, 1997; Cornwall & Jewkes, 1995). In addition, as discussed elsewhere in this manual, it is also becoming better understood and accepted that the knowledge and understanding of local residents and other stakeholders constitute a valuable, possibly essential, resource for the assessment and that the proponent and decision makers have a responsibility to design a participatory process that is effective and inclusive. In part, this recognition has come as a consequence of the conclusion by proponents and decision makers that such participation improves acceptability. A number of guides have been developed on public participation (or public involvement or public consultation as it is sometimes called) (Connor, 1995; Creighton, 1985), so the specifics of designing and conducting public participation are not addressed here. In general, public participation is most important and most challenging when the impacts are perceived to involve high stakes and high uncertainty (Ravetz, 1987), when multi-cultural populations are affected, when the proponent is perceived to be arrogant, aggressive and/or antagonistic, and when accountability to the public for managing and mitigating impacts is perceived to be unclear or inadequate (Bradbury, Branch, Heerwagen & Leibow, 1994).

In addition to development of a participation process for the overall assessment, as pointed out throughout this manual, social assessments are particularly reliant on the participation of the affected publics to help understand the existing culture, social structure and values, sense of place, and expectations and value judgements about the proposed action. These are key factors in social groupings and sectors' interpretations and responses to proposals for change, their resilience or vulnerability to the changes, and capacity to make the most of opportunities that the proposed actions might afford.

In scoping, as much as in the remainder of a study, it is worth assimilating the advice of Yankelovich, (1991:160–74) on assisting the public in developing their judgment about important proposed actions and policy alternatives. He identifies ten rules for engaging the public in dialogue that encourages this development. These rules are:

- On any given issue, it is usually safe to assume that the public and the experts will be out of phase. To bridge the gap leaders must learn what the public's starting point is and how to address it.
- Do not depend on experts to present issues.
- Learn what the public's pet preoccupation is and address it before discussing any other facet of the issue.
- Give the public the incentive of knowing that someone is listening . . . and cares.
- Limit the number of issues to which people must attend at any one time to two or three at most.
- 'Working through' is best accomplished when people have choices to consider.
- Leaders must take the initiative in highlighting the value components of choices.
- To move beyond the 'say-yes-to-everything' or 'say-no-to-everything' form of procrastination, the public needs help.
- When two conflicting values are both important to the public, resolution should be sought by developing alternatives that preserve some elements of each.
- Use the time factor as a key part of the communication strategy.

The Assessment Team and the Collaborative Framework

Environmental assessments are usually conducted as an interdisciplinary team effort. Team leaders and members therefore need to organize planning, teamwork, monitoring and reporting progress, and technical interactions to make the team work effectively. There are certain challenges in establishing and maintaining communication between social and physical science members of a large assessment team. In the scoping phase, it is essential to set up this teamwork, and to identify interactions among team members with different areas of specialization. For instance, anthropologists study people's symbolic and physical interactions with their environments. The interactions important to a particular society, such as subsistence hunting, will point the anthropologist towards those physical scientists dealing with the environmental characteristics concerned in the species hunted, their habitats and food (and water) chains. Systems analysis, common to both social and physical sciences, can provide a basis for communication. As the study progresses, techniques such as geographic information systems (GIS) can sometimes provide a common template and focus for discussion across different stakeholders and team members.

Taylor *et al.* (1995:79) point out that it is insufficient to have specialists working on their own small piece of the scoping or assessment and emphasize the importance of designing teams with the expertise to identify and address the interactions in the environment. They recommend initiating a 'specific process to link biophysical and social variables in a 'web' of cause and effects relationships . . .' where the team takes each proposed action (like burning a forest to reduce future fire risk) and examines the proximate and secondary–tertiary web of consequences (in increase/decrease terms).

This is particularly important to achieve a valid assessment of the impacts resulting from the interaction of humans and the natural environment (health impacts, impacts due to changes in resource use or the landscape, etc.). A valuable approach is to consider existing interactions and dependencies between people and their environment and strive to understand:

1 What symbolic or other cultural connections people ascribe to the environment, such as sacredness of landscape features, sense of place, subsistence uses of animals and plants – what types of disturbances to the place or its species would interfere with this relationship, and how would affected communities feel about this? Could there be secondary effects, such as undermining traditional beliefs?
2 What uses and dependencies are there for food, socialization in cultural knowledge, good health, and so on?

For instance, if a mining project is likely to contaminate groundwater, and local indigenous settlements use the groundwater as a water source, what are the health risks to the people? If surface water could be contaminated, which species could be contaminated as a result, and what will be the impact on their populations and the indigenous people who hunt them? What behaviour patterns put people in contact with this surface water (for example swimming or doing laundry)? If places or species which are culturally important to a people are damaged irrevocably, what could be the spiritual, economic and social effects?

A Framework for Social Impact Assessment

The framework shown in Figure 4.2 provides an analytical underpinning for scoping and, later, the social impact assessment. It provides an aid for identifying possible linkages between attributes of a proposed action and attributes of the social environment. Ethnographies, local knowledge, analysis of literature about the affected communities, type of intervention, and typical effects, as well as use of social change theories are necessary to trace the linkages. For instance, new mining operations in remote parts of Australia bring in large numbers of employees with different skills and characteristics for the construction and operational phases of the mine. According to the framework, this could have impacts on community resources and community social organization: – but how? Further information or past experience is necessary to appreciate the types of impacts that are likely to occur. It would be informative to know, for example, that in the past, Australian mine construction workforces of mainly single males sought the company of local Aboriginal women in remote areas, creating social tensions and potentially affecting social organization through births and distortion of linkages to traditional country. They also increased local Aborigines' access to alcohol, with serious effects on relationships within communities, and spent leisure time encroaching on Aborigines' sacred places, or hunting, fishing and recreation spaces which Aborigines preferred to enjoy alone. These potential impacts are now managed effectively by the mining companies. What has not been managed so easily is the sense of social, political and educational marginalization of Aboriginal people when they suddenly become a minority in their own land.

A key requirement for effective scoping and assessment of social impacts is an assessment team skilled in analysing the specific types of interactions that could occur between the proposed action and the social environment. Depending upon the characteristics of the proposed action, locale and potentially affected people, this can require a team that includes anthropologists or sociologists, specialists in regional and or resource economics, demography, facilities, services, and fiscal analysis, community and social change, public health, aesthetics and visual analysis, social psychology, and so on. There may be several different 'affected publics', which different disciplines will be best prepared to address. For instance, in the commissioned research supporting a public inquiry into proposed mining in the Alligator Rivers region of Australia, the impacts on Aborigines were studied by four teams specializing in social impact assessment, anthropological analysis (concentrating on the significance of sacred sites), archaeological analysis, and economic impacts on Aborigines. Impacts on tourism and the wider economy were studied under other consultancies (Resource Assessment Commission, 1991).

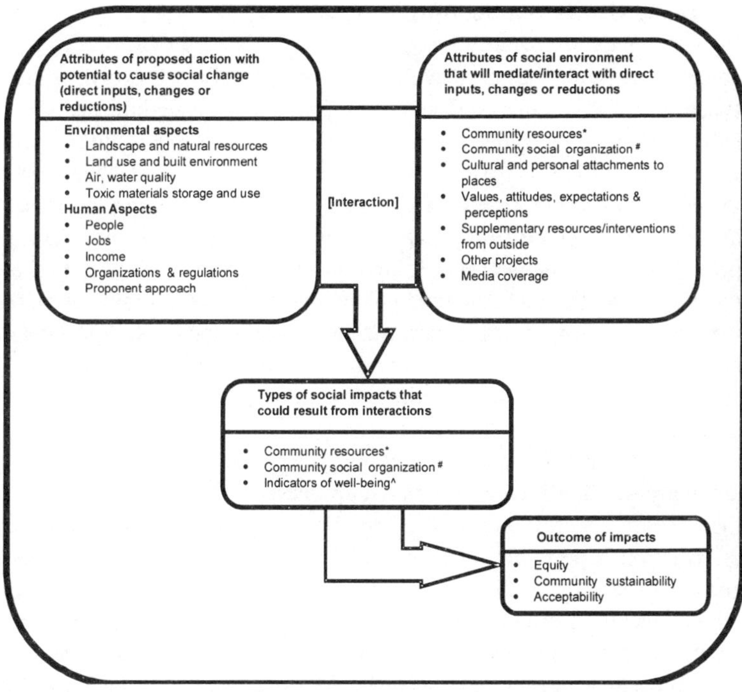

* Community resources =	# Community social organization =	^ Indicators of well-being = (reflecting issues/values)
• Physical environment and natural resources and their use • Historical experience • Demographic characteristics • Occupational/labour force characteristics • Facilities/services/ fiscal resources • Organizational & regulatory structure • Political skills and leadership • Cultural characteristics and values	• Diversity/complexity • Outside linkages • Distribution of resources/power • Co-ordination & co-operation/conflict • Personal interactions & relationships	• Health and safety • Sovereignty • Conflict • Co-operation • Employment • Cohesion • Satisfaction • Perceived risk

Figure 4.2 Framework for Initial Screening

Working through a Scoping Process

Impact assessment has been evolving and will continue to evolve as new types of activities and policies are proposed and better information is assembled about the range and significance of impacts that result. Indeed, this is one of the key reasons that scoping continues to be needed: past experience does not provide a reliable basis for anticipating the issues and impacts of current proposals. The same is true for the information provided in this manual: it can highlight only issues and impacts that have been identified to date (and it is undoubtedly not thorough in that). Consequently, the scoping process outlined in the following section should be used as a *guide* to the *analytic thought process* and participatory activities that can be used to help focus and prepare for a social impact assessment.

It is important to remember that both the scoping and the assessment are analytical, not merely descriptive, processes. Therefore, throughout the assessment, a continuing effort must be made to identify what information is pertinent to the analysis of the proposed action's social consequences and to avoid extensive reporting on information that is merely background and has little or no direct bearing on the assessment. However, also remember that it is important to document this process of refinement and focusing to provide a defensible, readily available record of the assessment process. It is frequently useful to be able to review this process when preparing reports and presenting information to the public. Also, if the proposed action is subsequently modified in the middle of the assessment (as is often the case), such documentation is useful in determining what modifications are needed.

Steps in a Scoping Process

We have the challenge here of describing scoping for an international set of jurisdictions, some with and some without public participation in scoping. Whether or not there will be a public scoping process, the research team typically prepares an initial analysis to refine and integrate their research tasks before commencing research.

Social assessments are often performed by social scientists on behalf of or under contract to a third party (lead agency, regulator, proponent, community, interest group). In addition, many if not most of the assessments will involve a team of specialists in different aspects of impact assessment. Consequently, social scientists often work as part of a team and need to conduct the following internally and externally focused steps:

1 Clarify the purpose and role of the overall assessment.
2 See how the overall assessment effort is organized and clarify the social scientists' role in it.
3 Conduct a preliminary social analysis that is co-ordinated with other aspects of the study.
4 Contribute to the design and conduct of the public scoping process (if any).
5 Analyse public input and develop a work plan for the social impact assessment.

Clarify the Purpose and Role of the Overall Assessment Assessment activities have different objectives and requirements at different stages of the particular decision-making process being implemented. The first step in an effective scoping process is to clarify the purpose of the assessment and the role it is to play in the planning and decision-making processes. In general, environmental and social impact assessments are conducted to:

1 Disclose information about proposed activities to those who might be affected by them and identify problems and issues associated with those activities and their implementation.
2 Help planners, decision makers and the affected publics predict changes that will result from the proposed activities and understand their meaning and significance.
3 Assess the ability and willingness of the affected communities or groups to adapt to those changes.
4 Identify mitigation and impact management opportunities or requirements.
5 Meet regulatory or policy requirements.

The type of proposal being assessed, which may range from a broad policy (strategic assessment) to an overall programme (programmatic assessment) or a specific project (site-specific assessment), can influence the purpose of the assessment as can its relationship to other assessments, for example as one of a 'tiered' set.

See how the Overall Assessment Effort is Organized and Clarify the Social Scientists' Role in it It is also important to understand the relationships among the decision-making, assessment and public participation processes and the social scientists' role and responsibilities in them. In particular, it is important to understand:

1 Why the assessment is being conducted (see above).
2 How the social assessment fits into the overall assessment effort.
3 The responsibilities of the organization or individuals conducting the assessment and their relationship to the project/policy proponents or planners, regulators and interested parties.
4 The legal and regulatory requirements governing the assessment, and other legislation that interacts with it.[5]
5 The schedule and budget available for the assessment.
6 The nature of the decisions to be made, by whom, and when.
7 How the public is to be informed and involved.
8 How the assessment is to be documented and information disseminated.

One of the greatest complaints of impact assessment specialists is the difficulty of ensuring that the assessment is empowered to address the critical issues and that the results will be presented clearly and considered seriously. If you wish to renegotiate any aspect of your professional role, including its integration with other parts of the assessment, this is a good time to do so. For instance, one of the team was hired by a government department to conduct a social impact assessment concerning an Aboriginal community housing project. That person negotiated with the department that they should report equally to the department and the affected community, to improve the information flow and the community's potential to adapt to the changes. This worked well: the community became proactive towards the changes and reconstituted its leadership in order to meet the challenges. Bellman (1993) offers some good advice for dealing with these types of issues.

Conduct a Preliminary Social Analysis that is Co-ordinated with the Other Aspects of the Team's Analysis The purpose of conducting a preliminary social analysis is to prepare for the public scoping activities or, if no public process will be conducted, to prepare for the analytic work. An important function of these initial screening steps is to help the social scientists think through the task they are undertaking and provide a structure for assembling information to help understand the nature of the problem being faced. If no public scoping activity is planned, the preliminary analysis will help the social scientists interpret and check the adequacy of their brief. They will need to co-ordinate among themselves and with other members of the team regarding study area, units of analysis/data aggregation, time periods, integration of findings and how other actions proposed for the study area are to be addressed. This is an iterative process – co-ordination with other members of the assessment team and interactions with the public are likely to identify new issues, different pathways, and additional interactions that will influence the framework of the assessment and other team members.

The assessment team may discover that it needs to add members with missing specializations.

A preliminary analysis typically includes:

1 Identifying and describing the attributes of the proposed action with the potential to cause social impacts.
2 Identifying the attributes of the social environment that need to be described to complete the scoping process.
3 Obtaining preliminary information about the potentially affected communities and social groups.
4 Working through the screening process (identifying the potential for interaction between the attributes of the proposed action and the existing social environment).
5 Summarizing the results in a presentation that will be useful to the public in the public scoping meetings.

At this stage in the scoping process the goal is to assemble key information about the proposed action, make a first estimate of the areas likely to be affected, including a preliminary determination of which communities, tribal nations or social groups will need to be addressed as separate units of analysis, and develop a preliminary analysis of potential social effects. Because the aim at this stage is to identify what types of social impacts might result, with a general idea of their geographic and social distribution and importance, the emphasis is on obtaining enough information to examine the interactions between the proposed action and the existing social environment. Consequently, although this step requires an understanding of the same mechanisms of social change that are needed for the impact assessment itself, it does not require the same detail in the development of forecasts or comparisons to baseline conditions.

Identify and Describe the Attributes of the Proposed Action with Potential to Cause Social Impacts It is essential to obtain or develop a description of the proposed action and to identify those attributes with potential to cause social change and impacts in any of three ways – directly, indirectly or cumulatively. Knowing the attributes of the proposed action can help focus the assessment both geographically and topically – i.e. which areas need to be examined, and what you need to know about them – as well as identifying the mechanisms and pathways by which interaction between the proposed action and the existing environment could result in social impacts of importance. The benefit of knowing this is that it helps to:

1 Identify what information is needed about the proposed action and the social environment.
2 Identify bio-physical/social interactions that need special attention.
3 Start designing the research and analytic methods needed to address the specific cause and effect relationships anticipated to be most important in the assessment.

Sometimes it is not possible to form a clear picture of the 'proposed action', for instance if information is withheld as 'commercial-in-confidence', or nebulous such as in climate impact assessment.

In general, social scientists are responsible for determining whether the proposed action could cause the following types of changes:

1 The conditions, use or access to the landscape and natural resources.
2 Land-use patterns and the built environment.
3 Air and water quality.
4 The storage or use of hazardous or toxic materials.
5 The number and/or characteristics of people in the affected area.
6 The number or types of jobs.
7 The level or distribution of income.
8 Private and government sector resources/infrastructure (e.g. housing, commercial resources, recreational resources); local, state, or tribal/indigenous people's government (e.g. revenues, facilities).
9 The organizational and regulatory context (e.g. changes in regulatory control, changes in policies, changes in social organizations and activities.
10 Relationship between the proponent and the affected population (e.g. proponent approach: antagonistic/aggressive, accommodating).
11 Cumulative effects (for instance tourism can follow the construction of roads into a remote town).

Figures 4.3 and 4.4 illustrate the *types* of questions social scientists will want to answer during the preliminary analysis. Answering these questions identifies not only the attributes of the proposed action that need to be described, but also many of the attributes of the existing social environment about which information will be needed. Branch *et al.* (1984) provide more detail on this process. For simplicity, these figures are based on the typical change patterns arising from large new developments in lightly populated areas. Different questions would be required for more complex impact assessment questions, such as the impacts of climate change.

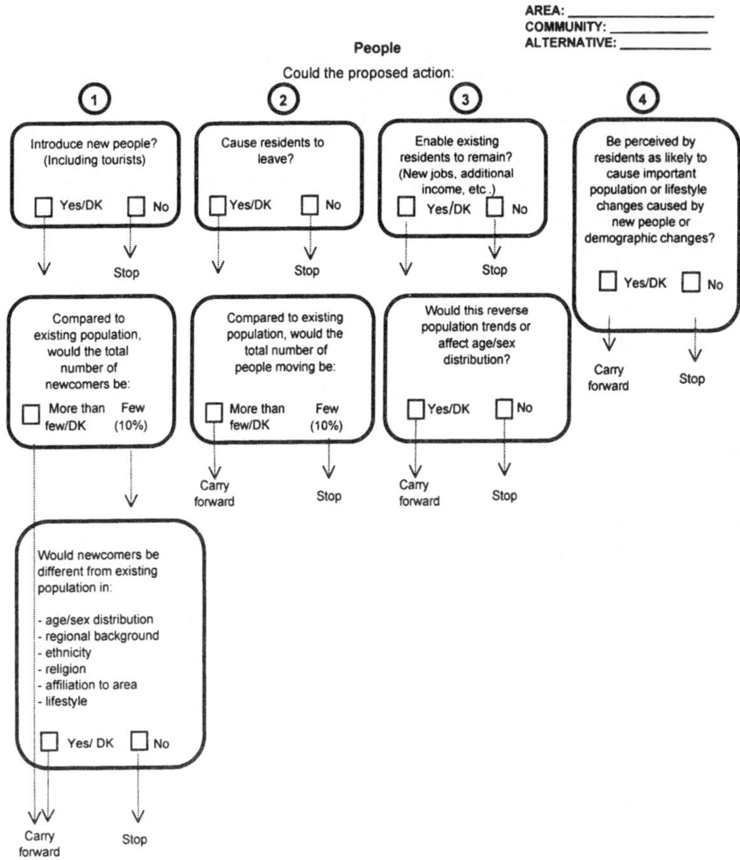

Figure 4.3 Identifying Potential for Impacts from Changes in People

This analysis provides the basis for focusing attention on the important analytic problems and determining the appropriate units of analysis for the study. At this stage of the assessment process, this analysis can often be done in more general, categorical terms, identifying the nature, general magnitude, approximate geographic location, and the general pattern of the potential changes (gradual and steady, intense and erratic) caused directly by the proposed action. It is often not easy to obtain an accurate

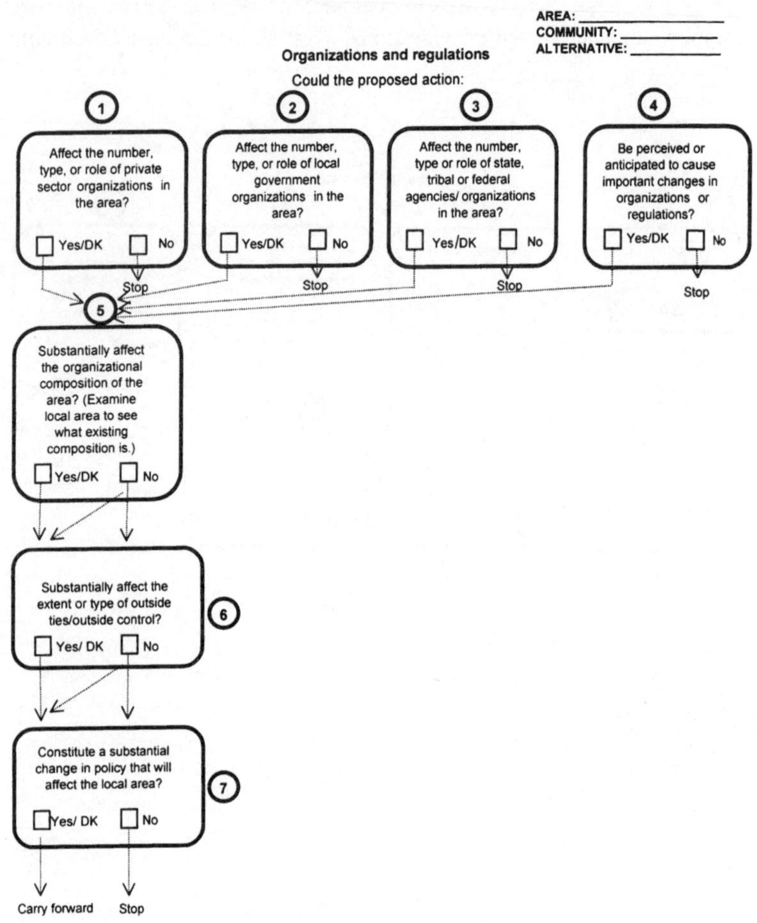

Figure 4.4 Identifying Potential for Impacts from Changes in Organizations and Institutions

description of these attributes of the proposed action, particularly as they vary across space and time. To obtain an accurate description of the proposed action it is often necessary to submit detailed information requests to the proponent and to carefully verify the information that is provided (for example, by comparing it with other, similar projects). However, for the scoping process, relatively general information can often suffice. What is learned about how difficult it will be to obtain accurate, sufficiently disaggregated information about the proposed action will be useful in planning the assessment effort. In addition, it may reveal whether the proponent is taking a co-operative or antagonistic approach toward the assessment and the affected communities.

Identify which Attributes of the Existing Social Environment need to be Described for the Scoping Process Once the attributes of the proposed action have been identified and described, the next step is to make a preliminary identification of which communities, geographic areas or jurisdictional units need to be included in the study area, which attributes of the existing social environment are important, and what information about those attributes is needed. The important characteristics of the existing social environment are those that will either affect the characteristics of the proposed action or the response made by the community to the proposed action, or be affected in an important way by the proposed action or by the responses made to it. As a general rule, at this phase, if there is doubt about the potential for impact it is best to carry a community or area and topical focus into the next phase of the assessment. Obviously, this step calls for judgement. Communities need not be geographically close to the location of a proposed action in order to be affected – for instance, historical displacement of indigenous societies in Australia, the USA and Canada means that people may no longer live within the places with which they have close spiritual affiliations. Depending upon the type of proposed action, the attributes of the social environment that may be pertinent to the assessment include:

1 Community resources:
   (a) physical environment and natural resources and their use
   (b) historical experience
   (c) demographic characteristics
   (d) occupational and labour-force characteristics
   (e) facilities, services and fiscal resources
   (f) organizational and regulatory structure
   (g) political skills and leadership
   (h) cultural characteristics and values.
2 Community social organization:
   (a) diversity and complexity
   (b) outside linkages
   (c) distribution of resources and power
   (d) co-ordination and co-operation or conflict
   (e) personal interactions and relationships.

3 Sense of place.
4 Values, attitudes, expectations and perceptions.
5 Supplementary resources and interventions from outside.
6 Other projects.
7 Media coverage.

The same references identified as useful concerning the theoretical frameworks also provide a more detailed definition and discussion of these attributes. The information already assembled about the proposed action and its potential to cause change should be used to help determine which attributes of the existing social environment are likely to be pertinent to the assessment of impacts, and therefore what information about the existing environment will need to be obtained. Different types of proposed actions will require assessments with different topical focuses, and hence require different information about the existing social environment. It is important to remember that the screening process is preparatory: its purpose is to help prepare for the public scoping process (if any) where additional information and perspectives will be obtained and the scope revised, and for the assessment itself.

Obtain Preliminary Information about the Potentially Affected Communities/Social Groups There is usually little time available to collect comprehensive information at the scoping stage. It is important to coordinate the information-gathering effort with other members of the assessment team, to avoid duplication of effort, contradictory assumptions, and inefficient or inappropriate use of community contacts. If possible, the social scientists should visit the study area and talk with representatives of the potentially affected communities and social groups, as well as those familiar with them, making sure to follow an appropriate protocol for contacting and interacting with them. This is especially important if indigenous people are involved. Depending upon the locale, information about the area as well as about the proposed action and the communities, and area residents' attitudes and perceptions regarding potential changes may be available. Examples of such data sources include:

1 Previous research on the locale, including ethnographies and local histories.
2 Studies of similar types of actions or similar communities.
3 Census data, including special censuses.
4 County comprehensive plans.
5 Clippings from local newspapers.

6 Employment and unemployment data (e.g. from the US Bureau of Economic Analysis or state employment offices).
7 Records of public meetings where the proposed action or similar actions have been discussed.
8 Records of public response to the proposed action or similar proposals.

Such sources should be identified and reviewed, to the extent that they are pertinent, before additional primary data are collected. Once this is done, members of the affected publics can be interviewed to determine how the problem of the assessment and the proposed action are being framed and to identify specific issues that will need to be addressed in the assessment.

Identify the Potential for Interaction between the Attributes of the Proposed Action and the Existing Social Environment It is now time to work through the interactions between the attributes of the proposed action and those of the existing social environment, ideally as a collaborative exercise with the other members of the assessment team. Having members of affected communities formally on the research team, or collaborating through a method such as action research, can be particularly helpful here. The 'webbing and chaining' process described by Taylor *et al.* (1995:80) is useful here. It takes the results of analyses such as those illustrated by Figures 4.3 and 4.4, which identify first-order changes, and traces them through subsequent cause-and-effect interactions to identify potential impacts and topics of inquiry. They emphasize the importance of involving members of the assessment team with different specialities in this process to ensure that interactions between biophysical and social variables are not missed. It is important to note that the purpose of this 'work through' is to identify the potential pathways through which impacts could be caused, thus helping to determine the appropriate focus for the assessment. The social assessment team can take the lead in working through the interactions between the attributes of the proposed action and the attributes of the existing social environment they have been working on, while other members of the team can take the lead in interactions that involve other attributes of the proposed action and the existing environment. Obviously, this is not a simple task and, in fact, it anticipates most of what is involved in conducting a social impact assessment.

Contribute to the Design and Conduct of the Public Scoping Process In the US, the social assessment team frequently have the opportunity to help design the public scoping process and may be called upon to serve as facilitators or participants in the public scoping meetings. Typically, considerable effort goes into the planning of these public meetings and the preparation of informational materials to support them (for example from the preliminary screening). The US regulations specify little about the nature of the public scoping process, requiring only adequate notice, accessibility, and accurate recording of the public's comments. CEQ guidelines do specifically require that indigenous people be provided an opportunity to participate. In recent years, there has been movement away from the traditional centralized, highly formal public meetings to more decentralized, smaller and less formal meetings that are designed to encourage discussion and interaction.

An effective *participatory* scoping process must include the range of people capable of giving both expert and locally informed opinion, it must provide appropriate information about the proposed action and the proposed assessment process to the public in a timely manner, and it must structure meetings and exchanges in a way that encourages and facilitates the expression of public concerns, issues and knowledge. Designing a process that achieves this is not easy, particularly in intercultural settings. Through their work on the Great Whale hydroelectric project, Mulvihill and Jacobs (1998) identified seven factors that are needed to make a scoping process effective in an intercultural setting:

1 Broadly accessible.
2 Clear to the proponent, but responsive to the intervenors (organizations or parties participating to represent their interests in the issue, such as indigenous groups, other local communities, and environmental organizations).
3 Capable of addressing competing world views (for instance in the scoping study for the Great Whale project, the Inuit and Cree peoples had entirely different definitions and understanding of the 'environment' and their relationships to it than the proponents and many of the non-native residents of the area).
4 Characterized by fairness, comprehensiveness and efficiency.
5 More analytical than encyclopedic.
6 Predisposed to accommodate an adequate, but not infinite, problem definition.
7 Receptive to both qualitative and quantitative input.

Even if the social scientists are not asked to play a major role in designing the public scoping process, they have a responsibility to make sure that indigenous groups, and any other categories of people likely to be vulnerable to impacts and marginalized in the assessment, are identified and taken into account in the design and planning. In addition, because of the work they have already done, the social scientists can help those designing the public scoping process anticipate the key issues and concerns of the affected publics, and encourage them to be prepared to answer questions that are likely to arise about the decision-making process, the relationship of the proponent and regulators to the affected communities, and the mechanisms for holding key participants (proponent, lead agency, regulators, assessment team) accountable to the potentially affected publics.

Social scientists are likely to be asked to help prepare informational materials for the public scoping process by summarizing the results of their preliminary screening process and integrating them with information from other members of the assessment team and the proponent. If no one on the social science team is experienced in this, reviewing some of the public participation and risk communication manuals (Creighton, 1985; Lundgren & McMakin, 1998) can help you be attentive to the information needs and communication preferences and abilities of your target audiences. Keep in mind that the public is watching the proponent, the lead agency and the assessment team to assess their openness, competence and commitment to the assessment process.

Analyse Public Input and Develop a Work Plan for the Social Impact Assessment It is important to make full use of the information provided by the public during the scoping process. In the US a complete inventory and detailed analysis of the public input is often prepared as part of the formal record. Because of their training, social scientists may be called upon to help with this process, or the responsibility may be given to someone outside the assessment team. To get full benefit from the information provided by the public, it is best for the social scientists to attend the public meetings and to see and hear them first-hand. It is also worthwhile to read the transcripts of the public input, if they are available. Mulvihill and Jacobs (1998) emphasize the importance of using care in the analysis of public input and of being sensitive to different ways of knowing and different definitions and values so that the assessment and decision making are not inappropriately biased toward the framework and values of the proponent and the dominant social groups.

Once the public's input has been analysed to determine its implications for social assessment, the social scientists need to meet with rest of the assessment team to work out the scope of the overall assessment and of the social assessment as a component within it. Then, drawing upon the public input, an understanding of the overall assessment, and the work already done in the preliminary screening, the social scientists should be in a good position to develop a work plan that lays out the information and data gathering, analysis, integration, and report preparation components of the social assessment.

Key Issues in Scoping for Social Impact Assessment

Several issues have been persistent problems for social assessment, in part because they have not been addressed adequately during the scoping phase of the process. These are particularly challenging because they require interdisciplinary interactions beyond the social sciences, and the topics may involve much uncertainty.

Addressing Human Natural Environment Interactions

Although many social assessments are conducted as components of environmental impact assessments, until recently the assessment process has often separated the social from the biophysical assessment and failed to address linkages and interactions between them. Taylor *et al.* (1995) and Craig & Ehrlich *et al.* (1996:62) have led the way in emphasizing the importance of these linkages and interactions to social assessment and the need to design the assessment process so that social and biophysical scientists/practitioners are working together to identify and analyse these linkages and interactions. Anthropologists, trained to study societies holistically, are well positioned to recognize such linkages. Taylor *et al.* (1995:78) recommend that when the social assessment is being conducted as part of an environmental assessment, 'the scoping needs to be undertaken from the basic proposition that all actions affecting the environment have social effects to varying degrees.' Identifying the need to address these linkages and interactions during the scoping phase of the project and specifically building this analysis into the tool selection, work plans and schedules of the different specialists would be a significant step forward. The increasing availability of tools and methods, such as systems analysis and GIS, that facilitate communication across disciplines should make this easier.

Dealing with Cumulative Impacts and the Concept of Sustainability

Impact assessment is both driving, and being driven by, evolving social definitions and images of sustainability and responsibility. These appear to be increasingly fundamental to the concept of impact assessment, which is being called upon to help decision-makers and community members develop a more systematic sense of desired ends against which potential impacts and feasible alternatives can be compared. The drive for sustainability is also providing part of the impetus for the progressive integration of impact assessment and planning (Armour, 1990), and of analysis and mobilization. It has also given new emphasis to the assessment of cumulative impacts (CEQ, 1997; Cernea & Kudar, 1997; Goodland, 1998).

The 1979 CEQ regulations for the US National Environmental Policy Act (NEPA), published in the US *Federal Register*, defined cumulative effects as: the impact on the environment which results from the incremental impact of the action when added to other past, present, and reasonably foreseeable future actions regardless of what agency (Federal or non-federal) or person undertakes such other actions' (40 CFR 1508.7) (CEQ, 1997:1), and specified that assessments should address them. In 1997, CEQ prepared further guidance on cumulative impact assessment that answered unclear aspects of the 1979 guidelines (Canter & Kamath 1995:312). This guidance identified the following principles for scoping for cumulative effects (1997:11):

- include past, present, and future actions
- include all federal, non-federal, and private actions
- focus on each affected resource, ecosystem, and human community
- focus on truly meaningful effects
- coordinate the assessment with other agencies/assessments.

In addition, CEQ laid out five steps for scoping for cumulative effects (1997:1–21):

1 Identify the significant cumulative effects issues associated with the proposed action and define the assessment goals.
2 Establish the geographic scope for the analysis (often broader than for a project-specific focus).
3 Establish the timeframe for the analysis (often longer than for a project-specific focus).
4 Identify other actions affecting the resources, ecosystems and human communities of concern (past, present and reasonably foreseeable future).
5 Identify the direct and indirect effects of both the proposed and other actions.

However, despite these guidelines, there is widespread agreement that cumulative effects are seldom adequately addressed in either the scoping or analytic phase of most assessments. Ross (1990) points out that one should also examine history for a sense of cumulative impacts affecting the communities and places under study. This is because the 'current conditions' for each social impact assessment task have been shaped by a history of past environmental and social effects. The Warmun Aboriginal community in north-west Australia described their current nature and ability to respond to new impacts – mining, tourism, and land use change – as deriving from their history of near-extermination a century previously, survival through co-optation to the cattle industry, demographic reorganization when award wages and other factors squeezed them out of that industry, then the unanticipated effects of 'equality' measures giving them access to welfare income and alcohol (Ross, 1990).

Summary

Scoping is a useful technique for ensuring that study resources are concentrated on the issues which truly need research, and will be important to decision making. However, it is not a technique that can be specified clearly: it relies a great deal on the skills and experience of those conducting it. Consultation about the identification of issues, whether or not through a participatory approach, is important to ensure that important issues are not missed, and the relative importance of issues is identified to all parties' satisfaction.

In any country, identifying the 'scope' of study is crucial. In the US system, which we have described in some detail here, scoping also serves purposes of public disclosure, involvement and initial documentation. Whether or not there is a participatory process for scoping, the analytic framework laid out in this chapter provides a process for basing study design on a preliminary analysis of the most important likely impacts.

References

Armour, A. (1990), 'Integrating impact assessment into the planning process', *Impact Assessment Bulletin*, 8(1–2):3–14.

Bellman, G.M. (1993), *Getting Things Done When You are Not in Charge*, New York: Simon and Schuster.

Blishen, B.R., Lockhart, A., Craig, P. and Lockhart, E. (1979), *Socio-Economic Impact Model for Northern Development*, Ottawa, Canada: Department of Indian and Northern Affairs.

Bowles, R.T. (1981), *Social Impact Assessment in Small Communities*, Toronto: Butterworth and Co. Ltd.

Bradbury, J.A., Branch, K.M., Heerwagen, J. and Liebow, E. (1994), *Community Viewpoints of the Chemical Stockpile Disposal Program*, prepared by Battelle Pacific Northwest Laboratories, Aberdeen, MD: Department of the Army.

Branch, K.M., Hooper, D.A., Thompson, J. and Creighton, J. (1984), *Guide to Social Assessment: A Framework for Assessing Social Change*, Social Impact Assessment Series No. 11., Boulder, CO: Westview Press.

Branch, K.M. and Ross, H. (1998), 'SIA in the Age of Complexity, Tight Budgets, and Participation', presented at the *International Association of Impact Assessment 1998 Conference*, Christchurch, New Zealand, April, pp. 21–4.

Brown, A.L. (1998), 'Decision-Scoping', in A.L. Porter and J.J. Fittipaldi (eds), *Environmental Methods Review: Retooling Impact Assessment for the New Century*, Atlanta, GA: Army Environmental Policy Institute, Georgia Institute of Technology, pp.135–43.

Buckley, R. (1998), 'Strategic Environmental Assessment', in A.L. Porter and J.J. Fittipaldi (eds), *Environmental Methods Review: Retooling Impact Assessment for the New Century*, Atlanta, GA: Army Environmental Policy Institute, Georgia Institute of Technology, pp.77–86.

Burdge, R.J. (1998), *A Conceptual Approach to Social Impact Assessment*, Middleton, WI: Social Ecology Press.

Carley, M. and Bustelo, E.S. (1984), *Social Impact Assessment and Monitoring: A Guide to the Literature*, Boulder, CO: Westview Press.

Canter, L.W. and Kamath, J. (1995), 'Questionnaire Checklist for Cumulative Impacts', *Environmental Impact Assessment Review*, 15:311–39.

Cernea, M.M. and Kudar, A. (eds), (1997), *Social Assessments for Better Development*, Environmentally Sustainable Development Studies and Monographs Series No. 16, Washington, DC: The World Bank.

Connor, D.M. (1995), *Constructive Citizen Participation: A Resource Book* (5th ed.), Victoria, BC: Development Press.

Cornwall, A. and Jewkes, R. (1995), 'What is Participatory Research?' *Social Science and Medicine*, 41(12):1667–76.

Council on Environmental Quality (1978), 'National Environmental Policy Act – Regulations', *Federal Register*, Regulations and Policy Guidance, 43(230):55, 978–56,007.

Council on Environmental Quality (1981), *Memorandum, Scoping Guidance*. Washington, DC: Executive Office of the President.

Council on Environmental Quality (1997), *Considering Cumulative Effects Under the National Environmental Policy Act*. Washington, DC: Executive Office of the President.

Craig and Ehrlich, Ross, H., Lane, M. and Northern Land Council (1996), *Indigenous Participation in Environmental Impact Assessment*, Agency Review of Commonwealth Environmental Impact Assessment Report Series, Canberra Commonwealth Environmental Protection Agency.

Creighton, J.L. (1985), *BPA Public Involvement Guide*, Portland, OR: Bonneville Power Administration, and Washington, DC: United States Government Printing Office.

Deitz, T. (1987), 'Theory and Method in Social Impact Assessment', *Sociological Inquiry* 57(1):54–69.

Edelstein, M.R. (1988), *Contaminated Communities: The Social and Psychological Impacts of Residential Toxic Exposure*, Boulder, CO: Westview Press.

Erickson, P.A. (1994), *A Practical Guide to Environmental Impact Assessment*, San Diego, CA: Academic Press.

Glaser, B.G. and Strauss, A. (1967), *The Discovery of Grounded Theory,* Chicago: Aldine Publishing Co.

Goodland, R. (1998), 'The Concept of Environmental Sustainability (ES)', in A.L. Porter and J.J. Fittipaldi (eds), *Environmental Methods Review: Retooling Impact Assessment for the New Century*, Atlanta, GA: Army Environmental Policy Institute, Georgia Institute of Technology, pp. 69–76.

Howitt, R. (1993), *Marginalization in Theory and Practice*, ERRRU Working Papers, 12, Sydney: Economic and Regional Restructuring Research Unit, Departments of Economics and Geography, University of Sydney.

Interorganizational Committee on Guidelines and Principles for Social Impact Assessment (1994), *Guidelines and Principles for Social Impact Assessment*, Silver Spring, MD: United States Department of Commerce, National Oceanic and Atmospheric Administration, National Marine Fisheries Service. Also published in *Impact Assessment*, 12(2):107–52.

Jain, R.K., Urban, L.V. and Stacey, G.S. (1977), *Environmental Impact Analysis*, New York: Van Nostrand Reinhold Company.

Leistritz, F.L. and Murdock, S.H. (1981), *The Socioeconomic Impact of Resource Development: Methods for Assessment*, Boulder, CO: Westview.

Little, R.L. and Krannich, R.S. (1988), 'A Model for Assessing the Social Impacts of Natural Resource Utilization on Resource Dependent Communities', *Impact Assessment Bulletin*, 6(2):21–35.

Lundgren, R. and McMakin, A. (1998), *Risk Communication. (2nd ed.)*, Columbus, OH: Battelle Press.

McGee, T. and Ross, H. (forthcoming) *Environmental Impact Assessment Review, SIA Theoretical Frameworks Revisited: A Cumulative Effects Case Study on Lead Contamination and Economic Change.*

Mulvihill, P.R. and Jacobs, P. (1998), 'Using Scoping as a Design Process', *Environmental Impact Assessment Review*, 18(4):351–69.

The National Environmental Policy Act of 1969 (NEPA), *Public Law 91–190*, pp. 852–59.42. United States Code.

Parsons, T. (1970), 'Some Problems of General Theory in Sociology', in J.C. McKinney and E.A. Tiryakian (eds), *Theoretical Sociology: Perspectives and Developments*, New York: Appleton-Century-Crofts.

Ravetz, J.R. (1987), 'Usable Knowledge, Usable Ignorance', *Knowledge: Creation, Diffusion, Utilization*, 9(1):87–116.

Rayner, S. and Malone, E.L. (eds), (1998), *Human Choice and Climate Change*, Columbus, OH: Battelle Press.

Resource Assessment Commission (1991) *Kakadu Conservation Zone Inquiry Final Report*: Canberra, ACT: Australian Government Publishing Service.

Ross, H. (1990), 'Community Social Impact Assessment: a framework for indigenous peoples', *Environmental Impact Assessment Review,* 10:1–2 and 185–93.

Ross, H. (1992), 'Opportunities for Aboriginal participation in Australian social impact assessment'. *Impact Assessment Bulletin*, 10(1):47–75.

Ross, H. (1994), 'Social impacts of climate change', in A.J. Jakeman and A.B. Pittock (eds.), *Climate Impact Assessment Methods for Asia and the Pacific*, Canberra: Centre for Resource and Environmental Studies, Australian National University.

Shirley, A.M., Hickey, T.E., Strong, K.W. and Sander, F. (1985), 'An Evolving Framework for Environmental Impact Analysis – Part I. Methods', *Journal of Environmental Management*, 21:343–58.

Swartz, L.L. and Reinke, D.C. (eds) (1999), *The NEPA Reference Guide*, Columbus, OH: Battelle Press.

Taylor, C.N., Bryan, C.H. and Goodrich, C.G. (1995), *Social Assessment: Theory, Process, and Techniques* (2nd ed.), Christchurch, New Zealand: The Caxton Press.

Wynne, B. (1996), 'May the Sheep Safely Graze? A Reflexive View of the Expert–Lay Knowledge Divide', in S. Lash, B. Szerszynski and B. Wynne (eds), *Risk, Environment and Modernity*, London: Sage.

Wood, C. (1995), *Environmental Impact Assessment: a Comparative Review*, Harlow, UK: Longman.

Yankelovich, D. (1991), *Coming to Public Judgment*, Syracuse, NY: Syracuse University Press.

Notes

1 This describes the commonwealth or national system. State systems differ in some details.

2 The project was withdrawn after the scoping phase was completed.

3 In which functions – such as adaptation, goal-attainment, integration and pattern-maintenance – are used to explain social structure and process (for example values, norms, roles and behavioural regularities) (Parsons, 1970).

4 We want to emphasize that this process was not completely linear. Some practitioners and some assessments were addressing or raising issues long before they achieved primary focus or the status of common practice.

5 For instance, in Australia heritage protection legislation, land rights and native title legislation also need to be considered for any SIA incorporating indigenous people's interests.

Part III
Assessment

–5–

Social Impact Assessment Tools for Mitigation and Project Development

Gary Simpson

Summary

A common problem with the Environmental Impact Assessment (EIS) process is that while stakeholders may reach in-principle agreement on a range of mitigation and development measures, the agreement is seldom translated into an action plan which clearly defines the respective roles and responsibilities of the parties in its implementation. The lack of attention to detailing action plans, particularly implementation and funding responsibilities, often leads to misunderstanding between the stakeholders and failure to adequately address core mitigation and development measures.

The objective of this paper is to introduce readers to tools for social and economic impact assessment and, in particular, the design of mitigation and development measures as part of the Environmental Review and Management Programme (ERMP) process. These tools focus on the use of a Scoping Matrix, Impact Assessment Profile and ERMP Project Submission Format. If properly utilized, these tools can provide stakeholders with a firm foundation for systematically analysing and negotiating strategic design, implementation, management and funding issues prior to project start-up.

The Environmental Impact Assessment Process

EIS encompasses a process which provides for both biophysical and socio-economic impact assessment. This paper focuses attention on social and economic impact assessment and, more specifically, on the process and procedures for documenting mitigation and development projects.

The starting point for negotiations between a developer (the proponent) and community and government stakeholders on environmental, social and economic issues is normally set out in the administrative and statutory requirements of Environmental Planning Acts.

A proponent cannot usually get approval to proceed with a development proposal until it has met the requirements specified under the Act. As defined in most Environmental Planning Acts, proponents are required to initiate a consultative process which culminates in the submission of an Environmental Impact Statement (EIS) to the relevant government agencies. A technical panel then appraises the EIS and public comment is also often invited. Subject to the findings and recommendations of the technical panel and the public, which are documented in an Environmental Impact Assessment (EIA), approval is then given to the proponent to proceed with an agreed development plan. This plan usually includes provision for the development of an Environmental Review and Management Plan (ERMP).

The procedural bases for conducting both EIS and EIA are detailed in Table 5.1. These processes vary from country to country but usually has common elements, as shown in the table.

Table 5.1 The EIS and EIA process

Steps	**Activity**
Screening	An initial assessment made by a government authority to decide whether a project requires further investigation in an EIA.
Scoping	Consultation with stakeholders to identify the key impacts requiring further investigation. Preparation of terms of reference for the EIS.
Assessing	The identification, analysis and evaluation of the significance of impacts.
Mitigation and development	Developing measures to prevent, reduce or compensate for impacts and/or to maximize benefits.
Reporting	Presenting the EIS report to the government and the public for comment.
Reviewing	Assessing the adequacy of the EIS report, taking into account stakeholder views and assessing the acceptability of the proposal in terms of existing plans, policies and standards.
Decision-making	Deciding whether the proposal can proceed and under what conditions.
Monitoring and managing	Implementing mitigation and development measures and monitoring impacts for compliance.

EIA and Stakeholder Perspectives

The scope within the statutory provisions of the EIA to adopt a comprehensive approach to the assessment of both the biophysical and social and economic impact of a development proposal will be of particular concern to potentially affected stakeholders.[1]

Most stakeholders require transparency in the description of benefits and risks prior to giving their support to the development proposal. While many in the community may be prepared to put up with, or to ignore, moderate levels of environmental degradation and social change, the decision to do so is invariably linked to perceptions of collective and/or personal social and economic well-being. If the benefits and risks are insufficiently well defined, it is unlikely that most stakeholders will voluntarily trade their existing physical and social environment for an uncertain package of benefits and undefined risk.

Stakeholders therefore look to the EIA process to provide them with the necessary support to ensure that there is a comprehensive and transparent analysis of the benefits and risks of a development proposal.

Decision Making

As stated above, the EIA effectively informs the decision-making process for the approval of a proponent's proposal. Central to this process is the submission by the proponent of an Environmental Review and Management Programme[2] (ERMP), which is usually an annex to the EIS report.

The ERMP is a programme for monitoring and managing the impacts during implementation and ultimately forms the basis for an agreement between the proponent and the state. The ERMP usually has provision to detail:

1 The activities which will be undertaken by the proponent, government and community to minimize risk and maximize benefits.
2 A schedule for their implementation.
3 Those agencies or persons responsible for implementation.
4 A monitoring program to assess performance.
5 Reporting and review procedures.

While the final decision to approve an EIS may be influenced by a range of political and economic factors additional to the data, the ERMP submitted by the developer will be central to influencing the decision-making process.

Decision makers are likely to have more confidence in an ERMP which is detailed and transparent in its approach to defining risks and benefits than one which relies on generalized statements of intent. If the ERMP is to have substance, it must be programme and project specific. That is, it should specifically address the issues identified as either risks or benefits in the EIS/EIA. This requires the adoption of a project planning approach to the formulation of the ERMP in which project design, implementation, financial and management issues are considered.

The cause of the proponent is also likely to be advanced if it can demonstrate that community and other stakeholders have participated in the design and development of the ERMP and have agreed to assist in the management of its implementation.

If the EIS is considered satisfactory by the government, approval for a development is usually granted on the condition that the ERMP is implemented, monitored and audited.

Impact Assessment

Introduction

The material presented in this discussion is largely drawn from documentation prepared by the United Nations Environment Program (UNEP).[3] As outlined earlier, the scoping phase is intended to establish a consultative process in which the principal stakeholders identify the key impacts requiring further investigation and develop terms of reference to address the outstanding issues.

The assessing phase of the EIA (Table 5.1) is when most of the work in impact assessment is carried out. Assessing usually involves three main tasks:

1 Further and more detailed work on impact identification, refining the understanding of the nature of the impacts, identifying indirect, cumulative and other impacts and ensuring identification of the likely causes of the impacts.
2 Detailed analysis of the impacts to determine their nature, magnitude, extent and effect.
3 Judgement of the significance of the impacts whether they matter and whether something needs to be done to reduce risk (mitigation) or enhance benefits (development impact).

Impact Characteristics

A range of variables can be taken into account when assessing environmental impact. Impacts can vary in a number of ways.

Nature Assessing the nature of the impact requires consideration as to whether it will have a positive or negative impact and whether the impact will be: (a) *direct*, occurring on or around the same time as the action that caused the impact; (b) *indirect*, resulting from changes that are less obvious and which may occur later in time or in a different location; (c) *cumulative*, impacts which can be added to the impacts from other sources.

Magnitude Assessing the magnitude of the impact requires consideration of whether the impact can be judged as low, moderate or high in nature.

Location/extent Assessing the location and extent of the impact requires consideration of the place and area covered by the impact.

Timing Assessing the timing of the impact requires consideration of whether the impact is evaluated as occurring immediately or as delayed, and whether it occurs during specific phases of the project proposal: for example, during project construction or during operations.

Duration Assessing the duration of the impact requires consideration of whether the impact is of a short-term, medium-term or long-term duration, and whether it is intermittent or continuous.

Reversibility Assessing the reversibility of the impact requires consideration of whether the impact can be assessed as reversible or irreversible in nature.

Likelihood Assessing the likelihood of the impact requires consideration of whether the predicted impact is confidently asserted as certain, likely or uncertain.

Significance Assessing the significance of the impact requires consideration of all of the impact characteristics described above and the importance or value attached to them. Ultimately, the significance of issues and their relative importance will involve the balancing of environmental, social and economic considerations.

Significance must be derived through an understanding of values and tolerance of impacts. Impact significance can be assessed as: (a) a*cceptable*, in that the impact is within the bounds of the tolerance levels of the community and/or government and does not require mitigation; (b) *requiring mitigation and other development measures*, to minimize risk or to maximize benefits; (c) *is unacceptable*, and requires either re-design or abandonment of the proponent's proposal. Assessment using these criteria is, however, complicated by the fact that development proponents, communities and governments will often have divergent values and tolerance levels. What is an acceptable level of impact for one stakeholder group may be unacceptable to another.

The Scoping Matrix

As previously outlined, an impact assessment should commence with a stakeholder scoping exercise to determine which impacts require further investigation. To facilitate this process it is often useful to develop a scoping matrix to determine the key impacts and their significance.

Table 5.2 illustrates an example of an impact scoping matrix which examines the projected impact of a mining project on the health of a rural community. The matrix has thirteen columns.

Structure of the Scoping Matrix

Column 1 — Impact parameter and reference number. Specify each of the impact parameters and allocate a reference number.

Column 2 — Status or incidence without project. Assess the current status/incidence of each impact parameter in a without-project situation. For example, an assessment of the incidence of malaria before the start of a project may reveal that the incidence of malaria in the project area is low but increasing.

Column 3 — With the project. Assess the status/incidence of the impact parameter with the proposed project. For example, the incidence of malaria may be projected to increase if the project goes ahead. If it is projected that there will be no significant impact as a result of the proposed project go to column 13.[4]

Column 4 — Cause. Refers to the projected cause(s) of the impact. For example, the projected causes of an increase in malaria may be related to an influx of settlers from

Table 5.2 The scoping matrix

	1 Impact parameters	2 Without project	3 With project	4 Cause	5 Effect	6 Nature	7 Magni-tude	8 Extent/ location	9 Timing	10 Duration	11 Reversibility	12 Likelihood/ risk	13 Signifi-cance
1	**Communicable diseases**												
1.1	Pneumonia	High											
1.2	Meningitis	Low											
1.3	Tuberculosis	Low											
1.4	Leprosy	Low											
1.5	Diarrhoeal disease	High											
1.6	Typhoid	Low											
1.7	Worm infestation	High											
1.8	Sexually transmitted disease	High	Projected increase	Income/ influx of single males	Increased morbidity/ social problems	Indirect	Moderate	Urban and rural areas	Construct-ion	Long-term continuous	Manageable with the exception of AIDS	Likely	Requires mitigation
1.9	Malaria	High	Projected increase	Popn. mobility	Increased morbidity/ reduced productivity	Direct	Moderate	Urban and rural areas	Construct-ion	Long-term continuous	Manageable	Certain	Requires mitigation
2	**Non-communicable diseases**												
2.1	**Injury**												
2.1.1	Alcohol and drug abuse	High											
2.1.2	Physical abuse	High											
2.1.3	Traffic accidents	Low											

	malaria-affected areas and the lack of an effective malaria treatment and control programmes.
Column 5	Effect. Refers to the projected effects. For example, an increase in malaria will contribute to personal health problems and reduce the productivity of individuals and households.
Columns 6–13	Proceed to define the projected impact characteristics in accordance with the criteria set out earlier in this chapter.

The scoping matrix is intended to be a worksheet to guide discussion on selection and assessment of the most significant impacts. Care needs to be exercised in its use as the inclusion of too many sector attributes in the matrix can result in significant time and resources being used to investigate issues which are of little significance or outside the scope of the proponent and stakeholders to reasonably address/influence.

The Impact Assessment Profile

Once the impact scoping matrix has been completed 'impact assessment profiles' need to be prepared for each of the impact parameters assessed as being potentially significant.

The Impact Assessment Profile expands on the principal issues identified in the Impact Scoping Matrix, assesses the significance of the impact, defines the scope for any mitigation and/or development activities, includes an analysis of any relevant cross-cutting issues.

Cross-cutting Issues

The design of mitigation and development measures should also take into account any cross-cutting issues which can affect project outcomes. They include: (a) participation; (b) cultural values; (c) poverty and equity; (d) gender.

Participation Participation is a process through which stakeholders influence and share control over development initiatives and the decisions and resources which affect them.[5] Experience suggests that the level of stakeholder participation in the design, implementation and monitoring of a project will significantly influence the outcome and perceptions of success. Projects which provide for participation of target groups particularly in the scoping and implementation phase are more likely to be successful than those which have been less inclusive of stakeholder groups.

Cultural Values Cultural values and interpretation are often important considerations in determining the response by indigenous communities and ethnic groups to issues of biophysical, social and economic impact. Anthropological and sociological research[6] undertaken by competent professionals is usually a prerequisite in the development of proposals associated with indigenous communities and minority groups.

Poverty and Equity Assessing the impact on poverty and equity requires consideration of the distribution of the benefits and risks within and between social groups. Equity may be defined by ethnicity, age and gender.

While there may be potential for communities, government and the private sector to benefit substantially from a development, the distribution of these benefits can be extremely uneven. Local communities and indigenous minorities, in particular, can be completely marginalized by more articulate, skilled and capitalized groups who monopolize the major employment, contracting and business development opportunities. Large amounts of money can be spent on administering community development funds rather than investing in community projects. Royalty payments to communities and local government are often diluted and delayed by bureaucratic and political inertia at the national level. The present generation of beneficiaries may consume the bulk of the benefits leaving very little for future generations. These distributional issues raise complex social and political questions and, depending on how they are handled, could make the difference between securing or losing the opportunity for achieving sustainable development outcomes.

In this context, the distribution of benefits and the question of equity become crucial issues, not only for communities and government, but for the developer as well. Failure to give adequate consideration to equitable distributional outcomes can prove costly to the future security of communities, government and the proponent.

Gender There will often be important differences in roles between men and women that may have a bearing on the outcome of mitigation and development measures. If these differences are ignored, the prospects for the success of the project may be adversely affected, and women may not have the opportunity to benefit from the project on equal terms with men.

There are three major areas where differences in roles between men and women within and outside the household may have an impact on the design and implementation arrangements for a project:

1 There are often significant differences in the allocation of time and work performed both within the household and in relation to economic activities which may impact on the delivery of technical advice and services.
2 There may be differences in the control over the use and distribution of assets and money.
3 There may be differences in roles with respect to decisions which influence the allocation of time and resources.

Sustainability

Sustainable development activities are those which meet the needs of the present without compromising the ability of future generations to meet their own needs and which seek to improve the total quality of life both now and in the future.

While project benefit streams (royalties, equity, employment, business opportunities and development grants) can offer significant returns, communities and governments often have major problems in identifying and managing sustainable investment strategies.

Generating sustainable development requires a collaborative effort on the part of the proponent, government and community stakeholders. Collaboration between the stakeholders must commence well before project start-up to have any impact on the major benefit streams. The issue of sustainability should therefore be a key consideration in the preparation of the EIS.

The issues surrounding the achievement of sustainable development are complex. However, a systematic analysis of the benefit streams and the options for their development at each stage of the proponent's proposed project cycle can assist stakeholders to focus on the opportunities and constraints to sustainable development. This analysis should also incorporate consideration of stakeholder roles and responsibilities in the management of the benefit streams, their capacity to design and implement sustainable development programmes and their human resource development and training needs.

Impact Assessment Profile Example

The following example is drawn from the scoping matrix referred to in Table 5.2 which identified that the proposed mining project could contribute to the increased incidence of malaria in the project area.

Impact Assessment Profile (IAP)

Proponent:	Clarke Kent Industries
Proposal:	Kryptonite mining
Location:	Southern province
Sector:	Health
Impact parameter:	Malaria
Stakeholders consulted:	Provincial Health Officer, Church Health Services and Clarke Kent Industries

1. Status or incidence without project
Currently malaria infection rates are low but increasing. Health centre clinic records indicate malaria only accounts for 15% of all illness treated on a monthly basis.

2. Projected status or incidence with the project
Provincial health authorities predict that the proposed mine will significantly add to the already increasing malaria transmission rates. This projection is based on a case study conducted into the incidence of communicable diseases, including malaria, in a mining community living at similar altitudes in the adjoining province of Bukidnon. This case study demonstrated that malaria infection rates doubled within two years of completion of the mining access roads.

3. Cause of projected impact
The proposed development of an access road to the coast will facilitate the influx of settlers and workers from lowland areas which have high malaria infection rates.

4. Effect of projected impact
It is anticipated that an increase in malaria will contribute to personal health problems and reduce the productivity of individuals and households.

5. Nature of impact
Positive or negative The increased rates of malaria are assessed as having an overall negative impact on the local tribal communities who have low resistance to malaria parasites.
Direct, indirect, cumulative Health authorities believe that the impact of malaria will be cumulative in that as more infected settlers and workers arrive in the project area they will progressively add to the already existing problem.

6. Magnitude
Low, moderate or high The magnitude of the impact of malaria is expected to be high in the first five to ten years of the project. However, infection rates may stabilise as the people develop a greater resistance to the disease.

7. Location/extent
Local, regional, national, global Those tribal communities living near the swamp are likely to be most affected. However, all communities living along the mining access roads are likely to experience some increase in infection rates.

The mining camp at Sesi is also likely to be a source of infection, as many coastal labourers who already have malaria will be rotated through this camp.

8. Timing
Immediate or delayed The full impact of malaria is likely to be delayed for up to two years pending completion of the access roads.
Phasing The mining construction phase is likely to pose significant malaria risk to workers, as this will be the period when employment will peak.

9. Duration
Short-term, medium-term, long-term, intermittent or *continuous* Given the development of chloroquine-resistant malaria strains, malaria is likely to be a long-term continuous problem for both the workforce and the surrounding tribal communities.

10. Reversibility
Reversible, manageable, irreversible Malaria is manageable in the project area providing there is an ongoing malaria programme.

11. Likelihood
Certain, likely, uncertain Based on the experience of other mines in the region an increase in malaria infection rates in the development and construction phase is considered certain.

12. Significance
Acceptable, requires mitigation, unacceptable Based on an assessment of the impact, characteristics mitigation and development measures will be required to ensure that the incidence of malaria is controlled in the project area.

13. Suggested mitigation measures
The following mitigation measures have been suggested for further development:

- Re-activate the Village Health Committee system
- Review provincial malaria control unit staff and resource requirements
- Establish indicator villages and conduct baseline survey
- Conduct a malaria awareness programme
- Conduct treatment programme at the Sisi base camp
- Initiate a bed net distribution programme for priority villages
- Ensure adequate supply of medicines to health services.

14. Cross-cutting issues

Participation The control of malaria in the project area will largely depend on the preparedness of communities to become involved in the design and implementation of awareness and eradication programmes. The Village Health Committee system should be reactivated.

Poverty and equity Low-income families are particularly affected by malaria especially if the productive capacity of the principle breadwinner is impaired by repeated illness. Low-income households should be targeted in the development of malaria-control programmes.

Gender In many villages men and women live in separate households. The design of malaria awareness and eradication programmes will need to cater for the specific needs of both male and female households.

Sustainability If malaria-control programmes are to be sustainable, communities must be prepared to contribute to the cost of maintaining the programme. The scope for introducing a head tax to fund health and other community services should be investigated.

Furthermore, the Malaria Control Unit within the Provincial Department of Health does not have sufficient trained staff or the financial resources to support an ongoing malaria programme. The Unit needs to be upgraded if it is to play an effective role in the control and treatment of malaria.

The Environmental Review and Management Programme Project Submission

Introduction

As indicated earlier in this chapter the proponent is usually required to submit an Environmental Review and Management Programme (ERMP) to address those impacts identified as requiring mitigation and/or development support. If the ERMP is to have substance, it must be programme and project specific and adopt a project planning approach in which project design, implementation, financial and management issues are fully considered.

In the discussion which follows a suggested approach to the documentation of ERMP project submissions is proposed which verifies and gives effect to mitigation and development measures identified in the impact assessment profile.

Design Documentation for Mitigation and Development Proposals

The impact assessment profiles (IAP) simply document the impact issues and assess their significance in terms of the need for mitigation and development measures. In order to give effect to these measures the IAP recommendations need to be translated into projects which:

- address clearly identified problems, opportunities and target groups;
- are technically feasible;
- have a realistic implementation schedule;
- are accurately costed;
- are manageable given resource and management capacity constraints;
- are environmentally, socially and economically acceptable;
- will provide sustainable benefits.

If these requirements are to be met it is important to standardize the documentation of mitigation and development proposals to facilitate the EIA review and decision-making process. Standardized project documentation will help decision makers to make choices between different project proposals. It will also provide a clear record of what was initially planned (the key outputs, activities and costs of each project) which will later help to guide implementation, and allow for monitoring of progress by comparing what was planned with what actually happens.

Documentation for mitigation and development projects is thus an important tool for both designing and managing the implementation, monitoring and evaluation of projects. A suggested approach to the design and documentation of ERMP submissions is detailed below.

Suggested ERMP Project Submission Format (PSF)

The Logical Framework Approach to Project Design There are many acceptable formats for project design. Government agencies, companies and community organizations often have formats which are tailored to suit their own physical and financial reporting systems. The format proposed here (Appendix 5.1) may need adjustment to suit specific requirements. However, irrespective of the format used, the project documentation must be completely transparent to assist those charged with project implementation to develop a physical and financial work plan, and to project manage, monitor and evaluate. A method which lends itself to transparency in the design, implementation, monitoring and evaluation of projects is the logical framework (logframe) approach. Logframes are used extensively by bilateral and multilateral aid donors such as the World Bank, the Asian Development Bank, United Nations agencies and the Australian Agency for International Development (AusAID).

The logframe seeks to develop a project hierarchy which:

- stipulates the goal or development vision of the project;
- identifies the structure or component parts of the project;
- details the objectives of each component;
- specifies the outputs or products to be achieved under each component;
- details the activities or work required to achieve each output;
- specifies the physical and financial inputs required to implement the activities.

Indicators for evaluating the impact of the project are built into the logframe at the objective and output level. The logframe matrix is complemented by the development of implementation and cost schedules which provide a framework for the physical and financial monitoring of the project.

The project example (Appendix 5.1) used here illustrates the level of transparency which can be achieved utilizing a logical framework matrix with implementation and cost schedules. Not all projects require this level of detail. However, the structure of the logframe can be adjusted to suit the scale of the project while providing a basic management tool for project monitoring and evaluation.

Project Narrative The logical framework approach needs to be complemented by a project narrative which includes:

1 A description of the problem or opportunity to be addressed.
2 A statement of the project goal, objectives and outputs, and from this, an analysis of the preferred project strategy.
3 Description of the financial and human resources required to implement the project.
4 Discussion of anticipated benefits.
5 Analysis of any special technical requirements.
6 Assessment of the overall scope for sustaining project initiatives and, in particular, the roles and responsibilities of the relevant project stakeholders.
7 Consideration of other special issues such as the gender, generation and poverty and equity dimensions of the project.

8 Sustainability.
9 Description of key assumptions and risks.

Appendix 5.1 details a proposed format for the formulation of EIA mitigation and development proposals. The format is intended as a guide and not as a blueprint. The format should be adapted to suit the particular project circumstances.

Conclusion

In undertaking environmental impact assessments it is important to remain focused on desired outcomes as they relate to mitigation and development measures. The combined use of the scoping matrix, impact assessment profiles and ERMP project submission formats provides a framework with which to maintain this focus.

Notes

1 Stakeholders may include: individuals, communities, government, other private sector developers and third-party interest groups such as Non-Government Organizations (NGOs).
2 Also often referred to as the Environmental Management Plan (EMP).
3 United Nations Environment Program (UNEP) Environmental Impact Assessment Training Resource Manual. Preliminary Version 1996. Prepared for UNEP by the Australian Environmental Protection Agency.
4 Note that while a project may be assessed as having no significant impact on a parameter (e.g. tuberculosis), there could still be a case for recommending remedial action be undertaken within the scope of the project to eradicate tuberculosis.
5 The World Bank Participation Sourcebook. The International Bank for Reconstruction and Development (1996).
6 Often referred to as 'social mapping'.

Appendix 5.1

(1) Logical framework
(2) Implementation schedule
(3) Cost schedules

Appendix 5.1.1. Logical framework matrix: project area health support programme

NO.	NARRATIVE SUMMARY	VERIFIABLE INDICATORS	MEANS OF VERIFICATION	ASSUMPTIONS
	GOAL To improve community awareness of primary health-care issues and access to treatment and referral services.	Operational Aid Post, MCH and Malaria services	Aid post, malaria and MCH records	That a Health Working Group (HWG) consisting of government, community and company representatives will be established to co-ordinate the programme
		Community health-care extension and awareness programmes	Extension and awareness evaluation reports	
	COMPONENT 1. **Malaria programme**			
1	**OBJECTIVE** To develop a malaria control programme through the distribution of bed nets	Annual malaria control programme funded and implemented by the Department of Health	Department of Health reports	Once the baseline survey has been completed and a bed net programme established, it is anticipated that there will be a progressive annual reduction in malaria infection rates. Annual surveys will be conducted to determine the rate of reduction
		Per cent of population using treated bed nets	Department of Health reports	
1.1	**OUTPUT** Malaria baseline survey	Per cent of population with malaria in indicator villages	Survey report	That the company will resource the Provincial Department of Health to undertake the baseline survey

NO.	NARRATIVE SUMMARY	VERIFIABLE INDICATORS	MEANS OF VERIFICATION	ASSUMPTIONS
	ACTIVITIES			
1.1.1	Establish survey methodology			
1.1.2	Select indicator villages and rural non-villages			
1.1.3	Conduct baseline survey.			
1.1.4	Analyse and publish results			
	OUTPUT			
1.2	2,000 bed nets distributed	2,000 bed nets distributed	Bed net distribution report. Distribution by village by household	That households will purchase bed nets and pay for re-treatment
	ACTIVITIES			
1.2.1	Utilize survey findings to develop and prioritize malaria extension programme			
1.2.2	Review community participation and cost recovery options			
1.2.3	Develop malaria awareness and education programme			
1.2.4	Initiate bed net distribution programme in priority areas			
1.2.5	Conduct follow-up treatment of bed nets			
1.2.6	Undertake periodic malaria surveys in indicator villages			

Appendix 5.1.2. Implementation schedule: project area health support programme

NO.	NARRATIVE SUMMARY	ACTION OFFICER	UNIT	TOTAL QTY.	1998				1999			
					1	2	3	4	1	2	3	4
	COMPONENT 1 Malaria programme											
	OBJECTIVE To develop a malaria control programme through the distribution of bed nets											
	OUTPUT											
1.1	Malaria baseline survey											
	ACTIVITIES											
1.1.1	Establish survey methodology	HWG			X							
1.1.2	Select indicator villages and rural non-villages	Malaria officer			X							
1.1.3	Conduct baseline survey	Malaria survey team			X	X						
1.1.4	Analyse and publish results	Malaria officer				X						
	INPUTS											
Personnel	Malaria officer		Months	2	1	1						
	Malaria survey teams		Months	1		1						
Training	Refresher courses		No.	1		1						
Other	Travel and allowances for malaria survey team		Lump sum	1		1						

NO.	NARRATIVE SUMMARY	ACTION OFFICER	UNIT	TOTAL QTY.	1998				1999			
					1	2	3	4	1	2	3	4
	Travel and allowances for malaria officer		Lump sum	1		1						
	Extension materials and supplies		Lump sum	1		1						
	OUTPUT											
1.2	2,000 bed nets distributed											
	ACTIVITIES											
1.2.1	Utilize survey findings to develop and prioritize malaria extension programme	Malaria officer					X					
1.2.2	Review community participation and cost recovery options	Malaria officer					X					
1.2.3	Develop malaria awareness and education programme	Malaria officer					X					
1.2.4	Initiate bed net distribution programme in priority areas	Malaria bed net teams					X	X				
1.2.5	Conduct follow-up treatment of bed nets	Malaria bed net teams							X		X	
1.2.6	Undertake periodic malaria surveys in indicator villages								X		X	
	INPUTS											
Personnel	Malaria officer		Months	4			1	1	1		1	
	Malaria bed net teams		Months	4			1	1	1		1	
Materials	Bed nets		No.	2,000			1,000	1,000				
	Community contribution		No.	2,000			1,000	1,000				
	Extension materials and supplies						1	1	1		1	
Other	Travel and allowances for malaria bed net teams		Lump sum	4			1	1	1		1	

Appendix 5.3. Cost schedule – $'000: project area health support programme

No.	NARRATIVE SUMMARY	Total qty	Units	Unit cost	Fund source	Budget code	1st	2nd	3rd	4th	Total	1st	2nd	3rd	4th	Total	Project total
	COMPONENT 1 Malaria programme																
1	**OBJECTIVE** To develop a malaria control programme through the distribution of bed nets																
1.1	**OUTPUT** Malaria baseline survey																
	INPUTS																
Personnel	Malaria officer	2	Months	1	Prov Gov		1.0	1.0			2.0						2.00
	Malaria survey teams	1	Months	1	Prov Gov			1.0			1.0						1.00
Training	Refresher courses	1		5	Prov Gov			5.0			5.0						5.00
Other	Travel and allowances for malaria survey team	1	Lump sum	5	Prov Gov			5.0			5.0						
	Travel and allowances for malaria officer	1	Lump sum	2	Prov Gov			2.0			2.0						2.00
	Extension materials and supplies	1	Lump sum	1	Prov Gov			1.0			1.0						1.00
						Sub-total	**1.0**	**15.0**			**16.0**						**16.0**

No.	NARRATIVE SUMMARY	Total qty	Units	Unit cost	Fund source	Budget code	1st	2nd	3rd	4th	Total	1st	2nd	3rd	4th	Total	Project total
1.2	**OUTPUT** 2,000 bed nets distributed																
	INPUTS																
Personnel	Malaria officer	4	Months	1	Prov Gov				1.0	1.0	2.0	1.0		1.0		2.0	4.00
	Malaria bed net teams	4	Months	1	Prov Gov				1.0	1.0	2.0	1.0		1.0		2.0	4.00
Materials	Bed nets	2,000		0.005	Company				5.0	5.0	10.0						10.00
	Community contribution	2,000		0.005	Community				5.0	5.0	10.0						10.00
	Extension materials and supplies	1	Lump sum	1	Prov Gov				1.0	1.0	2.0	1.0		1.0		2.0	4.00
Other	Travel and allowances for malaria bed net teams	1	Lump sum	5	Prov Gov				5.0	5.0	10.0	5.0		5.0		10.0	20.00
						Sub-Total			**18.0**	**18.0**	**36.0**	**8.0**		**8.0**		**16.0**	**52.0**
						Total	**1.0**	**15.0**	**18.0**	**18.0**	**52.0**	**8.0**		**8.0**		**16.0**	**68.0**
						Prov Gov	1.0	15.0	8.0	8.0	32.0	8.0		8.0		16.0	48.0
						Company			5.0	5.0	10.0						10.0
						Comunity			5.0	5.0	10.0						10.0

–6–

Social Mapping

Laurence Goldman

Introduction

In its broadest sense, social mapping refers to the process of collecting information about customary resource ownership and group formation. This task is most usually performed in response to requirements of government departments, landowners or developers who wish to mobilize resources in some way. Equally, however, the need for social mapping can be driven by specific problems such as the evaluation of competing resource claims by indigenes. Whether the catalyst for social mapping research then is the implementation of some scheme, such as landowner organizations or customary land registration, or resource project infrastructure, such as pipelines, townships or production facilities the mapping will effectively circumscribe a zone of impact. That is, it will delineate an area deemed susceptible to some immediate, cumulative or long-term changes as the result of an established or anticipated scheme. While social mapping is invariably conducted as part of a more encompassing social impact assessment (SIA), it can equally constitute a stand-alone project that is a precursor to, or in anticipation of, some future SIA.

Whatever the eventuality, carrying out social mapping entails an understanding of the cultural and historical factors which have shaped the relationship between humans and their environment. This incorporates a description of the group-to-ground grid (i.e. which social groups reside where and their pattern of distribution), the principles which underpin the social organisation of a given population, and the manner in which traditional ways of life will impinge upon, or in turn be affected by, the scheme or resource project which is a catalyst for the investigation. Filer (n.d.) has succinctly identified the foci normally expanded on in social mapping research:

1 The distribution of people between social groups.
2 The distribution of people between resources (including land).
3 The distribution of resources between people.
4 The distribution of power between people.

These rubrics subsume issues such as cultural heritage, sacred landscapes, political and economic forms of representation, gender-inflected patterns of behaviour, residential models, subsistence patterns and genealogical data, to name just a few of the parameters examined further below.

On the one hand, it can appear as if all that is required here is for a social scientist, for example an anthropologist, to conduct a general ethnographic inquiry. After all, researching such phenomena as kinship and descent structures has been the bread and butter of that profession for well over a century. Anthropologists are weaned on the tenet that these constitutive principles of human relationships – the different ways in which people relate to each other – provide a set of keys or blueprints that unlock patterns of political, economic and religious behaviour.

On the other hand, the anthropologist who conducts social mapping does so in the context of a wholly different and transformed set of relationships to that of conventional academic fieldwork. The veil of scientific neutrality becomes further clouded because the anthropologist frequently assumes, or is invested with, the identity of 'consultant'. Most often, they work for a contract fee, are subject to restricted time and resource constraints, and produce a report for the immediate benefit of commissioning agents who themselves invariably constitute a project stakeholder. That is, the commissioning agent may be a government department, a resource operator, or an interests group forming part of the target area population. The task of social mapping thereby seems encumbered by the need to address disparate audiences, to fulfill a broad spectrum of expectations, and to skilfully negotiate what are often competing sets of constraints and compromises.

Clearly, there are substantive issues of objectivity, advocacy and ethical practice attached to the conduct of any social mapping. This is especially so when investigating native title claims and complex indigenous land-ownership systems. Such issues are not, however, broached in this chapter. Rather, this chapter is more narrowly concerned with detailing why social mapping investigations are conducted, what topics are conventionally required in these reports, the different 'scales' of study that can be undertaken, how such objectives can be achieved and which are the best kinds of format to present and organize the data. In effect the discussions within constitute a social mapping roadmap to the innumerable kinds of decision-making moments and crises that typify this sort of endeavour. It is thus acknowledged that different cultural environments will inevitably generate context-specific problems – researching among North America Indians is clearly different from researching among Melanesians in Papua New Guinea. Because of variations in ethnicity, social complexity, population size and territory, we cannot hope to canvass here all possibilities. Rather, the argument is made that the principles which underpin social mapping, and which are described herein, are broadly generic in nature. In other words, what is presented below is an idealized schema that can be customized by researchers for particular geographic or social environments.

Importantly, and by way of introduction, it needs to be emphasized that a social mapping report is a quite different beast to the 'ethnographic monograph'. In the latter, topics are usually driven and selected by critical theory concerns. By contrast, the social mapping report is orientated to issues of an applied nature. It has to service a non-academic readership, and present as highly accessible and readable. In effect, this requires assiduous avoidance of jargon or discipline-specific terms of art. The range of skills or expertise required to perform such social mapping investigations may span disciplines as diverse as archaeology, human or political geography, environmental science, economics or human resource management. While anthropologists, then, certainly do not have a monopoly on the requisite knowledge base or skills, their specific enmeshment with kinship and descent systems often identifies them as the preferred class of social scientist for many social mapping jobs. Having said that, these skills can certainly be transmitted and acquired through instruction.

Social Mapping – Why Do It?

The extent to which there is an explicit acknowledgement of the need for information on customary social groups within an impact area can vary quite considerably. In some instances such recognition manifests a 'best practice' protocol – in order to gauge the impacts of some project or programme, answers are required to such basic questions as, 'which ethnic group lives here? How are they organized? What is their migratory history? Are they culturally related to other neighbouring groups?'. In other words, the compelling argument for a social mapping report may consist of nothing more than a commissioning agent's commonsense understanding that their ongoing community relations work requires certain minimum levels of information. At the other end of the spectrum, social mapping may be a mandatory legal requirement of all prospecting and development agencies. A recent example of this kind of legislation is that of the Papua New Guinea 'Oil and Gas Bill 1998' Part 111 (Petroleum Exploration and Development), Division 5, Section 47 – Social Mapping and Landowner Identification Studies. This bill stipulates that:

1 It shall be a condition of every petroleum prospecting licence that the licensee undertake social mapping studies and landowner identification studies in accordance with this section.
2 It shall be a condition of every petroleum retention licence that the licensee undertake social mapping studies and landowner identification studies in accordance with this section, to the extent that such studies have not been undertaken pursuant to a petroleum prospecting licence out of which the petroleum retention licence was granted.
3 Prior to first entry on to the licence area for the purposes of exploration pursuant to a petroleum prospecting licence or a petroleum retention licence, the licensee shall undertake –
   (a) a preliminary social mapping study; and
   (b) a preliminary landowner identification study,
   of the customary owners and the occupants of the land comprised in the licence area, with particular reference to that part of the licence area where the licensee's exploration activities are to be concentrated.
4 If a discovery is notified by a licensee under Section 32, and the licensee conducts a final feasibility study of the development or extension of a petroleum project for the production of petroleum from that discovery, the licensee shall at the same time conduct –
   (a) a full-scale social mapping study; and
   (b) a full-scale landowner identification study,
   of customary owners and the occupants of the land which will be comprised in the licence area of a petroleum development licence or licences which would pertain to the development of that discovery and the land within five kilometres of any facility which would be a dedicated project facility (other than a facility which would be situated on such a petroleum development licence) of the petroleum project or other areas which would be affected by the petroleum project if developed.
5 The Minister may by regulation prescribe the scope and method of a social mapping study or landowner identification study conducted in accordance with this section, and requirements as to reports of such studies.
6 Copies of any social mapping or landowner identification studies undertaken in accordance with this section (excluding any information which is confidential to the licensee or to the local groups of landowners) shall be provided to the Director.

A legal framework is hereby established which:

1 Makes social mapping mandatory for any prospecting activity.
2 Allocates responsibility for commissioning and funding such studies to the prospective licensee.
3 Establishes some guidelines in terms of circumscribing the impact zone to be investigated.
4 Makes submission of the document to a relevant government department, albeit with suitable caveats respecting confidentiality, legally mandatory.

The commissioning of a social mapping report may of course constitute a more complex process than simply establishing a bilateral agreement between a given investigator and commissioning agent. It can be subject to a nationally endorsed and constituted committee that oversees its conduct and frames its scope of work. This may extend to a determination of:

1 The terms of reference (TOR).
2 Accompanying personnel on fieldwork trips.
3 Requirements of recommendations on particular issues and to whom these should be routed.
4 Requirements about presentations of results and copies of reports deposited with particular institutions.
5 Proscription of a range of actions to be pursued after the formal contract has ended.

But irrespective of the kind or level of recognition accorded social mapping studies, the need for them is predicated on a few simple premises. Insofar as some landscape is associated with one or more social groups, it becomes incumbent on agencies both to negotiate with customary resource owners and to monitor possible social impacts of schemes in that area. For this to happen they need to formulate a good understanding of which interest groups are relevant, how they are organized at present, and what rights they may customarily exercise. These may be either continuous or discontinuous with the legally defined rights of supervening levels of government which exercise jurisdiction over their claimed resources. Social mapping then has a natural constituency within impact assessment studies. The first task for any prospective social mapper is to acquaint themselves with both the contractual and legislative requirements (see Chapter 2) governing the task at hand which will thereby identify what conditions or constraints are imposed upon the investigation itself.

Identifying a Target Area

Where a social mapping investigation is initiated under contract with given TOR, it is imperative that one of the TOR clauses stipulates an initial 'target area' (TA) defined as the geographic vector within which primary investigations will be undertaken. Importantly, circumscribing such an envelope is no easy task and must in part reflect the priorities and objectives of the social mapping research itself.

Consider the Following Scenarios:

Scenario 1 If the objective of the study is to establish customary landowning groups in accordance with a new national directive, consideration will have to be given to those people who are perhaps resident within a defined area as well as those non-residents who may have a claim to some resource but who choose to remain territorially outside a target area. Research either before or during the social mapping investigation may uncover a history of migration in which groups no longer resident in the area continue to exercise notional claims on the land. The researcher then faces the problem of establishing historical patterns of possession and grants of title or usage which may entail expanding the borders of the target area in ways not originally anticipated or allowed for. Succinctly put, the geographic boundaries cannot be precisely established prior to research, so that the 'target area' is effectively only a preliminary working concept.

Scenario 2 If the purpose of the social mapping is to assist in the identification of social impacts from project infrastructure, consideration will need to be given to the likely nature of these impacts – financial, migratory, demographic, ecological – and the timeframes in which one or more combination of these factors may impact – short-, medium- or long-term effects. These in turn will help define the geographic area over which impacts will be felt often differentially and unevenly. The target area is then constituted by minimal/maximal, or central/peripheral zones of impacts which have to be defined in more detail by the researcher in regard to the parameters mentioned above.

We can draw two important lessons from these observations. First, in the initial period of work the target area is continually being reassessed and monitored; its borders are fluid not frozen during the ongoing research. Second, the TA needs always to be articulated in consultation with the commissioning agent. That is, it must remain sensitive to the objectives of the study, and informed concerning the estimated ramifications some scheme might have as foreseen or predicted by the commissioning agent. Essentially, the TA one starts out with in a study – even if defined as a result of a prior scoping study (see Chapter 4) – may not remain the same once fieldwork has been initiated. Importantly, a map of the TA should be produced showing clearly the geographic boundaries in which the initial work will be conducted, as indicated for example in Figure 6.1.

Once a workable agreement as to the geographic area has been reached, the next task is to provide profiles of its ethnic, ecological, demographic and socio-cultural make-up.

Target-area Communities and Cultures

Prior to commencement of fieldwork proper, the social mapper needs to factor in a library research component, the aim of which is to conduct a thorough bibliographic search for materials pertinent to the TA and its inhabitants. Resources to be consulted should include (but are not limited to):

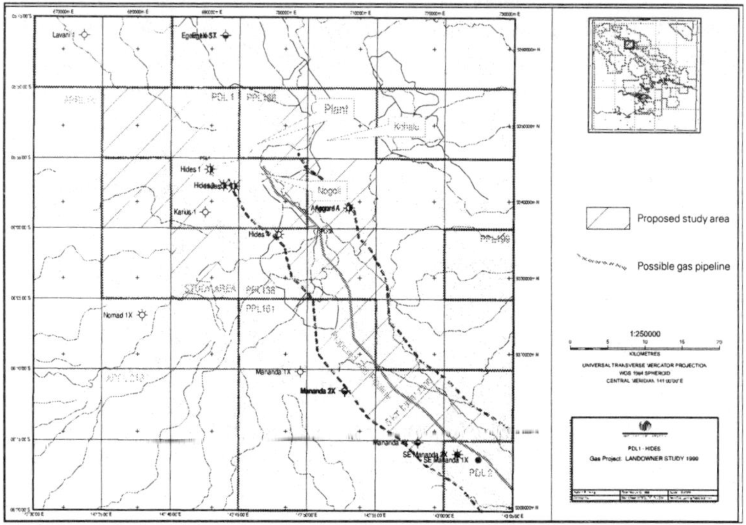

Source: Goldman, 1999b: 4

Figure 6.1 Proposed Social Mapping Area for Hides–Kutubu Gas Pipeline, Papua New Guinea

- libraries for anthropological, geographical, travel and linguistic publications;
- national archive centres including museums, government stations, mapping bureaus, or patrol posts;
- developers who have been or are currently operating in that area and who may hold files of relevance;
- non-government agencies such as missionaries, linguistic institutes and aid organizations who have had any contact in the area;
- any organization or resource bank (e.g. newspapers) with information on land, agriculture, livestock, customary land registration or census data.

This archival research establishes some baseline information about the TA and should include the collection of any maps, aerial photographs, etc. that are useful for tasks such as boundary demarcation. Because of the inevitable time constraints on any study, the ideal situation is one where an established ethnographer or regional specialist is commissioned. Thus, these experts always constitute a first line of contact. However, the available material for some areas may be thin on the ground or difficult to access. In such circumstances, the dangers posed a social mapping exercise are that of misinterpretation and misunderstanding through either lack of native language proficiency, and/or an inability to frame data within their proper cultural context. In many ways, then, the pre-fieldwork component can crucially determine the success or failure of the mapping venture.

Ethnic Group Composition

In this sub-section the principal tribal or ethnic identities of the customary landowners are defined. Because claimants to some resource may not always be obviously apparent – as for example in uninhabited borderlands (Prescott, 1987) – the social mapper is advised to situate the principal groups within a regional/national framework. This helps identify broad cultural patterns and may provide some insight into the pre/post-contact history as an explanation for subsequent trajectories of change. Thus, a map of the regionally important cultures should be produced. Figure 6.2, for example, shows those cultures which are regionally significant to the Gas Project proposed in Figure 6.1. The level of detail to be included in this section will vary in accordance with factors such as:

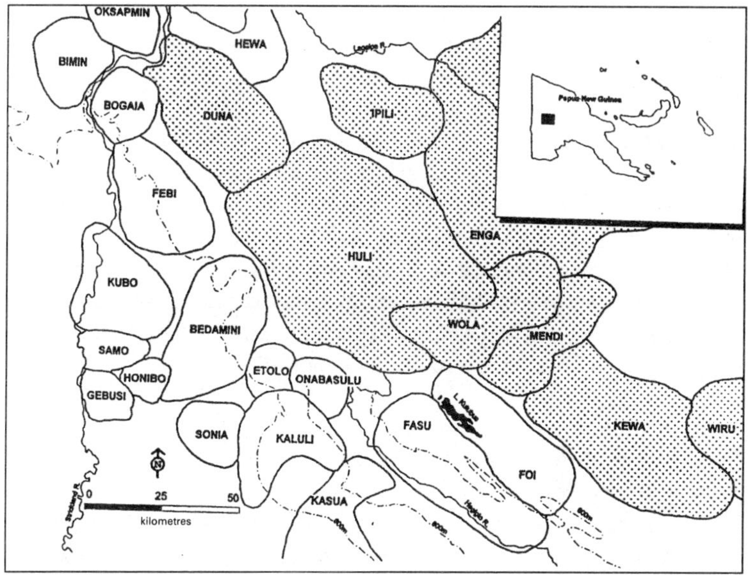

Figure 6.2 Southern Highlands Province Cultures

1 The scale of population involved.
2 The number of distinct ethnic groups in the target area.
3 The complexity of the history.

The following sub-section listings provide a general guide to the kinds of information most usually included in mapping reports.

Languages Spoken This will identify languages known and used, extent of bilingualism, the genetic relationships or phylum memberships of the languages and, most importantly, what these linguistic findings tell us about the proto-history of the populations and their origins. For example, in a situation of contested land claims, demonstrated linguistic connections may suggest migration from, say, inland to coastal regions within a specified time frame. This establishes a level of evidence that may indicate prior residence in the region or confirm indigenous migration myths. What is thereby illuminated is the concordance between one ethnic group's conception of regional ties and history, and the scientific knowledge that could support this. Descriptions within this rubric may extend to consider the sustainability of local argots or cants, implications of adopting a new 'lingua franca', or indeed language forms as symbols of cultural heritage.

Oral History Traditions Some reference to the group/groups' own oral/literary traditions about their origins and culture is required. Most usually this will articulate the belief system underpinning relationships between people and the sacred, cosmological and natural landscapes. Attitudes to resources and their symbolic value may be highlighted during the research. This section can also be utilized to talk about genealogical footprints – the way knowledge of ancestors and places is constructed and utilised to justify land/resource claims of currently non-resident groups.

History of Contact A brief description of the pre- and post-contact situations may be relevant in helping to explain current politico-economic structures. This history will typically consist of several distinct phases involving successive waves of professional and other visitors: religious organizations, scientists, tourists and travellers. This section allows for an assessment of the impact of these historical phases on changes in the socio-cultural fabric of the groups – populations, subsistence, customary trade and exchange, development trajectories and inter-tribal communication.

Literature Review While this task need not entail an exhaustive list of scholastic materials, some indication of the nature and breadth of the literature relevant to the TA should be included. Short descriptive paragraphs that indicate reference categories – ethnological, geographical, environmental, ethical etc., – may suffice. If there appears some major foci for dissension or debate in the literature, this should be included, together with an overview and statement of its relevance to the ongoing social mapping.

At the macro level of description, the above discussions are aimed at providing a rounded picture of the people and land – their history and culture – both retrospectively and prospectively in relation to projects, schemes or issues that have affected the region. The micro level of detail, described below, provides the kind of information which will help elucidate impacts across sectors such as education, subsistence, employment and training, business development, health, governance and communications.

Target Area Community Profiles

The following sections profile how the population is organized in terms of groups, representation, subsistence patterns and migratory history through the provision of both quantitative and qualitative data. Presentational formats will largely depend on the quantity and range of information selected, but more often than not tables can be utilized to project a range of parametric data as in the example given in Table 6.1.

For any social mapper there will always remain decisions as to just how much information one includes in a document that might otherwise be included within a fuller SIA. For example, does one incorporate infrastructure status of the community units in respect to health, education, communications, business development, trade, or political organization? Most commonly, inclusion of such information will likely reflect the purpose of the social mapping report itself and the types of recommendations one foreshadows.

A minimum expectation would be that the report provide indications of some gross demographic features of the TA population. That is, approximate total, age and gender make-up of the population, and the relative distributions across the TA in respect to density and/or locality. While it is uncommon for a social mapping report to conduct its own census by means of, say, a household survey (see Chapter 10), the baseline data resources available may provide indexes of morbidity, birth rates, and trends in population growth or decline. A brief comment on the accuracy or reliability of available figures may be necessary, but where figures are unavailable, an estimate should be attempted.

Depending on the specific political geography of the TA communities and the residential/settlement forms which obtain, for example, town, village, hamlet, household, indications of relevant national census divisions (e.g. rural, urban) and other supervening organizational levels should be included. Since the TA communities will likely be subsumed within a nested system of governmental zones – for example, the village within a province within a state within a nation – it can be useful to represent diagrammatically (e.g. in graph format) the TA demographics as a proportional representation of these higher order and inclusive divisions. In the context of a report which provides recommendations, say, about infrastructure projects and distribution of royalties or equities, comparative population size, density and growth trajectories will significantly impinge on the findings made. This is especially the case where the mapping covers only a segment of an ongoing or proposed resource

Table 6.1 Target village infrastructure and social organisation overview

Village	Infrastructure status					Councillor	Treaty status	Population			Clans/sections & totems
	Schools	Health	Power	Church	Water			1874–91[2]	1980[3]	1990[1]	
MASINGELE	Community/ elementary	Aid-post	Two generators	United	Well	Kable Mepasi	Non-signatory	4–500	—	300	Molobo [Eagle] Obetobe [Pig] Dariame [Bamboo]
MARI	Community	None	None	United	Well	Wek Takufar	Pending	—	—	129	Sangara Mbangu Maiawae
JARAI	None	None	None	United CLC	Tanks	Wek Takufar	Pending	—	—	65	Sangara Mbangu Maiawa
BULA	Elementary	Aid-post	None	United CLC	Well tanks	Mark Bize	Pending	—	—	86	Sangara Mbangu Maiawa
TAIS	Elementary	None	None	ECPNG	Well Tanks	Wek Takufar	Pending	—	—	126	Sangara Mbangu Maiawa
BUJI	Community	Aid-post	None	United	Well	Inkome Amadu	Signatory	250	174	198	Rirang Badlag Dodo Doagag Gaiman Tuang Ulekopa

Table 6.1 Target village infrastructure and social organisation overview *(continued)*

Village	Infrastructure status					Councillor	Treaty status	Population			Clans/sections & totems
	Schools	Health	Power	Church	Water			1874–91[2]	1980[3]	1990[1]	
BER	Elementary	None	None	United	None	Inkome Amadu	Signatory	—	94	85	Wibag Doagag Ulekopa Waragag
SIGABADARU	Elementary/ community	Aid-post	Five generators	United CLC	Well	Gao Warapa	Signatory	—	265	316	Bibra [Plant] Samoguad [Coconut]
MAWATTA	Elementary	No	Two generators	United	Well	Gamo Gagoro	Signatory	400	192	104	Dugarubi [Fish] Gaidai [Eel] Maruadai[Cassowary]

project. The twofold aim of this section then should be both to: provide an overview of TA demographics, and to indicate the relevance of the data in the context of current or anticipated operations in the area.

Ecology and Subsistence Patterns

As part of the overall TA profile, the social mapper is expected to briefly describe environmental factors such as mean average rainfall, temperature variation, seasonal changes and ecological diversity. What is the terrain like: premontane rainforest, karst, verdant swamp, desert, etc.? Are there important altitude zones and what associated flora and fauna need be identified? Prominent landscape features – major rivers, mountains, lakes – should also be included, especially if they serve as boundary markers or major resources.

Discussion may typically extend to consider the principal subsistence patterns of the populace. Importantly, the study needs to remain sensitive to variations that may subsist within the target area in terms of :

1 Age, gender, social category restrictions of populations to food resources.
2 Age, gender, social category conventions, habits in terms of food gathering.
3 Differential or restricted access of parts of the population to particular resources within the target area.
4 Available but unknown, unnoticed, unused or prohibited food resources.

Indications of food sourced at different zones – terrestrial, lower-higher canopy, streams, rivers, banks, pools, lakes, etc. – may be relevant along with seasonal fluctuations on account of water-level changes and other environmental conditions such as floods, drought or frost. Additionally, the profile of economic activity should address local and market trade, sources for household income and whatever other factors appear germane to a prospective SIA. Stipulating nutritional values, counts of subsistence crops per mound or garden, or producing inventories of floral or faunal resources is generally beyond the scope of detail required in social mapping reports.

Social Organization

For many social mapping ventures, this will be the key section which informs about the structural make-up of social groups and their enmeshment with spheres of ongoing social action. Simply listing the number of structural permutations would require almost a book-length treatment, so in what follows the focus is squarely limited on elucidating guiding principles.

The social mapper faces competing constraints between, on the one hand, making the descriptive account accessible to non-specialists – when the conventional terms of analysis would otherwise appear as so much incomprehensible jargon – while on the other hand not wishing to dilute or temper the presentation in the knowledge that the report will itself become part of ethnographic literature of the area. For a descent-based social milieu, issues to be addressed would be:

1 Do I have to go back to first principles in describing descent principles?
2 Do I have to provide kinship diagrams to explain findings?
3 How much genealogy will suffice and what issues of confidentiality have to be observed?

To illuminate some answers to these questions, I consider below a case example drawn from my own SIA work in Papua New Guinea.

Case Example – the Huli of Papua New Guinea

The Huli people of Papua New Guinea number some 90,000 and are at the centre of a number of large resource development projects in Papua New Guinea. These include:

1 Oil from the Lake Kutubu and Moran fields.
2 Gas from Hides and Moran which will feed the PNG–Queensland gas project.
3 Gold from the Porgera and Kare fields.

They are generally regarded to have one of the most complex group-to-ground ownership grids in the region. The TOR for the social mapping contract on the target area given in Figure 6.1 included the defined tasks of :

1 Describing the social structure.
2 Constructing a database which could serve future ongoing landowner and land boundary demarcation work.
3 Critically identifying the kind of strains in the system which present problems for the operator.

The immediate challenge was how to exhibit the Huli system in diachronic perspective so as to explain which descent or resident units could be targeted for registration as Incorporated Land Groups: groups regarded as owning land resources who might also serve as the recipients of ensuing benefit streams from oil, gas and gold revenues. The following details were incorporated into the social organization segment of the mapping report.

1 Local concepts of historical 'time' and the interface between humans and ancestral progenitors and spirits.
2 What is a patrilineal descent principle, the segmentary system of phratry, clan, sub-clan and lineage inclusive of local language terminology, and the nature of these groupings as 'corporations'.
3 Clan history as reflected in mythical oral charters, totemic associations, and the ascribed status and functions of descent group leader.
4 Average depth to genealogies and status/functions of this knowledge within community.
5 Exogamic practices and brideprice as they articulate economic and political relations.
6 Kinship and non-kinship categories and institutions as a basis for cross-cutting ties, residence and interpersonal obligations.

While much of the above presents as a relatively unproblematic descriptive task, there were three areas of required knowledge deserving of more in-depth treatment:

1 How the discriminated social categories occupied, owned or used land.
2 How claims to land were traditionally processed and argued.
3 Understanding the complex group nomenclatures as tests of authenticity to historical land claims.

The objectives were not simply to describe the systems, but to present the data in a way that non-anthropologists could access, to reveal the kind of tests that other researchers might utilize in follow-up work, and to explain how the recommendation that primary landowners constitute an Incorporated Land Group was arrived at on the basis of these findings. The following sections are abbreviated extracts from the final social mapping report (Goldman, 1999b).

1. Clan-to-Land Grids

Succinctly stated, on any piece of clan land there are a host of related and non-related people to the core of patrilineal descendants who form the principal land-owning corporation for that segment of territory. In essence all of these residents are indistinguishable in their everyday behaviour. However, the **Tene** are regarded as *primary* members in the sense of holding the freehold title, while the **Yamuwini** (non-agnatic cognates) are *secondary* members holding leasehold on their land in perpetuity. A third category are **Wali Haga** who are non-related guests such as friends. Another way of conceptualizing this relation is to think of the agnates as **Hosts,** and the other categories such as *yamuwini* as **Guests**. A good analogy is the following: the primary residents constitute the hotel owners, while the secondary residents occupy rooms as tenants or guests of the hotel owners, often in perpetuity. Their stay is open-ended. Importantly, while these *yamuwini* stay on the land for all intents and purposes like agnates, they can ideally be evicted by their hosts the hotel owners (Ballard, 1995:72; Goldman, 1993; Frankel, 1986:48). The kinship ties and associated obligations between the two resident categories explains why there is deviation from a one clan–one land model.

Traditionally, this first→second co-residence relationship was celebrated in rituals such that **Tene** held the head of pigs while **Yamuwini** held the tail. There is more than mere ethnographic trivia to this statement. Because in the fertility Tege rites of Ega Dole/Uri *Tene* & *Yamuwini* would conjointly act in this manner, it has spawned a rhetorical adage in land disputes such that a *tene* person may deny the *yamuwini* status of a claimant by asking the rhetorical question:

> *Iya ega uri ago angi harebali?*
> **So when did we go for Ega Uri?**
> (In other words, "we didn't both participate in this ritual rite so you cannot be my yamuwini")

This kind of indigenous test of historical co-residence can also be applied by investigators to similarly discern relative landowner status within a parish.

In land disputes, only the **Tene** conventionally are allowed to recount the corporate clan history (*malu*) because they were the true repositories of the clan mythology. Suffice to say at this stage then that **Tene** have precedence and priority in matters to do with clan land and history.

The second process which produces changes in the 'one clan–one piece of land' is that these secondary (*yamuwini*) members migrate from various Huli clans, and as they stay as guests on their hosts' lands for several generations a picture of 'groups to ground' emerges which shows a complex mosaic of Huli clan segments scattered across wide distances. In effect, the following scenarios start to emerge:

1 Incoming migrants establish themselves over a period of several generations often out-producing and surviving the host-clan agnates. Numerically, these migrant sections may compose anything from 1 to 99 per cent of the total parish population.
2 These migrant units will retain knowledge of, and share identity with, their natal clan – i.e. they remain **Tene** of, say, Clan A – but also constitute **Yamuwini** of Clan B to which they have moved. Thus any one clan in Huli may have several of its segments scattered in more than one area. If one then looks at any given selection of Huli clans, one finds a core *moon* living on its true ancestral land, and various *satellite* segments scattered across Huli land. These processes are illustrated in Figure 6.3.

Figure 6.3 depicts the Huli system showing how clan segments migrate out to other 'hotels' where they may co-reside both with their main hosts and other segments from other clans. The model also shows from the perspective of Clan C how these various migrant sections come to be categorized as either a secondary (*yamuwini*) member or a tertiary non-related member *(wali haga*) depending on whether relationships are traced to the host clan ancestors or not.

Recommendations were made in this instance that primary group status should be the constitutive principle for Incorporated Land Groups, which for each land parcel must subsume resident secondary members.

2. Processes of Land Dispute

Question 1: If everyone knows what the system is and how it works why do disputes occur and what are their sources?

Question 2: How is title to land evidenced and argued in Huli?

The answers to these two questions are in fact related but for the purposes of this exercise we shall try to separate out the issues involved.

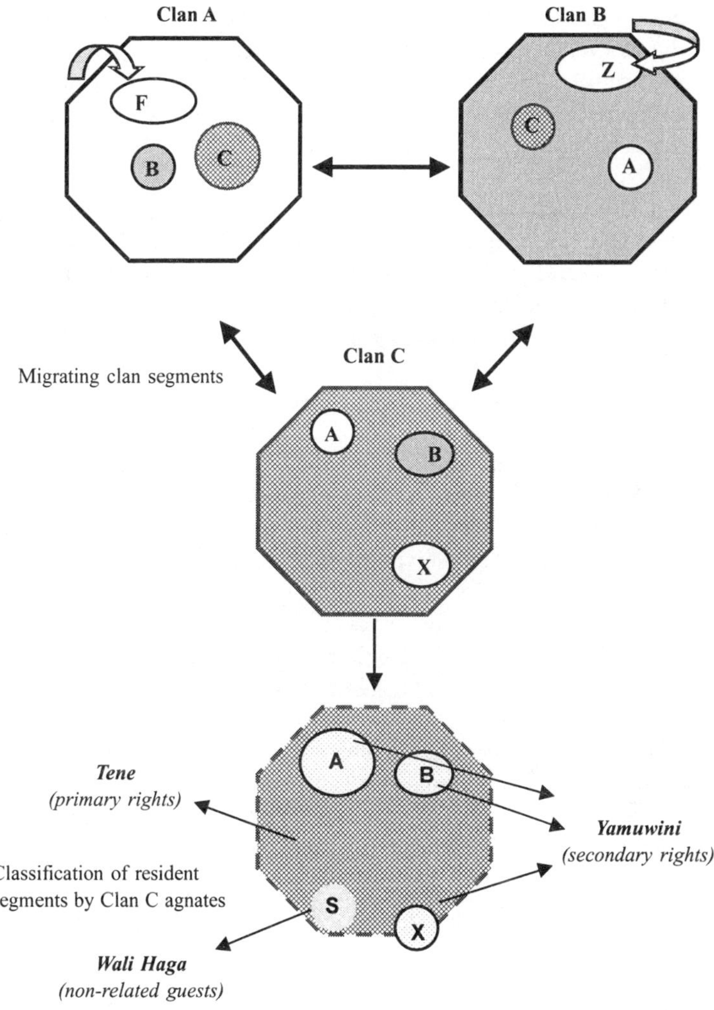

Figure 6.3 The Huli System over Time

Question 1 – Response The model of relationships depicted in Figure 6.3 suffices to explain an idealized situation with constituted hotels having various classes of guests as perpetual tenants in their hotel rooms. Importantly, we need to remember that boundaries between hotels may not always be, or have been, clearly demarcated. Three scenarios exist.

1 Because the clans evolve and establish themselves over time, historical charters which record group-to-ground grids will reflect clan specific perspectives. In other words it may be that neighbouring clans have different viewpoints on their boundaries: perspectives that can co-exist and never come to be challenged or tested until a resource dispute emerges.
2 In sparsely populated regions in which migrant groups independently re-settled there might be no valid history of inter-clan boundaries. In this circumstance, those groups who artificially fall within some zone such as a petroleum prospecting/development licence (PPL/PDL) may each independently generate accounts inadvertently in conflict with each other.
3 In the context of resource development where land assumes a previously unprecedented monetary value that can materially affect the wealth of individuals and families, the incentive is created for people to manipulate and massage their 'history' to opportunistically avail themselves of possible benefit streams. Accounts given to investigators typically fall into the following classes:
   (a) fabricated histories
   (b) false histories honestly given
   (c) histories which are incomplete because the knowledge was not handed down through the generations.

The above allows for predicted structural strains that will produce disputes in the target area. That is, despite the fact that the system and its categories are well understood by Huli, there is room to manoeuvre within the system by exploiting grey areas and re-categorizing oneself as a 'primary' rather than 'secondary' resident. We can then predict the following sets of possibilities with regard to how a dispute over land will be generated as illustrated in Figure 6.4.

1 Hotels will dispute with each other as to where their traditional boundaries exist with accounts that fall into the categories a–c given above.
2 Tenants who are secondary (*yamuwini*) or tertiary *(wali haga*) clan citizens will use accounts falling into the categories a–c above to establish themselves as independent hotel owners. That is, referring back to Figure 6.3 and Clan C, either/all A, B or S may assert that, contrary to C's claims, they constitute separate hotels within the area Clan C parish (see Figure 6.4)

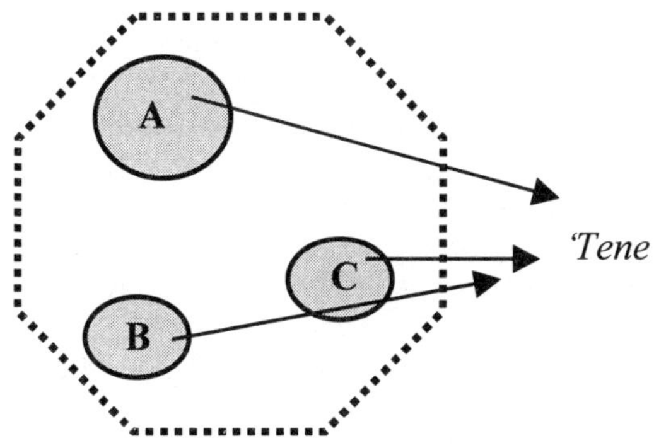

Figure 6.4 Land Claimants Contesting *Tene* Status

Question 2 – Response How do Huli clans assert title to land? As previously explained, each clan has its own charter (*malu*) which tells how the first ancestors lived and interacted on the land before humans existed. This account will often detail:

1 Ancestors and their travels/sojourns which explain how they arrived on the present land.
2 Significant events during this period which relate to landscape features such as rivers, drains, caves, trees, rocks, etc, and which usually explain how and why these are named as they are.
3 Significant marriages which resulted in the birth of the human progenitors of the clan.
4 How the land was divided both amongst members of the clan and perhaps other clans that were in the area.
5 The roll call of ancestors and the generations to the present.
6 Significant ritual events and history which identify sacred sites, ritual grounds and participation in fertility cults.
7 Ditches, drains, groves of hoop pines, etc.

As is found amongst Aboriginal Australians, the ties of people to place are rationalized and couched in the language of clan-specific histories. The tie to land is both a physical and a spiritual one. Land disputes are as much about conflicts over resources and the monetary benefits they bring, as they are about ownership of names, places, and ancestors which constitute clan identity.

This section thus commences to unravel what are frequently referred to as 'genealogical footprint claims' – resource claims based in genealogical history of residents. It described the kind of evidential criteria conventionally expected in land claim accounts.

3. Nomenclature Conventions as Tests of Authenticity

An outline of the very complex naming conventions which clans and clan members utilize to reference their identity was necessary for the following two reasons: (a) to understand the mechanisms by which groups attempt to re-position and re-categorize themselves in land disputes; (b) to reveal the kinds of tests that can be applied to determine the degree of authenticity of accounts which clans give as to their provenance and history in any particular area.

Clans may reference their identity in any of the following ways:

1. Totemic name They may refer to themselves by using their totemic ancestor name, so they call themselves 'x's children'.

No.	Clan name	Totemic name
50	URUA	*Gindi igini* – children of leeches
71	HAGU	*Tinagua igini* – children of rats
80	PI	*Urubungawe igini* – children of Raggiana Bird

Most usually this form of reference is utilised in political speeches as good poetic rhetoric.

2. Praise name Clans also have what may be called a 'praise' (*kai*) name again often utilized in political rhetoric and speeches made on grand ceremonial occasions such as pig feats and during the sharing of pig meat (see Goldman, 1983:262).

No.	Clan name	Praise name
63	TOBANI	*Walu Pubu*
65	WIDA	*Bauwaya*
64	PINA	*Wataga Pina*
54	KELA	*Ngoari Kela*

These appellations are very much clan specific and we will see later how many of the incoming clan segments from non-Huli areas have attempted to assimilate their own clans to the Huli system by creating atypical versions of this naming practice. What we notice is that for 63 and 65 the praise term does not incorporate the clan name but in 64 the clan name Pina is part of the praise name. Very often the praise name derives from some landscape feature associated with that clan, for example, a river or mountain name, and sometimes the praise term will be partly made up of a patronym term described below. Sometimes too, the praise name will be made up of the host (*tene*) + guest *(yamuwini*) names, as in **Hiwa-Koma** where Hiwa is the precedent clan who hosted (i.e. gave land) to Koma. So there is no systemic rule about how these praise terms were generated for each clan other than that they do not change and are conventionalized across Huli clans.

3. Patronyms These are prefix names utilized only by the agnates of a clan. That is, they reference that person's agnatic identity – true father's line – as descent from an ancestor. Irrespective of where a person ends up residing, this agnatic status never changes. To mark this identity an individual x (man or woman) will be referred to by others utilizing the agnatic prefix which belongs specifically to that clan or phratry of which the clan is a member.

No.	Clan name	Individual patronym
54	KELA	*Ngoari x*
66	KOMA	*Hubi x*
58	HORA	*Dau x*
92	TORO	*Gambe x*

As with most naming systems in Huli, there is nothing coincidental about the choice of terms: most usually a meaning can be found that explains their presence. For 54 Kela, this clan is part of the Tani phratry and *Ngoari* comes from Mt *Ngoari*ba in the Tani area. Similarly, for the immigrant 92 Toro clan from Tsinali, *Gambe* is the name used for the small pitpit which they brought to the Huli land. For 58 Hora, *Dau* comes from the tree *Ira Dau Mali* which provides the red beads used by Huli for decoration and rattles.

Because these nomenclatures intimate a conventional system of reference – that is, the three types of names are standardized, known throughout Huli, and do not/should not change over time – they provide an important means with which to verify clan accounts and test for bogus claims. In other words, when a clan of, say, Tani phratry attempts to call themselves by some other patronym, one knows immediately that the account being given is either proffered in ignorance or an attempt to mask one's true heritage.

The content in the above descriptions is less important here than the presentational reliance on diagram aids, choice of appropriate analogies, and relationship between data and applied problems of generating tests for authenticity in accounts. This example social mapping report covered an area of approximately 1,200 square kilometres (see Figure 6.1) and identified in excess of 100 primary landholding clans and some 300 secondary clan segments. The information was collated and formatted into an Microsoft Excel database, an extract of which is given in Table 6.2.

Genealogies

It may be apposite, depending on the social categories discriminated by the researcher, to include a section on genealogical issues. While again this will depend on the size and social complexity of the groups under investigation, it is important the consultant seize the opportunity to communicate conventional anthropological truths about genealogies in respect to the limitations of and sensitivities to this kind of data.

Genealogical information is always responsive to situational exigencies. Genealogies are not stable enumerative lists but malleable political instruments which evolve and transform. In many ways, genealogies exist only in their performance, as delivered to an audience for political purposes and agendas. It is rare then for genealogies to always present as unchanging delineations of ancestors in relation to land. Moreover, these artefacts are never merely a listing of ancestors: names are recounted as always enmeshed with, and anchored to, resources such as land and sea.

Given limited time and personnel resources, most social mapping reports provide only skeletal genealogies of a small and sample percentage of the groups identified. The objective is often to provide a blueprint for ongoing work by the commissioning agent. Figure 6.5 shows the place of this task within ongoing processes of land demarcation and landowner group identification. Equally, genealogical information may relate to specific issues of resource ownership discussed elsewhere in the findings of the report. In such cases the diagrams can be customized to present more than one layer of information. In the example in Figure 6.6, Ballard

Table 6.2 Example of Landowner Group Information Layout

Phratry	Tene Clan	Kai'Name	Sub-Clan-Lineage	Yamuwini	Ancestors	#ILG No.	Leaders	No.
HULI PROVENANCE								
				Tambaluma				
				Pobe			Dagibe	
							Mone,	
	DAGIMA	*Ngoari*	Wagia	Gambara			Henry	53
		Dagima					Hadu	
				Alo				
	Ngoari x'			Imini				
				Kuora	Yari			
TANI			Wabiago	Hiribi	Yalo			
Ira (tree) *wuale*				Himabe				
(will be planted)								
				Dambaluma				
				Dabamu				
Yari (cassowary)				Tangi				
igini (sons)			Telabe	Piriya				

(1995) is able to depict phratry related clans, number of generational descendants, references to other genealogies in his study, and the generational depth where Huli distinguish between ancestral spirits and the first human progenitors. The rule of thumb in these sections is to impress upon the reader the following points:

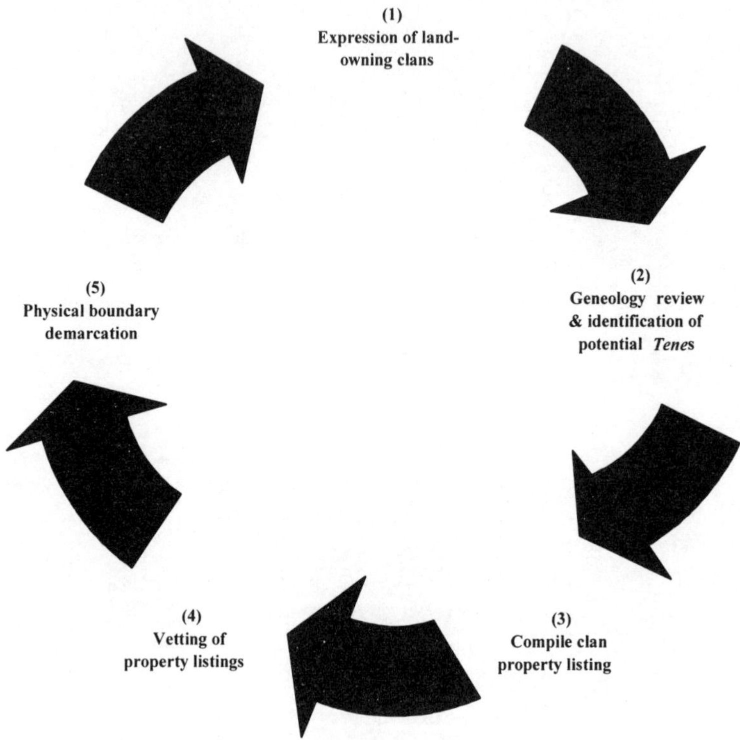

Figure 6.5 The Land Demarcation Process

1 The need for understanding higher-order segmentary divisions – the big picture – rather than the minutiae of individual memberships.
2 That it is rare for two genealogies on the same unit, even when given by the same informant, to exactly match in oral traditional societies. There are many computer programs available for formatting genealogies, for example Corel's Family Tree Maker, and as a last resort, any word processing package has the requisite symbols to allow for acceptable presentation. In this section recommendations can be

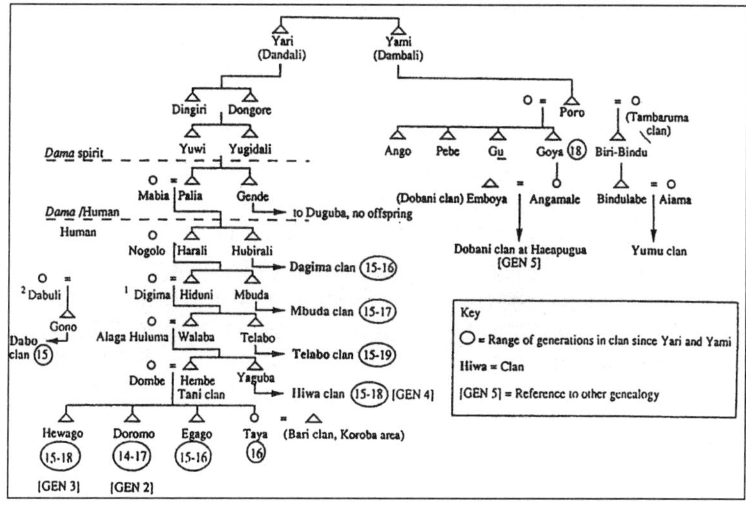

Source: Ballard, 1995: Appendix B6, p.11.

Figure 6.6 Genealogy 14: Tani

included in respect to issues such as future conduct of genealogical reports as well as the attendant confidentiality and ethical issues about what is often regarded as secret and sacred knowledge:

(a) Is genealogical evidence given in confidence and how far is this likely to be respected by commissioning agents and their personnel? If either by commission or omission there is a risk that such data may fall into inappropriate hands, the investigator has an ethical responsibility to make recommendations in this regard. If ancestral names have to be hidden out of respect for the wishes of the informant, the deceased and/or the group, decisions will have to be made about their inclusion in the report.

(b) If time does not allow for a full genealogical report, recommendations need to be made about genealogical collection and data gathering as an ongoing process.

Migration Models and History

As indicated previously, the social mapping report should represent the present group-to-ground circumstances as the consequence of merging historical trajectories that may include the following:

1 Traditional migration patterns.
2 Inter-tribal relationships.
3 History of contact.
4 History of resource development.

These discussions are normally intertwined with explanations about how this history allows for understanding about resource claims, disputes and trigger issues in the community. Explanation for present circumstances may need to move from macro to micro explanatory models. For example, in the Huli, population growth and dispersal is believed (Ballard, 1995) to have been triggered by the sweet potato revolution some time in the sixteenth to seventeenth century. This allowed both people and pigs to rapidly increase leading to dryland pressures, warfare and subsequent migration (Figure 6.7). Clan maps can then be produced to reveal central and peripheral locations of clan and clan segments which testify to these out-migrations. Somewhat differently, Figure 6.8 depicts the south coast Omati basin in Papua New Guinea and the proposed PNG–Queensland Gas pipeline route. What is illustrated is how this superimposed infrastructure unit will traverse abandoned villages whose owners are now displaced after successive waves of out-migration from Goaribari Island. This kind of social mapping work, then, has the capacity to uncover potential land claimants to any right-of-way compensation, and any further benefit streams associated with compensation for garden destruction, sacred sites, fauna and environmental pollution, etc.

Mapping Findings

This section essentially presents indications at various levels of detail about how the identified social groups are distributed on the land. Maps are conventionally provided which locate boundaries, frontiers, borderlands (Burton, 1991; Prescott, 1978) and other demarcated zones. The format chosen is really going to depend on what prior resources exist, what competencies the researcher has, and what can be achieved within the timeframe of the study.

Let us look at the typical range of information required to be included:

1 Plotting of the discriminated social categories within the target area.
2 Sacred sites, material culture heritage indicated on map.
3 Significant political divisions indicated, e.g. rural/urban census divisions, regional/provincial/state lines.
4 Major landscape features.

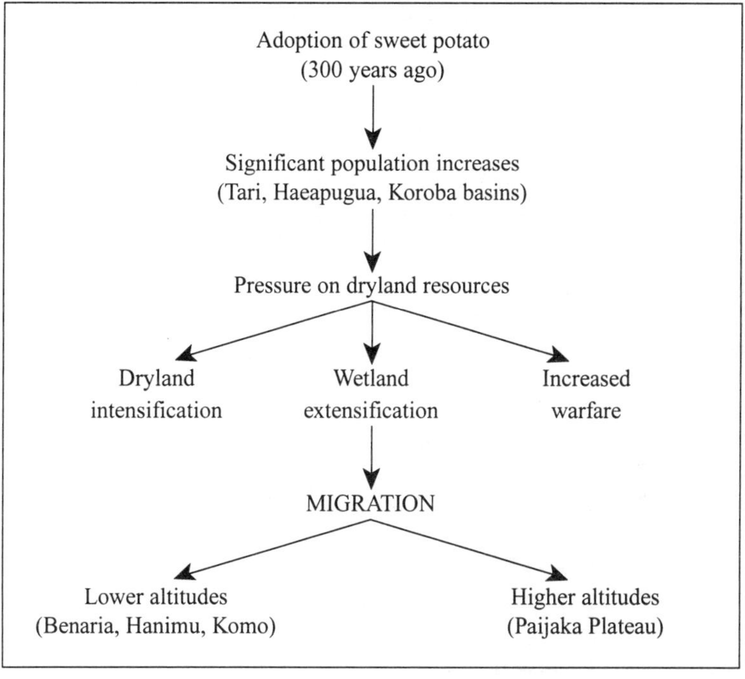

Figure 6.7 An Historical Model for Huli Migration (see Ballard 1995)

5 Disputed areas indicated.
6 Major service infrastructure across health (hospitals, aid-posts), education (schools), communications (roads, airports, railways) and religion (churches).
7 Resource development infrastructure: wells, pipelines, mines, development or processing plants, and so on.
8 Place names in local language.

Clearly, using geographical information system (GIS) computer programs (such as MapInfo or ArcView) allows for a level of detail and accuracy which all reports should aspire to. These programs permit the mapper to make definitive geographical identifications which can be linked with information databases on clans (see Table 6.2), ecology, demography, sacred sites, etc. But if these presentational resources are not available, for whatever reason, other techniques for illustrating findings can suffice.

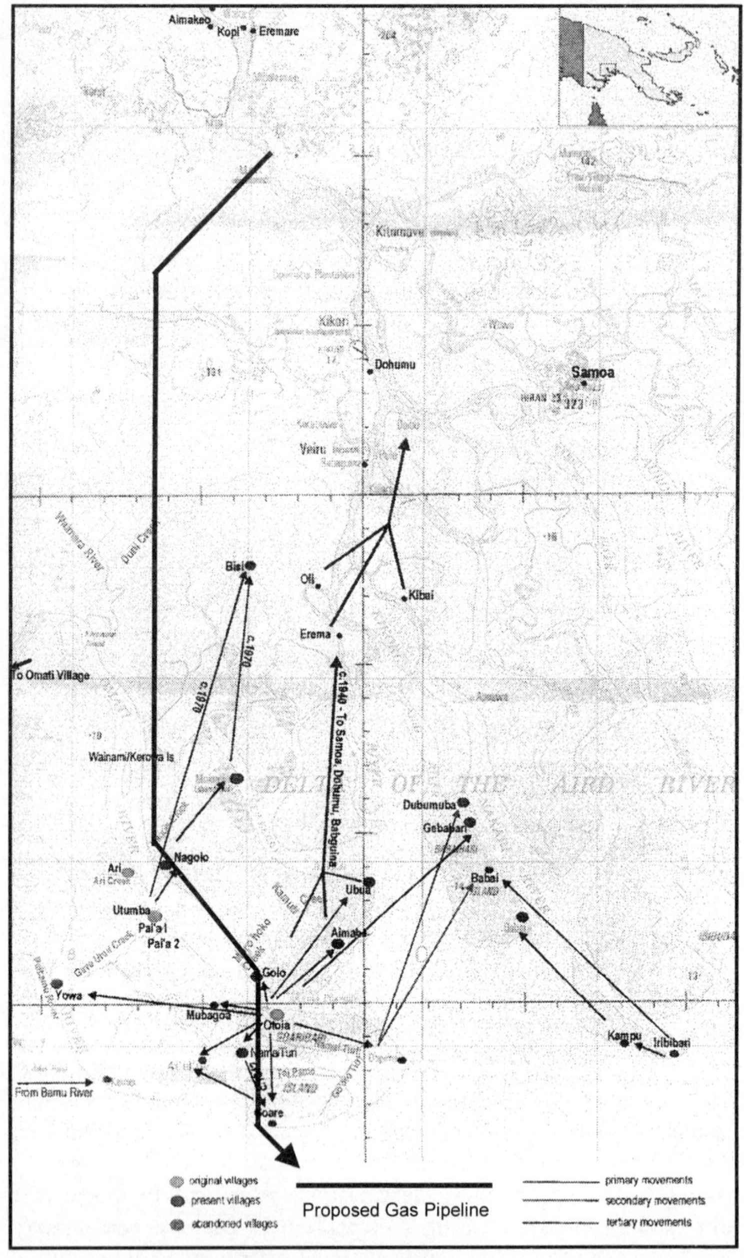

Figure 6.8 Traditional Omati villages and migration history

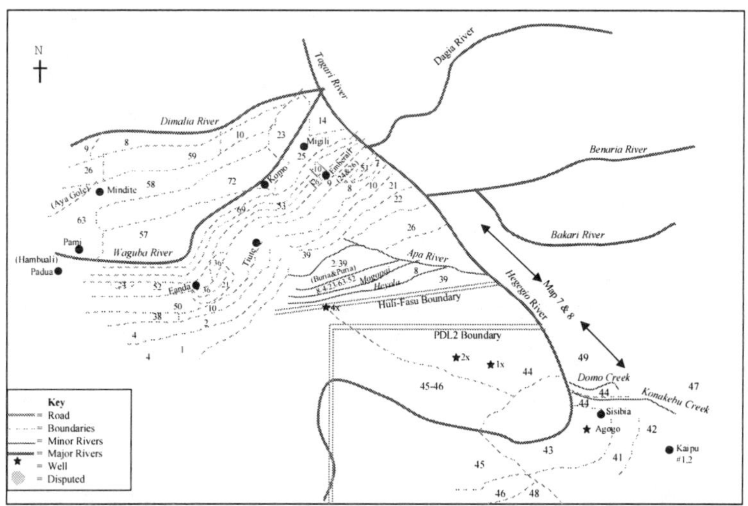

Figure 6.9 Example Presentation of Social Mapping Findings

Scanning of maps and superimposition of data can be resorted to, or free-hand not-to-scale drawings using a processing package such as CorelDraw or Microsoft PowerPoint.

Figure 6.9 represents a sector of social mapping for the project outlined in Figure 6.1. It was produced using CorelDraw and indicates major rivers, clan groups numerically indexed, areas likely to be disputed between landowners, cultural boundaries and petroleum development licence zones. Because the size of the target area to be covered was 1,200 km^2 of often inhospitable terrain, extreme accuracy of boundary determination using geographical positioning system (GPS) instruments would have required several years to complete.

The point to emphasize here is that decisions must be made by the prospective mapper as to what is realistically achievable in the allocated time, what is required for ongoing operations and decision-making, and what can be left for future work. The example in Figure 6.9 is merely indicative of a minimal acceptable standard in the circumstances. Importantly, the mapper is then obliged to articulate in the report the constraints and limitations such as the following:

1 Maps such as the above portray an amalgam of perspectives. They are not frozen landscapes of certitude but an approximation of viewpoints about boundaries which landowners may wish to see as fluid. They

reflect present exigencies as much as versions of past history. Defining such boundaries on the ground will inevitably involve 'negotiation' and any decision which is reached will likely stand only so long as acceptance has a consensus basis. That is, agreements here are no more than pauses in negotiation.

2 These approximate maps thus portray the relative distribution of people on the ground in terms of who is adjacent to whom.
3 The maps also reflect decision making by the social mapper in terms of which groups get to be represented on paper given the identification of more than 300 clan segments. In the above example, since the previous recommendation of the investigator was to formally register only primary (*tene*) groups (who exercise responsibility for their incumbent tenants), only primary clans were represented on the maps.

The map findings can then be amplified in the text with discussions of land disputes, boundaries, and likely scenarios in the target area as a consequence of any introduced scheme or development.

Sacred Sites, Material Culture and Cultural Heritage

As indicated above, attention may need to be given in the report to issues of cultural heritage and, more broadly, what are now frequently referenced as sacred geographies: ritual landscapes. As with issues of genealogy, what is raised here is the spectre of the social mapper as an information gatekeeper needing to exercise discretion and judgement on what must remain confidential and what can be sanitized for more public consumption. Equally, there will be definitional quandaries as to what constitutes, say, a sacred site within the context of a particular culture, and what kinds of checks and constraints can be utilized by researchers and others when certifying the authenticity of any such claim. This is a complex field which cannot be covered fully here, but clearly there will be a need to make the commissioning agent aware of what the interface is between national legislation on cultural heritage, and what indigenes view as important cultural symbols. The following is a preliminary list of some germane questions:

1 What is defined as national cultural property and is this consonant with indigenous classifications?
2 What evidential tests can be called upon to verify claims where a fiscal value is attached to such artefacts and where there are ownership disputes between various parties?

3 What contemporary levels of significance are attached to these sites or items, and what measures need to be taken to preserve both the knowledge about and the existing status of these cultural phenomena?
4 What is the existing level of awareness among the community about laws governing sacred sites and material culture items?
5 What responsibilities must or should a developer assume where development has the potential to affect heritage either by disturbance, damage, or creation of an inimical environment. That is, which bodies must reports be made to in the event of archeological deposits or finds, skeletal materials, ritual shrines, etc.?

Social mapping reports need not always entail a full-scale archeological investigation, though circumstances may dictate one be conducted. A full listing and discussion of all heritage phenomena should be included. As hinted at above, there will be grey areas in terms of what might pass as a sacrilegious act and what may not be sacrilegious but which will inevitably affect cultural heritage. For example, there may be a host of previously important ceremonial places used for initiation rites long since abandoned. Such sites may now have been built on and there may be only a few older men who retain any knowledge of their location – places which include plants, lakes, pools, wells, holes, caves, trees or almost any landscape feature. In such circumstances, options have to be listed as to what can be regarded as a community consensus view, what might be an acceptable level of physical disturbance, and what options exist for relocation, preservation or associated infrastructure development.

Status Summary Sections

The social mapping report may further be required – or find it judicious – to incorporate a number of sections which present status summaries or synoptic overviews across a range of issues. These may include, but are not limited to, items such as the following:

1 The developer's current achievements and directions in respect to community relations, lands work, etc. in the target area.
2 Current levels of political, legal and community representation, leadership, institutions, networks, and organizational capacities.
3 Infrastructure levels, distribution, adequacy and shortfalls.
4 Aspects of governance from local to national levels which directly impinge on the trigger issues within the community.

Table 6.3 Community-expressed demands for benefit infrastructure

	UPGRADES & IMPROVEMENTS						INSTALLATION, REBUILDING AND FINANCING						
VILLAGE	School	Aid-post	Water services	Teachers' houses	Solar lighting/ power	Boats/ motors	Treaty status	Roads/ telecom-muni-cations	Water tanks	Business projects	Sewing machines etc.	Fishing nets/refri-geration	Churches/houses community halls/sports facilities
MASINGELE													
MARI													
JARAI													
BULA													
TAIS													
BUJI													
BER													
SIGABADARU													
MAWATTA													
TURETURE	Community briefing and consultation by the councillor had not occurred prior to our visit and people were unwilling to express any opinions in his absence												
MABUDAWAN													
PARAMA													
SUI													

	UPGRADES & IMPROVEMENTS					INSTALLATION, REBUILDING AND FINANCING							
VILLAGE	School	Aid-post	Water services	Teachers' houses	Solar lighting/ power	Boats/ motors	Treaty status	Roads/ telecom-muni-cations	Water tanks	Business projects	Sewing machines etc.	Fishing nets/refri-geration	Churches/houses community halls/sports facilities
KATATAI													
KADAWA													
KIBULI													
KUPERE													
GNAO													
SEBE													
KULALAE													
DRAGELI													
WAIDORO													
WAMRONG													
IRUPI													
KUNINI													

Key to priorities: *High priority* *Medium priority* *Not listed* *Low priority*

5 Community attitudes, interests, and expectations concerning benefit streams. Table 6.3 is an example of community expressed demands in respect to the proposed PNG–Queensland Gas Project (Goldman, 1999a).
6 Community and regional planning strategies in light of projected benefit streams associated with the project or scheme – fiscal management, human resources and training, roles and responsibilities of stakeholders.
7 Ongoing benefit streams defined and listed – royalties, equities, trust/future trust funds, compensation types and rates, loans (revolving credit, etc.), telecommunications, scholarships and training, housing, roads, agricultural projects, etc.
8 Social issues (see Chapter 5): gender, development, inequity, conflict, education, migration, etc.
9 Major risks or sources of conflict. These may include items such as the following (Filer, 1998).

- Loss of cultural heritage in the project impact area.
- Unequal distribution of project-related benefits between local stakeholders.
- Mismanagement or misappropriation of cash benefits to local landowners.
- Forms of community organisation which discriminate against some project impact area people.
- Breakdown of traditional mechanisms of social control.
- Divergence between legal and customary definitions of resource ownership.
- Actual measurable damage caused by development to local resource base.
- Exclusion of local stakeholders from process of measuring and monitoring damage.
- Unexpected or unplanned changes in physical dimensions of project or scheme.
- Exaggerated fears of environmental damage amongst impact area people.
- Excessive expectations and demands by local stakeholders.
- Social and ecological disruption caused by influx of outsiders to project impact area.
- Inadequate planning or design of relocation schemes for local landowners.
- Disruption caused by relocation of local landowners.
- Mismanagement and failure of local business spin-offs from resource development.
- Recruitment and accommodation of the project workforce.
- Substance (alcohol, drugs etc.) abuse in the project impact area.
- Failure of government agencies to honour commitments.
- Confusion over the division of powers and responsibilities between government agencies.
- Lack of opportunity or capacity of government agencies to mediate between stakeholders.

- Inconsistency between compensation agreements or benefit packages across projects.
- Failure of developer to honour commitments.
- Overlapping boundaries between resource development or management projects.
- Addition of new development projects/impacts to existing project area.

There is a fuzzy fine line here between what would be the conventional scope of work and issues to be covered within a social mapping report and what might otherwise be incorporated into a separate chapter or chapters on social issues within a more encompassing SIA. To some extent, the TOR governing the social mapping will circumscribe the tasks to be completed. Other chapters in this book thus deal with some of the above topics in respect to scope for risk mitigation and benefit maximization strategies. The point to be made here is that accompanying any discussion of the above items there should be a list of recommendations.

Summary

What emerges from the above discussions is the insight that social mapping reports can service a number of key tasks in respect to both SIA and ongoing operations in the target area by all stakeholders. On one level they become additions to the resource literature on the region which provide social status summaries for a particular place and time; they become part of the historical legacy of documentary evidence and data. On another level, mapping reports can also function as blueprints for ongoing and future work concerned with the interface between community and resources. That is, they can set agendas and guidelines for such tasks as landownership registration, or for the landscape of negotiation about benefits, contracts, infrastructure agreements, memorandums of understanding, etc. The priorities are less those of decision making than providing an informed context in which decisions can be reached in respect to the impacts and social harmony trajectories associated with resource mobilization.

In effect, any social mapper is part social scientist, part social engineer, part social worker and part social conscience for the community represented in the work. These roles have to be choreographed and stage-managed in a manner that retains the credibility and independence of the investigator. At the same time, as Liebow (Chapter 8) clarifies, the investigator as anthropologist brings to the task a preconception that, in articulating the cultural milieu, the resources for problem-solving are thereby illuminated, if not identified. This does not compel one to deny that cultures are always in dynamic states of evolution – change is inevitable with or without the extraneous project/scheme impact scenarios. Nor need the researcher claim adherence to a view that cultures are somehow specimens to be pickled and preserved for romanticists. However, the very sensitivity to understanding how culture defines the context in SIA work invokes the belief that the bitterness of cultural loss, in the long term, will be remembered well after the sweetness of material gains made in the short term.

References

Ballard, C. (1995), *The Death of a Great Land. Ritual, History & Subsistence Revolution in the Southern Highlands of Papua New Guinea*, unpublished PhD Thesis, Canberra: Australian National University.

Burton, J. (1991), 'Social Mapping', in P. Larmour (ed.), *Customary Land Tenure: Registration and Decentralisation in Papua New Guinea*, Monograph 29, Papua New Guinea: IASER, pp.195–215.

Filer, C. (1998), *Social Impact Assessment in the Mining & Petroleum Sectors*, unpublished paper, Papua New Guinea: National Research Institute.

—— n.d. *Social Mapping Guidelines*, unpublished paper, Papua New Guinea: National Research Institute.

Frankel, S. (1986), *The Huli Response to Illness*, Cambridge: Cambridge University Press.

Goldman, L.R. (1983), *Talk Never Dies. The Language of Huli Disputes*, London: Tavistock.

Goldman, L.R. (1993), *The Culture of Coincidence and Accident and Absolute Liability in Huli*, Oxford: Oxford University Press.

Goldman, L.R. (1998), *Omati Social Mapping Report*, Kutubu: Chevron.

Goldman, L.R. (1999a), *Papua New Guinea South-West Coast Cultural Interests Report*, vols. 1 and 2, Kutubu: Chevron.

Goldman, L.R. (1999b), *Social Mapping Report on Land Sectors within PDL1, PDL2, PPL138, PPL161*, Hides: Oil Search.

Prescott, J. (1978), *Boundaries and Frontier*, London: Croom Helm.

Prescott, J. (1987), *Political Frontiers and Boundaries*, London: Allen & Unwin.

–7–

Cultural Heritage and Resources

Richard Stoffle

A Native Americans Social Impact Assessment (SIA) is virtually unique because it is negotiated rather than just conducted. In SIA projects the study evaluates the potential impacts of a proposed action on human social, cultural and economic values. The study may be stratified by ethnic group, but even so there is little expectation that somehow the study will stimulate a permanent connection between the involved ethnic groups, the project and the Federal regulatory agency that is overseeing the project decision. Exceptions to this are long-term projects that contain continual community monitoring. On the other hand, virtually all Native American SIAs will leave the regulatory agency, the project and the involved tribes as future partners. For this reason, this chapter talks about conducting Indian SIAs with an eye on past and future relationships between the tribes, the Federal agency, and even the SIA team.

SIA projects potentially impact Native Americans in many ways (Geisler, Green, Usner & West, 1982). Indian tribes, communities and individuals experience all of the same impacts that other people do (Stea & Buge, 1982:190–4), and the analysis of such impacts should proceed along standard lines as suggested in the Guidelines and Principles for Social Impact Assessment (National Oceanic and Atmospheric Administration, 1994). When Indian people write about these issues they define themselves as specially impacted because their communities have already lost most of their traditional productive base, have lost large percentages of traditional populations, and are recovering from the pressures of a dominant society that sought to rationalize conquest by denigrating traditional languages, culture and social organization. The Federal policy of forced acculturation was rejected and apologized for by the United States Congress in the American Indian Religious Freedom Action of 1978. This event alone set up Indian people as special in future agency actions and in SIAs (CEQ NEPA – regulations Federal Register Vol. 43 No. 230:44978–56007). Indian tribes are further recognized as the aboriginal land holders of the territorial United States and thus are considered to be dependent nations within the United States (Deloria & Lytle, 1984). Today, Indian concerns tend to be highlighted throughout various sections of environmental impact study (EIS) documents. Whole new sections, such as Environmental Justice, specially address Indian issues. Still, when we think of Indian SIA studies, cultural issues come to mind.

Native American Cultural Resources

Indian SIAs are complex because they are protected by specific Federal laws, congressional actions and presidential orders. Sometimes Indian SIA studies are glossed by a term that refers to a single type of study. In fact, even though a Federal agency has selected one law as the specific driver for an Indian SIA study, all of the various laws still apply and should be considered in the EIS. The five types of studies are:

1 Cultural landscapes – National Register Bulletin 30.
2 Traditional cultural properties – National Register Bulletin 38.
3 Sacred sites – Executive Order 13007.
4 Native American Graves Protection and Repatriation – 1989, 43 CFR 10.
5 American Indian Freedom Act – 1978, 92 Stat. 469.

It is important to remember that each type of study considers different aspects of Indian culture. Choosing the most appropriate ones will critically impact the outcomes of the study and the willingness of the Indian tribes to participate.

Indian cultural resources are complex because Indian people have lived so long on their traditional lands. This is a simple process of human adaptation (Rappaport, 1990). As a general rule of thumb, the longer a human group lives in a place, the more it comes to know about the place and to translate this knowledge into increasingly abstract culture phenomena (Bennett, 1976:265–305). Today, we call the spatial aspects of this cultural cognition of the environment a 'cultural landscape', and it has both physical and spiritual dimensions. Cultural landscapes involve, from the most to the least abstract (a) holy lands; (b) song and story scapes; (c) regional landscapes; (d) ecoscapes; (e) landmarks (Stoffle, Halmo, & Austin, 1997).

Our study team has selected the concept of cultural landscapes as the overarching analytical frame in an Indian SIA because it best reflects how Indian people view their cultural resources (Dewey-Hefley, Zedeno, Stoffle, & Pittaluga, 1998:15). This frame permits the assessment of impacts on the relationships between places and objects (Zedeno, Austin & Stoffle, 1997:125–7). Often SIA research ends with the identification of objects and places and their potential project impacts. If the SIA team uses a cultural landscape frame, then both types of impacts are assessed. This has important implications for the Record of Decision as well as for mitigation and monitoring.

Local cultural resource studies consider identification and assessment of impacts to the following:

- archaeology sites;
- petroglyphs;
- human burials;
- plants;
- animals;
- minerals;
- water.

The air as a living organism has recently been identified in a major EIS as a variable to be assessed (Department of Energy, 1996). Cultural resource studies also can consider impacts to Native American cultural practices (like a traditional healing ceremony) that are not tied to specific places. Ideally, each of these cultural resources should become the subject of a separate study so that native groups can send persons with special knowledge about the topic. In practice they tend to be folded into a single study thus challenging the SIA team and the Indian people to do it all at once.

Our study team has responded to the challenge of doing all types of Indian cultural resource studies at once by developing a series of data collection forms each with a specific purpose. In addition, we qualify our SIA text with the understanding that Indian cultural resources are more complex than our narrowly defined SIA efforts can reveal. All of our data collection forms emerged out of studies where data were gathered through open-ended interviews. The forms were created because Indian people told us later that they felt constrained by the presence of other people around during the interviews. The forms are a practical solution to conducting simultaneous interviews at the same location, and permit the systematic collection of data with each tribal representative having a private interview. We have found it optimal to have two Indian people for every one SIA interviewer.

At this time our SIA team has developed unique forms for the study of plants, animals, archaeology sites and petroglyphs. In addition, we have developed forms for the study of places and cultural landscapes. The forms have been refined in response to comments by Indian people, Federal agencies, and the academic community. Some forms have been used dozens of times, so have become really quite useful. Other forms are very much in process, and we are looking for better ideas for how to collect complex data. Forms are printed as an appendix to each SIA report and are available for use and review by other SIA teams.

Location is critical in interviews. Sitting in people's homes and talking about things far away in space and time is a bad idea. Early SIAs were conducted with this type of interview, but today our SIA team would reject a study design that totally relies on this procedure. If you want to talk about something or some place, the SIA interviewer and the Indian person must be looking at the thing or sitting at the place. This is easy to achieve for plants, water, archaeology sites, petroglyphs and landmarks, but difficult if studying animals and isolated caves.

Consulting with Native Americans

Formally working with Native American tribes is called consultation, and here is presented a model for that consultation. The model describes nine ideal steps for developing a consultation relationship with Native Americans who are culturally affiliated with lands being studied. These steps are suggested on the basis of the past experiences of the SIA team and on the analysis of other consultation relationships. Examples of relationships between Native Americans and Federal agencies are used throughout so the model will be as instructive as possible. These steps suggest how a process might occur, but they need not always be followed in order to achieve an acceptable consultation. Instead, the nine steps suggest a logical sequence of decisions and actions that normally would be involved in developing a consultation relationship. It is important that the SIA study team work with the involved Indian tribes to design a consultation relationship that reflects their needs, the needs of the responsible Federal agency and the protection requirements of the cultural resources under consideration. The ideal steps are:

1 Defining consultation.
2 Establishing cultural affiliation.
3 Contacting the tribes.
4 Having an orientation meeting.

5 Forming a consultation committee.
6 Conducting site visits.
7 Developing mitigation recommendations.
8 Maintaining ongoing interactions and monitoring.
9 Terminating consultation.

These consultation steps are discussed in their logical sequence of occurrence. The first consultation step is to decide what type of consultation relationship is desired. The second step is to specify, using cultural and historical research, which Native people or peoples have traditional ties to the lands being studied. The third step is to establish government-to-government relationships between formally recognized American Indians tribes and Native Americans with special Federal standing and the SIA study team. The fourth step is to have an orientation meeting, where the SIA study team begins to meet and talk with Native Americans. The fifth step is to form a Native American consultation committee and establish mutually agreed-upon procedures for its operation. The sixth step is to bring Native American cultural resource experts to the lands being studied so that traditional cultural resources can be identified related to sites, and initial management recommendations can be made. Mitigation recommendations come as a seventh step followed by ongoing interactions and monitoring as an eighth step. Finally, because some consultation relationships do not last, a ninth step involves terminating the consultation relationship.

The following model for developing a consultation relationship is presented here on the assumption that there is no pre-existing relationship between the Federal agency and the tribes. Most SIA projects occur when there are no current relationships with Native Americans, but some Federal agencies or private corporations do have working relationships with Native Americans at this time. Many of these relationships are working well from the perspective of both the Native Americans and the land manager. Few of these relationships are established using all of the nine steps described here, but all nine steps are potentially relevant to any relationship.

Defining Consultation

Federal land managers have a stewardship responsibility to consult with Native American people regarding cultural resources found on Federal lands and on other lands affected by a Federal activity. The Federal government requires that all of the lands held by its various agencies be managed in certain ways; some ways defined by legal obligations, others defined by treaties, and still others reflecting the desire of the Federal agency to involve Native people in the management of their ancestral resources. Increasingly Native Americans have been asked to identify their cultural resources located on these lands and to suggest culturally appropriate management practices.

'Consultation' is a term that is commonly used to describe a process by which Native American peoples with traditional ties are identified and brought into discussions about cultural resources on Federal or Federal-activity-affected lands. Consultation involves a fundamental decision on the part of the Federal land agency to share some decision making with Native Americans. Native people are asked to share in the decision to identify resources needing protection, decision to prioritize which cultural resources will be protected first, and the decision to select from among a variety of management practices those that most appropriately protect the cultural resources in the context of other resource uses. Native peoples are asked to share in the long-range planning and monitoring of these cultural resources and the lands that hold them.

According to scholars who study consultation (Cernea, 1991; Dobyns, 1951; Parenteau, 1988:5–10), the quality and success of the consultation process depends directly on the degree to which decision-making power is shared. Arnstein's (1969) studies demonstrate that any consultation process can be characterized as falling on a scale from 1–8 where participation without shared power is called 'manipulation' and where sharing power even to the point of negotiating with the agency is called 'partnership'. The primary decision that a Federal agency must make is how much decision-making power can be and will be shared with Native people. Once the range of decision-making sharing is established, it should be clearly identified at the outset of the consultation so that it can become a part of the Native people's decision to participate in the consultation.

General Consultation More and more Federal agencies are becoming involved in general consultation with Native Americans. This establishes a permanent relationship with Native American groups who have cultural ties to the lands and resources managed or affected by the actions of a Federal agency. General consultation should be based on extensive research concerning cultural resources that Native groups identify as being located on lands of concern. General consultation should be based on a strong information foundation.

A major advantage of general consultation is that it can occur in the absence of a specific project proposal, which is evaluated under specific laws usually as part of an NEPA. Often the laws that govern specific project studies add third parties to discussions between the Federal land managers and Native people, which can confuse and limit discussions. General consultation occurs when it is desired by the Federal land manager and the Native people and is neither limited by time nor issue. It is the perfect social environment for discussing a complex relationship designed to protect cultural items of greatest significance. Another advantage of general consultation is that it produces a strong information base for identifying cultural resources for both the Federal agency and for Native people.

Through various cultural studies, the Native people build a set of recommendations that suggest how to best manage these resources. Most Native American cultural resources located on Federal lands or effected by the Federal actions will become known through the process of general consultation. This will reduce the number of times that Federal actions will have to be stopped and modified because of unanticipated discoveries of cultural resources. If Federal actions activities were to impact cultural resources not previously identified, procedures would be in place for informing the Native people about the discovery and those Native people would have procedures for helping the Federal agency minimize adverse impacts on the newly discovered cultural resources.

General consultation is the only way to build true and stable partnerships between Federal agencies and Native American people. Often project-driven SIAs bring Federal agencies and Native people together for the first time, and afterwards they decide to move to general consultation as a means of resolving problems before projects precipitate specific cultural resource decisions. The initial SIA team can be retained to facilitate these further studies.

Native people approach cultural resource management from what has been termed 'holistic conservation' (Stoffle & Evans, 1990). They respond positively to holistic studies that bring into consideration as many factors as possible, so the Federal agency can better understand the complex interrelationship between cultural resources and other aspects of Native life ways. Interestingly, the new Federal initiative for ecosystem management closely reflects the philosophical orientation of Native peoples. According to Gore (1993:300) '. . . some people now define themselves in terms of an ecological criterion rather than a political subdivision'. For example the people of the Aral Sea and the Amazonian Rain Forest define themselves in terms of these all-important ecosystems. In March 1994, eighteen United States federal agencies demonstrated their ecosystem management activities to the United States Congress

(Morrissey, Zinn & Corn, 1994). By 1996 (Yaffee, Phillips, Frentz, Hardy, Maleki & Thorpe, 1996) there were hundreds of ecosystems projects most involving extensive SIA components. Native people have responded in a positive way to Federal agencies that are willing to consider cultural resources from an ecosystem perspective.

Specific Consultation There is always the need to conduct specific consultation regarding cultural-resource issues associated with actions on Federal lands. For example, when general consultation has identified all types of cultural resources, ground-disturbing activities may unexpectedly unearth a human burial or an object of great Native ceremonial significance. The Federal agency may wish to use some portion of their reserve lands for an activity that was not considered during general consultation. Also, the United States Congress may pass new laws regarding the management of cultural resources that potentially would alter the existing relationship between the Native people and the Federal agency. One such law is the Native American Graves Protection and Repatriation Act (NAGPRA), which specifically requires certain types of information to flow between the Federal land managers and Native American people.

Specific consultation is limited by the scope of the specific law that is being complied with and the proposed activity that is being evaluated. Native people often are frustrated by specific consultations because they are limited to those project-specific issues and cultural resources that are being assessed. The Federal agency's responses are too often limited by third parties that legally participate in the assessment. None-the-less, a series of SIA consultations can produce the base from which to build general consultation.

Establishing Cultural Affiliation

There are many ways that Native American peoples have established cultural affiliations to lands held or affected by a Federal agency. At the most general level Native Americans established these ties because they lived on the land long enough for a culturally shared connection to occur. So the basic question asked in cultural affiliation is, 'what Native American people or ethnic groups lived here?'

The nature of the relationship between Native American people and the land is cultural. The concept of culture (LeVine, 1984:68, 72, 79) implies that a phenomenon is shared in that it represents a consensus on a wide variety of meanings among members of an interaction community;

that it is connected and ultimately comprehensible only as a part of a larger organization of beliefs, norm, and values; that people who share a culture make sense of new information in terms of a cultural rationale which is founded on a single collective formula. Simply put, the connection between Native Americans and lands held or affected by a Federal agency is abstract, complex and non-trivial. Assessing this relationship is best accomplished by professionals trained in the study of cultural systems, in consultation with potentially culturally affiliated Native American people.

Most laws, regulations and guidelines that cause Federal land-holding agencies to consult with Native Americans do not define what is meant by the term cultural affiliation. Some laws do define this concept; for example, the term is defined very specifically by the NAGPRA. It is important to note that when a Federal agency adopts a broad definition of cultural affiliation for most kinds of cultural resource studies they can still narrow the consultation process when needed for NAGPRA and then resume Native American interactions based on the broader definition. Flexibility is needed when establishing consultation relationships with Native Americans.

How long must a people have lived on the land in order to establish a cultural affiliation? The length of time Native Americans have spent on the land will vary from groups who perceive they have lived there since the beginning of creation to groups who have had a brief but culturally significant experience on the land. Native American cultural affiliations are created by the supernatural at the beginning of time and by historic events such as a military battle that lasted only a day. When periods of time are chosen as the frames for viewing cultural affiliation, three broad divisions emerge:

1 Traditional period.
2 Aboriginal period.
3 Historic period.

It is important to remember that Native Americans may use other definitions of time including a pre-human time, which is without measure and is thus time-less.

Traditional-period Affiliation Native American people have lived on the North American continent for at least 14,000 years according to some scholars (Dincauze, 1991; Haynes, 1987) and as much as 30,000 years according to other scientists (Dillehay, 1991; Grayson, 1988; Meltzer,

1989; Whitley & Dorn, 1993). Despite various scientific interpretations of their origins, most Native Americans believe they were created as a people in North America given birthright ties to a holy land. Often Native American people have a specific cave, spring, valley or mountain where they were created. Similarly, the people of Polynesia, including Hawaiians, emerged from an earlier people known as the Lapita, who spread eastward into the Pacific from their homelands in northwestern Melanesia. The Lapita people were a marine people who began their eastern journey to new islands about 1600 BC and arrived in the Hawaiian islands about AD 300 (Abbott, 1992:1–4; Cuddihy & Stone, 1990).

Native American peoples have lived in many locations during the thousands of years that the Americas have been occupied. Because native peoples moved or were moved, most portions of their traditional land have been occupied by peoples of different cultures. When such movements have been retained in the memory of the living native people, they often have cultural attachments to places where they no longer live. Oral history can accurately convey certain types of information over thousands of years, as illustrated by the Hebrew and Islamic peoples of the Middle East. Like other peoples with oral traditions, Native Americans retain their attachments to sacred places over long periods.

Aboriginal-period Affiliation The term 'aboriginal' is used here to refer to those people who are recognized by the United States government as having possession of land at the time it was lost to the United States. For many Native American groups, this transfer involved a treaty negotiated between their people and the government of the United States. For many other Native American people, however, they simply were moved away from their aboriginal lands without formal transference of title. These two unique processes of land-loss produced two types of aboriginal period cultural affiliations for Native Americans, which are termed here treaty-tribes and land-claim tribes.

'Tribe' is used here to refer to the aboriginal inhabitants of territory lost to the United States federal government. The term tribe is commonly used as a gloss for a variety of Native American social structures that existed aboriginally. Actually, few aboriginal Native American peoples were organized as a tribe, if the technical meaning of this term is used. Most cultural anthropologists would call aboriginal Native American people an 'ethnic group'. In the following discussion the term 'tribe' is used as meaning something like an ethnic group. It is important to make this distinction because not all of the people from any particular Native American ethnic group participated in the 'tribalization process'.

Representatives of the United States government often organized Native American ethnic groups by region, a process that often occurred without the full participation of the people. Normally some ethnic group members were left without any tribal membership. Today, there are many Native people who do not belong to a formally recognized tribe or Native organization. These people are usually referred to as not 'federally acknowledged' peoples; none-the-less, they remain Native peoples. Some of these Native people are seeking federal acknowledgement and others are not. The cultural concerns of not 'federally acknowledged' people need to be considered during most types of Native American consultation.

1 **Treaty-tribes.** Native Americans who lost control over some or all of the lands they occupied at the beginning of the historic period to the United States government are called here 'treaty-tribes'. The term is a useful distinction for Federal agencies seeking to understand cultural affiliation because there are a variety of primary references listing United States federal treaties, specifying the lands considered under the treaty, and identifying the Native American group involved in the treaty. While it is relatively easy to identify treaty lands and tribes, most aboriginal lands were not transferred to the United States by treaty.
2 **Land-claims tribes.** Most Native American people can be classified as land-claims tribes, because they lost control over their lands to Euroamericans, but no treaty was ever signed. In most cases, these Native Americans simply were moved off aboriginal lands by force and non-Indian settlers (Sutton, 1985) occupied the lands. The United States federal government created the Indian Claims Commission (ICC) in 1946 (60 Stat. 1049) charging it with adjudicating the claims of Native Americans for lands lost. After three decades of legal action, a map was prepared that listed the lands considered and the associated Native American people. The ICC produced a multicoloured foldout map entitled 'Indian Land Area Judicially Established' as part of its final report (ICC, 1978; Sutton, 1985:12–13). This ICC map is a useful (but not definitive) tool for identifying the cultural affiliation for most Native Americans to aboriginal lands.

To summarize, both treaty and ICC documents can be used to begin to determine which Native American ethnic groups occupied certain lands when these were lost to Euroamerican society through encroachment or the Federal government through treaty. It must be remembered, however, that both treaties and ICC processes only establish which Native American group lived on a segment of land at the time it was lost to non-Indian peoples, and do not identify pre-existing Native groups who lived on the land. Furthermore, few land areas were covered by treaty and few treaty lands were surveyed to make reference maps geographically accurate. The ICC process also did not address lands jointly used or claimed by more than one Indian ethnic group, so that many lands were not designated as belonging to any Indian ethnic group (Sutton, 1985:112). Finally, treaties and ICC claims rarely specified the contemporary Native American group or tribe who would be culturally affiliated with the land in question. Given these limitations, the process of establishing cultural affiliation should include a search of treaties and ICC documents, but it should not be limited to Native ethnic groups found in these documents.

Historic-period Affiliation Probably the time of greatest movement for Native American peoples was during the historic period when the Euroamerican frontier expanded into lands held by Native Americans. The historic period began at different times for different Native American groups and the encroachment on Native lands resulted in both total dislocation and gradual dislocation. In many instances, however, when Euroamericans arrived in a place the Native peoples moved. After forced relocation, Native people retained cultural attachments to their aboriginal lands, while culturally re-establishing their way of life in new lands. In the new lands they gathered plants, killed animals, planted crops, gathered clay for pottery, had babies and died. In other words they continued to live as coherent cultural groups. When they interacted with the new lands through traditional ceremony they formed new cultural affiliations.

Native people often were repeatedly relocated; thus they became culturally affiliated with many places. The Shawnee people, for example, were moved from southern Michigan to Ohio where they lived and died; then they moved near to Kansas City, Kansas, where they lived and died; then they moved to Oklahoma where they live today. When asked about cultural affiliation to places where they had lived in Kansas, Ohio and Michigan, the Shawnee tribal council expressed concerns for these and other places where they had resided during their forced migrations (Stoffle, 1990), because in these places their ancestors are buried and the places represent critical junctures in Shawnee cultural history.

Some Navajo people were relocated in the 1950s, in response to pressure from the United States government, to the Colorado River Indian Tribes reservation, which is located on the lower Colorado River in the Mohave Desert. Two generations later, descendants of these Navajo people had attached themselves to these lands that were the aboriginal lands of both the Mohave and the Chemehuevi Southern Paiute. During recent

SIAs, these Navajo people expressed concerns for places in the Mohave Desert that were made sacred when they worked there as railroad workers (Drover, 1985) and for plants in the Mohave Desert now used in medicinal ceremony and rug weaving (Cultural Systems Research, 1987:129–31). Navajo people only used these places and plants after being relocated to the lower Colorado River, but the places and plants were used by the Navajo people in a traditional way, thus qualifying as sacred items under the National Historic Preservation Act.

Perhaps one of the most complex cultural resource issues that emerged during the historic period occured when one native ethnic group was relocated to lands formerly occupied by another native ethnic group. This process was not restricted to the historic period, but it seems to have occurred most often then. A recent study of petroglyph sites in Wyoming and Montana (Francis, Loendorf & Dorn, 1994) used chemical dating techniques to show that over thousands of years different native peoples made petroglyphs on the same rock panel. The Navajo Nation expresses claims to prehistoric Pueblo sites because the sites are used by Navajo medicine men to gather arrowheads, pottery, rattles, and even the skin and bones from pueblo burials for use in Navajo ceremonies (McPherson, 1992:105–22). Some Navajo people express claims to prehistoric Pueblo sites because the Navajo people believe they are biologically and culturally related to these Pueblo people. These cases of sequential use and cultural affiliation demonstrate that places, artefacts, and even bodies can have multiple and even conflicting native cultural affiliations.

Contacting the Tribes

Cultural affiliation studies basically establish which Native American ethnic groups potentially have traditional-, aboriginal- or historic-period ties to lands held or affected by a Federal agency. The term 'ethnic group' means people who share a common culture. Perhaps an example will serve to clarify the complexity of moving from ethnic affiliation to that of contemporary Native American organizations that actually would be contacted about the consultation. One can speak of the Southern Paiute people as an ethnic group who aboriginally occupied a territory extending from the north in Utah along the right bank of the Colorado River through the Grand Canyon, and to near Blythe, California. This is a north–south distance of more than 600 miles. The southern portion of their aboriginal lands extended from the Colorado River west into the Mohave Desert almost to Death Valley. The boundary of these aboriginal lands was established in the Indian Claims Commission hearings. Near the present-day community of Las Vegas, Nevada, is Nellis Air Force Base, which is clearly within the aboriginal boundary of Southern Paiute Lands.

Nellis Air Force Base wants to consult with the Southern Paiute ethnic group regarding cultural resources on Department of Defence (DOD) lands, but this ethnic group lost most of its corporate functions between the 1840s and the 1860s as Euroamericans encroached on the major riverine and spring oases. Traditionally the Southern Paiute ethnic group was politically, economically and socially integrated based on agriculture, natural food gathering, and trade. Social disintegration, which was manifested in Southern Paiutes having a simpler form of social organization, occurred due to drastic population reduction caused by dozens of lethal disease episodes and Euroamerican encroachment on key agricultural portions of the ecosystem. By the late 1890s the United States federal government had established a series of small reservations to support Southern Paiute people. In the twentieth century, more small reservations were established where most, but not all, Southern Paiute people were registered so they could have access to federal resources. In 1934 the United States government provided Indian people on reservations an opportunity to organize and become officially recognized as tribes. Thus various economic and political processes created a series of Southern Paiute tribes out of what aboriginally were local divisions of the Southern Paiute ethnic lands. Today, there are nine Southern Paiute tribes recognized by the United States government. In addition there are about 300 Southern Paiute people living in the four-ethnic group (Southern Paiute, Navajo, Hopi and Mohave) composite tribe called the Colorado River Indian Tribes. Furthermore, the Pahrump band of Southern Paiutes is a local group that has never been federally recognized as a tribe even though its members continue to occupy its portion of aboriginal territory. Finally, most Southern Paiute tribal chairs belong to the Southern Paiute Chairmen's Association, which attempts to provide ethnic-group level integration across a wide range of issues.

Who among all these Southern Paiute people should be involved in consultation relationships at Nellis Air Force Base? There is no legal answer, but there is a practical one. Ethnic groups ultimately hold the culture of their people (Stoffle, Halmo, Evans & Olmstead, 1990a; Stoffle, Halmo & Evans, 1999). Not every member of an ethnic group will know about all aspects of this culture, so it is necessary to talk with persons who have specialized knowledge. Where are these people? They are scattered throughout the various tribes and unrecognized groups. If all tribes and organizations that represent Southern Paiute people are contacted during the consultation, potentially each will bring needed experts to visit the study area and identify places and things of cultural importance. The output of a broad-based consultation should be the fullest understanding of Southern Paiute concerns on Nellis Air Force Base lands. A more restricted consultation will leave out noted Southern Paiute cultural experts and produce an uneven quality in the cultural resource assessment. This could cause time and dollar-costly delays in agency actions, because decisions would be based on incomplete information.

Officially the United States government prefers to deal with Native American groups on a government-to-government basis. The President, in a Memorandum of 29 April 1994, recently reaffirmed the well-established Federal position entitled 'Government-to-Government Relations With Native American Tribal Governments'. The National Congress of American Indians, which is the national association of tribal chairs, also supports government-to-government relationships. Such a relationship recognizes the 'dependent nations-within-the-nation' status of American Indian tribes (Deloria, 1985). This relationship should be the foundation of all consultation. The consultation will be incomplete, as discussed above, without a procedure for additional ethnic-group inputs from non-tribal government sources. It is suggested, therefore, that federally unrecognized native groups, Native American organizations and pan-Indian organizations be added to the consultation when it can be demonstrated that they do represent special ethnic-group perspectives relevant to the cultural resource management issues of concern to the DOD installation. Finally, individuals from the native ethnic group who otherwise would not be able to share important cultural insights can be added to the consultation as 'interested parties'. The recommendations of interested parties and non-tribal Indian organizations, however, must be subsumed under the recommendations of the officially recognized tribal governments.

Having an Orientation Meeting

Contacting potential culturally affiliated tribes and Native American organizations should be done in a manner appropriate to the consultation. If it is to be a project-specific SIA consultation, the information given to Native people should reflect that project. On the other hand, if a general consultation is desired then a very different essay and set of materials are needed. Although project-specific SIA consultations can lead to a mutual decision to begin general consultation, the orientation meeting should have a clear-cut purpose and deal only with the issues actually under consideration at the time.

In general, letters, maps and diagrams appropriate to the issues to be discussed should accompany the initial communication with Native American groups and tribes. Such letters describe the agency that is making the contact and the purpose of the contact. Recently, a video-letter was used to inform almost two dozen tribes about an assessment of cultural affiliation and concerns for Chaco Culture National Historical Park (Stoffle, Evans, Zedeno, Stoffle & Kesel, 1994:11). The video letter was about seventeen minutes long and began with the park superintendent discussing the goals of the study. Photos of places in the park that were the focus of the study followed this. Clear instructions for becoming involved in the study closed the video. The video-letter was well received by the Indian government leaders who said it permitted them to make an informed decision about whether or not to send representatives to the park.

Letters alone generally are an insufficient basis for most tribal governments to gain sufficient understanding of an issue under discussion so that the government can respond to a project, and many letters therefore are not answered. Follow-up telephone calls are always necessary to provide further information, but most tribal governments require that a consultation request, for their people's time and perhaps tribal resources, be made in person. Cultural resource specialists and agency personnel should meet in person with tribal councils (or their officially chosen representatives) to explain the project and answer questions.

Members of tribal governments and Native American organizations tend to be unfamiliar with legal aspects of cultural resource questions, although they generally believe decisions about such issues to be highly significant. This presents an information-gap problem for most Native government leaders. One solution to the information-gap is for the United States federal agency to invite government leaders to visit a portion of the study area as part of an orientation meeting. During the meeting government leaders can learn first-hand about what is being discussed and have the opportunity to exchange cultural resource views and strategies with other native leaders. The native government's need to know before making key cultural resource decisions should be respected and addressed by the consultation process.

Forming a Consultation Committee

The decision to form a Native American consultation committee can be the key to the success of the consultation when many tribes and Native

American groups are culturally affiliated with the lands under consideration. The consultation committee stands as a meta-organization between the tribal governments and the Federal land managers. The committee is composed of and chaired by native people. As such, the consultation committee is able to resolve certain issues relating to the process of consulting. In the early stages of consultation, for example, the committee may resolve issues such as how many days are needed to complete an ethnobotany study or it may decide how best to prepare progress reports to be submitted back to native governments. By meeting together and acting in unison, native people belonging to different tribes and ethnic groups are able to draw on common information and to speak with a single voice. The clarity and consistency of the Native American requests will influence the Federal agency's ability to respond effectively and acceptably.

The consultation committee may be asked to resolve problems that would otherwise be impossible for either the agency or the tribal governments. After the consultation committee comes to understand both the laws that are driving the consultation process and the management needs of the agency, the committee may be asked to determine when sufficient information has been collected so that recommendations can be made to both the tribes and the agency. If there are disagreements among the tribes or ethnic groups, the consultation committee can be asked to resolve these in closed executive session. Halmo (1994) has recently studied the benefits of a consultation committee participating with the Department of Energy (DOE) to understand the cultural-resource impacts of the underground atomic testing programme on the Nevada Test Site. He concludes that this programme's success came largely because of the consultation committee's efforts to adjust the process to meet the needs of three major native ethnic groups represented by seventeen tribes and native organizations.

Conducting Site Visits

'What is out there?' is the fundamental question that must be addressed in any consultation. The answer will not come directly from tribal governments, but they will send cultural experts who can identify various cultural resources located on the Federal lands under study. Native government leaders can appoint representatives to a consultation committee, and during the operation of that committee a native based inventory of cultural resources can be planned.

Native American cultural resource studies should be conducted separately whenever possible because tribes and native groups will send different types of cultural specialists depending on what is to be studied. The native person who can speak at length about archaeological sites may know little about the traditional use of plants. A native person who specializes in fishing ceremonies may have little knowledge of petroglyphs and curing ceremonies. Native cultures, like all cultures, are differentially held in the minds of specialists.

The term 'study' is used to separate research that is needed to prepare a cultural resource inventory from what are sometimes described as Native American tours. Occasionally, Federal agencies will simply bring Native Americans to the lands under discussion and ask them individually or in a group what is out there. These tours are usually organized and conducted by agency personnel who are not professionally trained in scientific methods associated with cultural resource studies. The agency tour guides rarely have a hypothesis about what resources may be present and so naively believe that they can simply ask for information and the Native American will completely share all pertinent information. In an extreme case, a senior environmental manager of a DOE facility suggested that native representatives be taken to a high hill overlooking the thousand-square-mile facility, asked as a group 'What is out there?', and then taken to dinner. In his opinion, all Native American cultural resource concerns could be addressed in one day. Native American tours were more common decades ago before there was an extensive body of research about how to conduct studies with Native Americans and what to expect from such studies.

Forming a Study Design Native Americans have become aware of the quality of information that is needed to make convincing policy recommendations on Federal lands, so they are demanding to participate in the formulation of study designs that are both culturally and scientifically valid. A recent analysis of Native American research studies suggests that the design of the study can directly influence the findings and the recommendations (Stoffle & Evans, 1990). An analysis of eleven projects suggests that Indian people will have greater impacts on land-use decisions if the study design permits them to identify and select for special protection those places, plants and archaeology sites that have the highest cultural significance, a process that has been called 'cultural triage' (Stoffle & Evans, 1990:97). When it is difficult for Indian people to demonstrate how to move from cultural concerns to land management recommendations that protect the most cultural items, it becomes the responsibility of the scientist to help make this translation. For example, it is possible to calculate the cultural significance of individual Indian plants so that specific places where the plants grow can be assigned and valued, and protection can be afforded to those places with the highest plant scores (Stoffle, Halmo, Evans, & Olmstead, 1990b:427–9).

Defining Basic Concepts It is essential that all parties to a study agree on what is to be studied. It is common for Indian people, agency personnel and study scientists to assign different meanings to the same term. One of the most commonly misunderstood terms is 'sacred'. The concept of sacred is really a non-Indian concept that creates a division between the sacred and the profane: most Indian people do not believe such a division exists. Indian cultures, and there are hundreds of variations, contain many ceremonies designed to assure proper behaviour towards and communication with the natural environment, other humans and the supernatural, 'the mysterious presence'. These ceremonies literally translate everything touched by an Indian person into a sacred object. For example, a Shoshone Indian women who makes willow baskets will keep the shavings that have been produced by smoothing the split willows. Eventually, she prays over these shavings and returns them to a natural area near her camp. The Shoshone woman considers these willow shavings as sacred. Indian people also have ceremonies associated with great life transitions – birth, first menses, and death – which use and create sacred objects that are more generally recognized by others, such as Euroamericans. Finally, there are sacred objects that are specifically defined by United States federal laws such as NAGPRA. So the concept 'sacred' could refer in any given discussion to many categories of items, some defined by law, some defined and mutually recognized by Indian and non-Indian alike, and some exclusively perceived as sacred by Indian people.

Great care must be taken in the formulation of study concepts and when discussing the meaning of these concepts with native government representatives. If someone asks a native person to come to Federal lands and identify places and things that are sacred, the person is likely to respond that all is sacred. If on the other hand, the Indian person is asked to identify which objects in a museum collection are needed in a current religious ceremony as defined by NAGPRA, the person will be able to make a discriminate decision. The answer is often framed by the question, but it can also be influenced by the amount of time the native person has to share her/his cultural resource perspective and her/his confidence that deeper cultural resource insights will have more protective influence than simple holistic conservation statements.

Assuring Participation The Federal agency and SIA study team must approach the study of cultural resources with caution when seeking Native American participation in land-management decisions, because Native Americans will weigh the potential benefits from increased protection against the potential that if cultural resources become known they will be threatened. In one study (Stoffle, Jake, Bunte & Evans, 1982:124) a Kaibab Paiute elder indicated he wanted to protect traditional trails, but that he would not reveal their location because once known they could be followed to hitherto undiscovered Indian camps. Native people often say that revealing Indian plant usages causes the plants to be taken by non-natives who profit from sale of the plants. The curing power associated with certain places can be reduced if the place and its function become known to other ethnic groups, including other Indian people. Agency personnel should be aware that native experts who are sent to identify cultural resources are subject to ethical conflicts, emotional stress and even fear of reprisal. Native experts express concern about violating traditional norms against sharing knowledge with outsiders. Concern is also expressed over how other tribal members and even future generations of tribal members will evaluate the sharing of information. Basically, the question they ask is whether or not more good than harm will come from sharing cultural knowledge (Greaves, 1994).

When Native American tribes and organizations send experts to represent cultural concerns they expect that the shared information will be used to set policies to better protect cultural resources. To accomplish this the identifications of the experts must be systematically recorded so they can be written into a scientifically and ethnically acceptable report. In general, interviews should be conducted in private so that the native person does not have to share the information with others. An interview form should be prepared in advance with the assistance of the consultation committee or informed native people so that similar questions are asked of each expert and there is a place to record their answers. Tape recorders can be used as backup, but only used with the expert's permission. Experts' confidentiality should be assured unless they wish to go on the record regarding some aspect of the study.

Group interviews can be conducted when individual interviews are either not desired or impossible to conduct. Group interviews tend to produce consensus data, which means that members of the group talk over possible answers and provide one answer to the interviewer. The weakness of group interviews is that some people are not willing to express their opinions in the presence of others. The strength of group interviews is that people have the opportunity to talk over a response while in the field. Focus group interviews are a special type of group interview but they require special preparation and training for the focus group facilitator.

Presenting the Findings The report presenting the findings of the consultation process being discussed should be more than a pure description of what was said by the native experts. Some attempt should be made to translate the thoughts of native experts into information that can be used by agency land managers. In general, native concerns should be contextualized by providing findings from published historical and ethnographic literature that demonstrate how the expressed cultural concerns fit into the overall culture of the ethnic group. Translation into management information and contextualization will help achieve the goals of building Native American concerns into land management policies.

The report should receive a technical review by the native experts and members of the consultation committee before being sent for draft review by the agency. This will assure that the report does not contain confidential information and that the information it does contain is accurate. When the technical review is complete, the report should be given a draft review by the agency. Then the draft report should be sent to the Native American group or tribal government for official review and approval. Final reports should be available to other agencies seeking to achieve similar goals and in need of case data for developing or refining their own consultation processes. The public has a right to know about significant land management decisions made by Federal agencies, even if these are in consultation with Native Americans and have some element of confidentiality that will continue to be respected, so the final report and perhaps portions of the information (not the data) used to make the decision (Ruppert, 1994) should be available to the public.

Developing Native Mitigation Recommendations

Cultural resource technical reports should focus on the cultural resources under study and should not attempt to make government-level policy recommendations. Technical reports are the basis for proceeding with mitigation discussions and eventual recommendations from the native governments to the Federal agency. Policy decisions occur after the native recommendations are combined with what the land management agency can and will do to incorporate Native American recommendations. It is important that this point in the decision-making process has been thoroughly considered by the agency before the consultation began – see the earlier discussion of decision making and consultation.

Native Policy recommendations should derive from three sources:

1 Native experts during the on-site interviews.
2 Consultation committee.
3 Native organizations and tribal governments.

These three sources of recommendations represent a hierarchy of decision-making authority that is inversely related to the degree of information about the resource. Native experts are knowledgeable about the cultural resource and, because of their on-site experiences, are aware of factors that could have either adverse or positive impacts on its protection. Native experts are charged, by their tribes and organizations, with identifying what is out there and making preliminary recommendations. The report should consolidate all of the native expert recommendations by place and resource and these should be presented to the consultation committee. Committee members have a long-term relationship with the project and are generally aware of what is possible in terms of agency resource management. It is up to the committee to consider the recommendations of the native experts and, if possible, resolve conflicting recommendations and add recommendations. The final cultural resource decision recommendations in a government-to-government relationship belong to the tribal council and advisory board of a native organization. They tend to follow the advice of their appointed Native experts and consultation committee members; however, they can add or modify recommendations.

Recommendations that have passed with some consensus through this hierarchy of Native decision making should be seriously considered by the agency. The strength of the recommendations depends in part on whether or not the Indian recommendations remain within the Federal laws that govern land-management decisions. In addition, the Native recommendations should be within the agreed upon limits of power-sharing decided upon by the installation when the consultation process began. If the recommendations are within these limits, then credible cultural resource recommendations should be adopted by the agency.

Maintaining Ongoing Interactions and Monitoring

'Partnership' is a term often used to describe the desired outcomes of consultation relationships between Native Americans and Federal agencies. Partnerships require shared power, mutual respect and mechanisms for sustaining a long-term relationship. Partnerships can be established when the Native American people and the Federal agency establish (a) mutual trust; (b) a common knowledge base; (c) a cultural resource management plan; (d) a monitoring plan.

Mutual Trust When people get to know each other through face-to-face interactions they lay an understanding base that can be used to establish what is called 'trust'. The term 'trust' is not being used here to refer to the legal trust relationship that exists between the United States government and American Indian people. Instead, the term trust is used as it is more generally understood, as confidence in the honesty, integrity, reliability and justice of another person or organization.

People do meet, but Federal agency–Native American consultation occurs within the context of government-to-government relationships. One of the great dynamics of mutual trust is differences between the people-to-people and agency-tribe relationships. First and foremost Indian people must believe that their participation in consultation is more likely to protect cultural resources than would say nothing at all. Decision making should be shared (insofar as it is appropriate and possible) and the decisions must have some identifiable positive impacts – see 'monitoring' below.

Trust derives from the history of relationships between the Department of Defence installation and its personnel and Native Americans. This history may go back to a time with the Native peoples were at war with the United States federal government. Trust also derives from more recent interactions about agency policies. It is important to address these issues early in the consultation process. In fact, it is likely that Native people will raise these issues as stipulations before they are willing to proceed with consultation. Concerns about past relationships are often raised in holistic conservation statements made by native elders and leaders in early consultation meetings. Stipulations are not debatable by the agency, who instead will have its own stipulations it may wish to express at this time. Trust cannot be negotiated – when it begins with clearly expressed stipulations and becomes an organizational element in developing a process of consultation – trust can emerge from long-term interactions. Trust must be earned and mutually shared.

Any consultation relationship will depend in part on the individuals involved. Friendly and professional relationships have the potential of overcoming any negative historic relationships between the native people and the agency. Unfortunately, personnel change in both native organizations and agencies. Thus, mechanisms should be in place to assure that consultation partnerships can survive personnel changes.

A Common Knowledge Base A primary goal for every Federal agency–Native American consultation is to create or contribute to a common knowledge base that is shared by both. Native groups send their most knowledgeable experts to identify cultural resources: these thoughts should not be lost. United States Federal agencies cannot afford to forget what has been told them by native groups. Similarly, most agencies have archaeology, botany and animal studies that can be shared and used by native groups. The challenge is to develop a single, shared pool of information that can be used by both the agency and the native people to know what is out there and to understand what is happening to it.

Geographic Information Systems (GIS) are being used by many United States federal agencies and native groups to inventory and keep track of resources distributed across an extensive landscape. GIS systems are expensive and difficult to use, but innovative interactive multimedia data systems that can draw upon some GIS-like components are being developed. An ideal data base could be used simultaneously by the native people at their homes and agency. This is likely to require the development of a multimedia program that can use and make easily accessible the products of the GIS data analysis. The GIS and multimedia system should be updated easily when new information comes from native expert visits or science studies. It should contain photos, video, sound clips, maps and text. Finally, the GIS and multimedia system should restrict access to certain portions of the database to reflect both the agency and the native concerns for selective distribution of data and information.

Cultural Resource Management Plan United States federal land management agencies produce overall land use plans that include specific plans for wildlife, plants and cultural resources. A Native American cultural resource management component could be developed in each of these plans. Possibly more difficult, but none-the-less important, would be to include Native American cultural resource management comments in discussions of minerals and water.

The recommendations produced by the hierarchy of Native American decisions (experts, consultation committee, tribal governments) should be organized to reflect how the information can be incorporated into installation management plans. Early co-ordination with the consultation committee should produce both information and recommendations that fit how the installation manages natural and cultural resources.

Monitoring Plan There must be some way of knowing whether or not Native American consultation has influenced the condition of cultural resources contained on the lands under study. Because it is impossible to constantly monitor all cultural resources located on the study lands, monitoring timeframes and monitoring locations must be chosen. Basically the timeframe issues are:

1 How fast are culturally significant changes occurring to any specific cultural resource?
2 Does the quality, quantity, or distribution of medicine plants change seasonally, annually, or over a period of years?
3 Damage due to erosion or vandalism to archaeology sites may be occurring sporadically; monitoring should occur at least once a year with more sensitive sites monitored more often.

Monitoring locations should be decided in terms of how well they represent a certain cultural resource. Monitoring samples should be selected with full input from the Native people. Monitoring techniques will vary, from ground level photography of petroglyph panels to remotely sensed data from satellites showing the distribution of plants. When ground disturbance is to occur, native monitors may be hired to oversee activities. The results of all monitoring efforts should be provided to the members of the consultation committee and native governments at regular intervals. Regular feedback on the condition of cultural resources is the only way to maintain an ongoing relationship with Native peoples.

Terminating Consultation

Today most Federal land-managing agency initiatives to establish Native American consultation relationships are intended to be ongoing because Native people's views will become part of the information base for making, monitoring and adjusting ongoing land-management decisions. Still some consultations are designed to end. These may be project-specific SIA consultations designed to provide a narrow range of findings for the evaluations of a project or action proposal. Sometimes the Federal agency itself is transferring title such as happens during Military base closures. Whatever the reason for termination, how it occurs has implications for both the involved native people and the United States federal agency.

Making Analogues Anyone who has made a presentation before a tribal council or native governmental body has experienced some council or audience member standing up and talking at length about some other project that occurred many years in the past that did not end in a positive way. Most presenters want to say, 'That is not what I am talking about, it occurred a long time ago and I (or my SIA study team) was not involved'. The point being made by the Native Americans, however, is well taken – 'we have seen your kind before and here is the summation of those experiences'. In most cases native people lump most United States federal agencies and SIA study teams together, so the mistakes of one agency or SIA study team are transferred to another.

'Project Analogues' is the technical term used to discuss the process of evaluation of a current proposal in terms of past proposals. For example, during the SIA of the Superconducting Super Collider (SSC) for the State of Michigan it was discovered that local people responded to this new and unique proposal in terms of how the involved state and United States federal agencies had behaved with past projects (Stoffle, Traugott, Harshbarger, Jensen, Evans and Dury, 1987:37–54; Stoffle, Traugott, Jensen & Copeland, 1988). So the proposed SSC, a massive and generally positive project, was being evaluated in terms of how the Michigan Department of Natural Resources had conducted a public access for hunters programme, a state utility had handled a cross-county pipeline project, a cement company had dealt with air pollution, and state politicians had proposed a prison for the area. These small-scale and highly localized projects were not similar in any respect to the SSC proposal, but the local people drew upon them as historic analogues for deciding whether or not to trust the State of Michigan and private business and support the SSC proposal.

Keeping Relations Relations between the United States Federal agencies and Native Americans began long ago and are often recounted as a bitter history of adversarial relationships. All lands currently held or affected by Federal agencies once belonged to a Native American ethnic group. Nevertheless, many Native peoples have served in the Armed Services and worked for Federal agencies and they have begun to establish positive relationships. It is important at this moment in the history of relations between Native Americans and the United States Federal government to create positive analogues, so each SIA and general consultation effort is important. No positive action of the agency or SIA study team will go unrewarded, because Native Americans respond well to being involved in decisions about their traditional resources. Even small-scale and terminal SIA consultations have the potential to be a positive analogue.

References

Abbott, I.A. (1992), *La'au Hawai'i: Traditional Hawaiian Uses of Plants*, Manoa, HI: Bishop Museum Press.

Arnstein, S.R. (1969), 'A Ladder of Citizen Participation', *Journal of the American Institute of Planners*, 216–24.

Bennett, J. (1976), *The Ecological Transition: Cultural Anthropology and Human Adaptation*, New York: Pergamon Press.

Cernea, M. (ed.) (1991), *Putting People First: Sociological Variables in Rural Development*, New York: Oxford University Press.

Cuddihy, L.W. and Stone, C.P. (1990), *Alteration of Native Hawaiian Vegetation: Effects of Humans, Their Activities and Introductions,* Honolulu: University of Hawaii Cooperative National Park Resources Studies Unit.

Cultural Systems Research, Inc. (1987), *Cultural Resources Surveying: Ethnographic Resources Candidate Site Selection Phase*, California Low-Level Radioactive Waste Disposal Project, prepared for United States Ecology, Inc., Menlo Park, CA: Cultural Systems Research, Incorporated.

Deloria, V. Jr. (1985), *Behind the Trail of Broken Treaties: An Indian Declaration of Independence*, Austin, TX: University of Texas Press.

Deloria, V. Jr. and Lytle, C. (1984), *The Nations Within: The Past and Future of American Indian Sovereignty*, New York: Pantheon Books.

Department of Energy (DOE) (1996), *Final Environmental Impact Statement for the Nevada Test Site and Off-Site Locations in the State of Nevada*, Vol. 1 Appendix G: American Indian Assessment, Las Vegas, Nevada: United States Department of Energy, Nevada Operations Office.

Dewey-Hefley, G., Zedeno, N., Stoffle, R. and Pittaluga, F. (1998), 'Piecing the Puzzle', *Common Ground* (Winter/Spring): 15.

Dillehay, T.D. (1991), 'Disease Ecology and Initial Human Migration', in T.D. Dillehay and D.J. Meltzer (eds), *The First Americans: Search and Research*, Boca Raton, FL: CRC Press, 231–66.

Dincauze, D.F. (1991), 'Review of Monte Verde, A Late Pleistocene Settlement in Chile, by T. Dillehay', *Journal of Field Archaeology*, 18:116–19.

Dobyns, H. (1951), Blunders with Bolsas, *Human Organization*, vol. 10 pp. 25–32.

Drover, C.E. (1985), 'Navajo Settlement and Architecture in Southeastern California', *Journal of California and Great Basin Anthropology*, 7(1):46–57.

Francis, J., Loendorf, L. and Dorn, R. (1994), 'AMS Radiocarbon and Cation-Ratio Dating of Rock Art in the Bighorn Basin of Wyoming and Montana', *American Antiquity*, 58(4):711–37.

Geisler, C., Green, R., Usner, D. and West, P. (1982), *Indian SIA: The Social Impact Assessment of Rapid Resource Development on Native Peoples* Monograph No. 3, Ann Arbor, MI: The University of Michigan, Natural Resource Sociology Research Lab.

Gore, A. (1993), *Earth in the Balance: Ecology and the Human Spirit*, New York: Plume.

Grayson, D.K. (1988), 'Perspectives on the First Americans', in R. Carlisle (ed.), *Americans Before Columbus: Ice Age Origins*, Pittsburgh, Ethnology Monographs No. 12, Department of Anthropology, University of Pittsburgh, pp.107–23

Greaves, T. (ed.) (1994), *Intellectual Property Rights for Indigenous Peoples: A Sourcebook.* Oklahoma City, OK: Society for Applied Anthropology.

Halmo, D.B. (1994), 'With One Voice: Collective Action in Cultural Impact Assessments', *Practicing Anthropology*, 16(3):14–16.

Haynes, C.V. Jr. (1987), 'Clovis Origin Update', *The Kiva*, 52:83–93.

Indian Claims Commission (ICC) (1978), *Indian Claims Judicially Established*, Washington, DC: The Commission.

LeVine, R. (1984), 'Properties of Culture: An Ethnographic View', in R. Shweder and R. LeVine (eds), *Culture Theory: Essays on Mind, Self, and Emotion*, Cambridge, England: Cambridge University Press, pp.67–87.

McPherson, R. (1992), *Sacred Land Sacred View: Navajo Perceptions of the Four-Corners Region*, Provo, Utah: Brigham Young University.

Meltzer, D.J. (1989), 'Why Don't We Know When the First People Came to North America?', *American Antiquity*, 54:471–90.

Morrissey, W.A., Zinn, J.A. and Corn, M. (1994) 'Ecosystem Management, Federal Agency Activities', in *CRS Report for Congress*, Washington DC: The Library of Congress.

National Oceanic and Atmospheric Administration (NOAA) (1994), Guidelines and Principles for Social Impact Assessment, *National Marine Fisheries Service*, prepared by the Interorganizational Committee on Guidelines and Principles for Social Impact Assessment. NOAA Tech. Memo, NMFS-F/SPO-16, 29pp.

Parenteau, R. (1988), *Public Participation in Environmental Decision-Making*, Montreal: University of Montreal Press.

Rappaport, R. (1990), 'Ecosystems, Populations and People', in E. Moran (ed.), *The Ecosystem Approach in Anthropology*, Ann Arbor, MI: The University of Michigan Press.

Ruppert, D. (1994), 'Buying Secrets, Federal Government Procurement of Intellectual Cultural Property', in T. Greaves (ed.), *Intellectual Cultural Property Rights for Indigenous Peoples: A Source Book*, Oklahoma City, OK: Society for Applied Anthropology, pp.111–28.

Stea, D. and Buge, C. (1982), 'Cultural Impact Assessment on Native American Reservations: Two Case Studies', in C. Geisler *et al.* (eds), *Indian SIA*, Monograph No. 3, Ann Arbor, MI: The University of Michigan, Natural Resource Sociology Research Lab, pp.177–99.

Stoffle, R.W., (ed.), (1990), *Cultural and Paleontological Effects of Siting a Low-Level Radioactive Waste Storage Facility in Michigan: Candidate Area Analysis Phase*, Michigan, MI: Institute for Social Research, The University of Michigan.

Stoffle, R.W. and Evans, M.J. (1990), 'Holistic Conservation and Cultural Triage: American Indian Perspectives on Cultural Resources', *Human Organization*, 49(2):91–9.

Stoffle, R.W., Jake, M., Bunte, P. and Evans, M. (1982), 'Southern Paiute Peoples' SIA Responses to Energy Proposals', in C. Geisler et al. (eds), *Indian SIA*, Monograph No. 3, Ann Arbor, MI: The University of Michigan, Natural Resource Sociology Research Lab, pp.107–34.

Stoffle, R.W., Traugott, M., Harshbarger, C., Jensen, F., Evans, M. and Drury, P. (1987), *The Superconducting Super Collider at the Stockbridge, Michigan Site: Community Support and Land Acquisition*, Ann Arbor, MI: Institute for Social Research, University of Michigan Press.

Stoffle, R.W., Traugott, M.W., Jensen, F.V. and Copeland, R. (1988), *Social Assessment of High Technology: The Superconducting Super Collider in Southeast Michigan*, Ann Arbor, MI: Survey Research Center, Center for Political Studies, Institute for Social Research, University of Michigan.

Stoffle, R.W., Halmo, D.B., Evans, M.J. and Olmstead, J.E. (1990a) 'Calculating the Cultural Significance of American Indian Plants: Paiute and Shoshone Ethnobotany at Yucca Mountain, Nevada', *American Anthropologist* 92(2):416–32.

Stoffle, R.W., Halmo, D.B., Evans M.J. and Olmstead, J.E. (1990b), *Native American Cultural Resource Studies at Yucca Mountain, Nevada*, Ann Arbor, MI: Institute for Social Research, University of Michigan.

Stoffle, R.W., Evans, M.J., Zedeno, M.N., Stoffle, B.W. and Kesel, C. (1994), *American Indians and Fajada Butte: Ethnographic Overview and Assessment for Fajada Butte and Traditional (Ethnobotanical) Use Study for Chaco Culture National Historical Park*, Tucson: Bureau of Applied Research in Anthropology, University of Arizona.

Stoffle, R.W., Halmo, D. and Austin, D. (1997), Cultural 'Landscapes and Traditional Cultural Properties: A Southern Paiute View of the Grand Canyon and Colorado River', *The American Indian Quarterly*, 21(2):229–49.

Stoffle, R.W., Halmo, D.B. and Evans, M.J. (1999), 'Puchuxwaraat Uaapi (To know about plants): Traditional Knowledge and the Cultural Significance of Southern Paiute Plants', *Human Organization* 58(4): 416–29.

Sutton, I. (ed.) (1985), *Irredeemable America: The Indians' Estate and Land Claims*, Albuquerque, MI: Native American Studies, University of New Mexico Press.

Whitley, D.S. and Dorn, R.I. (1993), 'New Perspectives on the Clovis Versus Pre-Clovis Controversy', *American Antiquity*, 58(4):626–47.

Yaffee, S., Phillips, A., Frentz, I., Hardy, P., Maleki, S. and Thorpe, B. (1996), *Ecosystem Management in the United States: An Assessment of Current Experience*, Washington, DC: Island Press.

Zedeno, N., Austin, D. and Stoffle, R. (1997), 'Landmark and Landscape: A Contextual Approach to the Management of American Indian Resources', *Culture and Agriculture*, 19(3):123–29.

Appendix 7.1

LANDSCAPE QUESTIONS
ETHNOGRAPHIC INVENTORY OF OJIBWA NATURAL RESOURCES IN THE WESTERN GREAT LAKES

University of Arizona Interview Forms

Interview number ______ Date _____ Respondent name _______

Ethnographer's name______________ Tape number __________

Study areas site number__________

(1) Were there Indian villages in relation to this PARK AREA?

1 = Yes 2 = No 8 = Don't know 9 = No response

(2) If yes, were the villages in this park connected with villages elsewhere in the GREAT LAKES AREA?

1 = Yes 2 = No 8 = Don't know 9 = No response

(3) If yes, how were these connected?

(4) Do you know what Indian people lived at or used the villages at or near the PARK AREA? (Ethnic group)

(5) Do you know what the Indian people did when they were at or near the PARK AREA?

1 = Yes 2 = No 8 = Don't know 9 = No response

(6) If yes, what kinds of activities:

* fishing
* hunting
* farming
* mining activities
* gathering plants
* gambling
* ceremonies
* political meetings
* political meetings
* others (specify)

(7) Do you know of Indian land trails that were connected with the PARK AREA?

1 = Yes 2 = No 8 = Don't know 9 = No response

(8) If yes, can you tell me something about those trails – like

* where did trails go
* why did Indian people travel these trails
* were these trails somehow special to the Anishinabe? How?

(9) Do you know of Indian water trails that were connected with the PARK AREA?

1 = Yes 2 = No 8 = Don't know 9 = No response

(10) If yes, can you tell me something about those water trails – like

* where did the trails go
* why did Indian people travel the trails
* were these water trails somehow special to the Anishinabe? How?

(11) Do you know of any song trails or story trails associated with the PARK AREA?

1 = Yes 2 = No 8 = Don't know 9 = No response

(12) If yes, can you tell me something about these songs and/or stories

(13) Do you know of any migration places or stories connected with the PARK AREA?

1 = Yes, places 2 = Yes, stories 3 = Yes, both
4 = No 8 = Don't know 9 = No response

(14) If yes, can you tell me something about those migration places or stories?

(15) Do you know of any ceremonies that were conducted at or near the PARK AREA?

1 = Yes 2 = No 8 = Don't know 9 = No response

(16) If yes, can you tell me something about these ceremonies?

* Ceremony #1 – place ______ , when ______, why______
* Ceremony #2 – place ______ , when ______, why______
* Ceremony #3 – place ______ , when ______, why______

(17) Do you recall or have you heard about events in Anishinabe history that occurred at or near the PARK AREA?

1 = Yes 2 = No 8 = Don't know 9 = No response

(18) Will you tell me something about those events?

* Event #1 – date ______ , place ______ , what happened?
* Event #2 – date ______ , place ______ , what happened?
* Event #3 – date ______ , place ______ , what happened?

(19) Is there a connection between the PARK AREA and the Mountains in the GREAT LAKES AREA?

1 = Yes 2 = No 8 = Don't know 9 = No response

(20) If yes, what mountains and how are they connected to the PARK AREA?

* Mt. #1: name in English _____, name in Anishinabe _____ , how connected?
* Mt. #2: name in English _____, name in Anishinabe _____ , how connected?
* Mt. #3: name in English _____, name in Anishinabe _____ , how connected?

(21) Is there a connection between the PARK AREA and the river and lakes in the GREAT LAKES AREA?

1 = Yes, rivers 2 = Yes, lakes 3 = Yes, both
2 = No 8 = Don't know 9 = No response

(22) If yes, what river or lake is connected to the PARK AREA and how?

* River/lake #1: name in English ___ , name in Anishinabe ___, how connected?
* River/lake #2: name in English ___ , name in Anishinabe ___, how connected?
* River/lake #3: name in English ___ , name in Anishinabe ___, how connected?

(23) Is the PARK AREA connected to the Anishinabe creation place/ story?

1 = Yes 2 = No 8 = Don't know 9 = No response

(24) If yes, how is it connected? And where is the creation place?

(25) Are there any connections between the Anishinabe creation place and other places in the GREAT LAKES AREA?

1 = Yes 2 = No 8 = Don't know 9 = No response

(26) If yes, where are those places and how are they connected?

(27) Is the PARK AREA connected to any places or events in the GREAT LAKES AREA that we have not already talked about?

1 = Yes 2 = No 8 = Don't know 9 = No response

(28) If yes, what other connections would you like to talk about?

* Connection #1 – place ____ , event ____ , connection ____
* Connection #2 – place ____ , event ____ , connection ____
* Connection #3 – place ____ , event ____ , connection ____

(29) Is the PARK AREA connected to any places or events in traditional Anishinabe history that we have not already talked about? (Use traditional map here)

1 = Yes 2 = No 8 = Don't know 9 = No response

(30) If yes, what other connections would you like to talk about?

* Connection #1 – place ____, event____ , connection ____
* Connection #2 – place ____, event____ , connection ____
* Connection #3 – place ____, event____ , connection ____

Methodology for Administering this Instrument

1 Read questions ahead of time so you familiarize yourself with the topics and order of questions
2 Look at the map packets before administering the instrument, have them ready and in order when you begin the interview.
3 Make sure to show the maps when appropriate and let the person think and study them. Don't hurry the process: you have a half-day to spend with each person.
4 Ask questions slowly and let the person think about them.

Appendix 7.2

ETHNOGRAPHIC INVENTORY OF OJIBWA NATURAL RESOURCES IN THE WESTERN GREAT LAKES REGION

University of Arizona Interview form

***** NOTE: You must record a response for every question asked in order for data to be correctly coded*****

Interview number: ____________ **Tape number** _______________

Ethnographer's name_____________________________________

1. Date: ______________

2. Respondent's Name: ___________

3. Tribe/organization: ____________ 3a. Ethnic group: __________

4. Gender: Male Female

5. Date of birth: —/—/—

6. Place of birth (*Town, Reservation*):____ 6a. US state of birth____

7. Study area site number (*ethnographer fill this in*): ____________

8. What is the name of this place in English? ________________

9. What is the name of this place in Anishinabe (*Ojibwa*)?

    ____

10. Please describe the geography of this area or elements which stand out.

11. Would Indian people have used this area?

    1 = Yes   2 = No   8 = Don't know   9 = No response

12. (IF YES) Why or for what purpose would Indian people have used this area?

    1 = [permanent] living   2 = hunting
    3 = fishing   4 = gathering food
    5 = [seasonal] camping   6 = ceremony/power
    7 = other   8 = Don't know
    9 = No response

13. What characteristics make this place good or suitable for the activities you just mentioned? (*OR* why did Indian people perform these activities at this specific place?)

    ____

    - living
    - hunting
    - fishing
    - gathering food
    - [seasonal] camping
    - ceremony/power
    - other

14. Is this place part of a group of connected places (*Is this place connected to others?*)

    1 = Yes 2 = No 8 = Don't know 9 = No response

15. (IF YES) What kinds of other places might this place be connected with and where are they?

    1 = Comment given 8 = Don't know 9 = No response

15a. (IF ANSWERED 1 to 5a.) Comments given:

16. (IF COMMENT GIVEN) How is this place connected to the others you mentioned?

    1 = Yes 8 = Don't know 9 = No response

16a. (IF ANSWERED 1 to 6a.) Comments given:

Place Features

(Explain you will now begin asking questions about the physical features of the place)

17. Which, if any, of the following features is an important part of why this place is significant to Indian people?

Feature type	1 = Yes	2 = No	List and describe each specific feature, like waterfall, wild rice, bears
17a. Source of water			17aa.
17b. Source for plants			17bb.
17c. Source for animals			17cc.
17d. Source for fish			17dd.
17d. Evidence of previous Anishinabe use, e.g. archeological remains, historic structures			17dd.
17e. Geological features, e.g. mountain, spring, landmarks			17ee.

For each feature please fill out appropriate feature page

Feature Type A: Water Source

(*List specific feature from table above*)

___

18. Would Indian people have used this (*Name the feature*)?

    1 = Yes 2 = No 8 = Don't know 9 = No response

19. (IF YES) Why or for what purpose would Indian people have used this ________ feature(s)?

    1 = Food/drink 2 = Medicine 3 = Ceremony
    4 = Other 8 = Don't know 9 = No response

19a. Comments:

20. How would you evaluate the condition of the _______ feature(s)?

    1 = Excellent 2 = Good 3 = Fair 4 = Poor 9 = No response

21. Is there anything affecting the condition of the ___ feature(s) ___?

    1 = Yes 2 = No 8 = Don't know 9 = No response

22. (IF YES) What, in your opinion, is affecting the condition of ____?

Feature Type B: Plant Source (List features from table on page 227)

___

23. Would Indian people have used the plants at this particular site?

    1 = Yes 2 = No 8 = Don't know 9 = No response

24. (IF YES) Why or for what purpose would Indian people have used these plants?

    1 = Food　　2 = Medicine　　3 = Ceremony
    4 = Making things　　8 = Don't know　　9 = No response

25. Comments (if given):

26. How would you evaluate the condition of these plants?

    1 = Excellent　2 = Good　3 = Fair　4 = Poor　9 = No response

27. Is there anything affecting the condition of these plants?

    1 = Yes　　2 = No　　8 = Don't know　　9 = No response

27. (IF YES) What, in your opinion, is affecting the condition of the plants?

Feature Type C: Animal Source (List features from table on page 227)

---

28. Would Indian people have used the animals at this place?

    1 = Yes　　2 = No　　8 = Don't know　　9 = No response

29. Why or for what purpose would Indian people have used the animals in this site?

    1 = Food　　2 = Medicine　　3 = Ceremony
    4 = Clothing　　5 = Tools　　6 = Exchange/trade
    7 = Other　　8 = Don't know　　9 = No response

29. Comments:

30. How would you evaluate the condition of these animals/habitat?

    1 = Excellent　2 = Good　3 = Fair　4 = Poor　9 = No response

31. Is there anything affecting the condition of the animals/habitat?

    1 = Yes   2 = No   8 = Don't know   9 = No response

32. (IF YES) What, in your opinion, is affecting the condition of the animals/habitat?

Feature Type C: Fish Source (List features from table on page 227)

33. Would Indian people have used the animals at this place?

    1 = Yes   2 = No   8 = Don't know   9 = No response

34. Why or for what purpose would Indian people have used the animals in this site?

    1 = Food   2 = Medicine   3 = Ceremony
    4 = Clothing   5 = Tools   6 = Exchange/trade
    7 = Other   8 = Don't know   9 = No response

34. Comments:

35. How would you evaluate the condition of these fish/habitat?

    1 = Excellent   2 = Good   3 = Fair   4 = Poor   9 = No response

36. Is there anything affecting the condition of the fish/habitat?

    1 = Yes   2 = No   8 = Don't know   9 = No response

37. (IF YES) What, in your opinion, is affecting the condition of the fish/habitat?

Feature Type D: Evidence of Previous Occupation or Use (specifically)

38. Would Indian people have used this site and/or artefacts?

    1 = Yes   2 = No   8 = Don't know   9 = No response

39. Why or for what purpose would Indian people have used this site and/or artefacts?

1 = Living	2 = Hunting	3 = Gathering
4 = Camping	5 = Ceremony/power	6 = Exchange/trade
7 = Other	8 = Don't know	9 = No response

39a. Comments:

40. How would you evaluate the condition of this site?

1 = Excellent   2 = Good   3 = Fair   4 = Poor   9 = No response

41. Is there anything affecting the condition of this site?

1 = Yes   2 = No   8 = Don't know   9 = No response

42. (IF YES) What, in your opinion, is affecting the condition of this site?

Feature Type E: Geologic Features (specifically)

---

43. Would Indian people have visited or used this ____(feature) ____?

1 = Yes   2 = No   8 = Don't know   9 = No response

44. Why or for what purpose would Indian people have used this _____ (feature) _____ ?

1 = Seek knowledge/power	2 = Communicate with other Indians
3 = Ceremony	4 = Communicate with spiritual beings
5 = Teaching other Indians	6 = Territorial marker
7 = Other	8 = Don't know
9 = No response	

44. Comments:

45. How would you evaluate the condition of the ____(feature) ____?

    1 = Excellent 2 = Good 3 = Fair 4 = Poor 9 = No response

46. Is there anything affecting the condition of the (feature)?

    1 = Yes 2 = No 8 = Don't know 9 = No response

47. (IF YES) What in your opinion, is affecting the condition of (feature) ?

Management and Access Recommendations

48. How would you evaluate the condition of this place?

    1 = Excellent 2 = Good 3 = Fair 4 = Poor 9 = No response

49. Is there anything affecting the condition of this place?

    1 = Yes 2 = No 8 = Don't know 9 = No response

50. (IF YES) What in your opinion is affecting the condition of this place?

Above you identified specific features at this site. What would be your recommendation for protecting each specific feature?

51. Water source:

52. Plant source:

53. Animal/fish source:

54. Traditional use feature:

55. Geological feature:

56. What would be your recommendation for protecting this place?

57. Do you think Indian people would want to come to this place?

    1 = Yes 2 = No 8 = Don't know 9 = No response

58. (IF YES) Why would Indian people want to come to this place?

–8–

Environmental Health

Edward Liebow

Introduction: A Special Instance of Measuring Change

If flood control dikes are built along a river's edge, and early flood warning measures are instituted in low-lying communities, will these actions noticeably reduce exposure to cholera and other water-borne pathogens?

Out of a lengthy list of abandoned factories – many of which may be leaking solvents, lubricants, and other toxic chemicals into the ground – does the lingering threat to health posed by each dictate which get cleaned up soonest, or do we let the market decide?

If hazardous industrial wastes are shipped off to a proposed regional incinerator in a sparsely populated rural area, will nearby farmers be hurt by market perceptions that their crops are unsafe to eat?

These predicaments reflect a nearly universal condition of modern existence: practically every corner of the planet is filled with environmental contamination, even the sparsely populated arid interior regions of our continents. What's more, this contamination and more systemic environmental degradation are often the legacies of internal colonialism of the largest scale. From the Maralinga and Woomera military ranges in the Australian outback to the shores of Lake Baikal in Eastern Russia, from the collapsing aquifers in the Middle East to the uranium mill tailings piles in the American South West, promoting global and national interests comes with a locally borne burden.

The burden of environmental degradation often is a threat to human health and safety, and it challenges health care institutions and notions of equity as well. It is advisable to understand the potential health consequences of decisions that may result in environmental change, as some of the environmental changes inevitably are not sustainable.

Assessing environmental health impacts, then, is a special instance of change analysis. It is predictive, it is interpretive and, because it is interpretive, it depends on collaboration to achieve validity and acceptance among affected populations. The general aim is to predict changes in health status and health care institutions resulting from proposed government or non-government organizations' (NGO) actions (policies, programmes or projects) while still in the planning stage – that is, before the purported effects have occurred. Most assessments are concerned with specific interventions usually in the form of publicly funded economic development projects (i.e. investments in energy, water, transportation, or telecommunications systems).

Strictly speaking, in contrast with the more familiar 'evaluation research', which gauges the changes resulting from programmes already in operation, the impact assessment enterprise is anticipatory.[1] That is, a profile of a given population's health status at a given time is followed by one or more profiles formulated for a specific future time period, reflecting changes predicted to occur. Differences between the initial profile and predicted futures are then measured. In this manner, previously unanticipated consequences of a development proposal can be identified, and strategies for coping with such consequences can be devised.

In practice, assessment of environmental health impacts has turned, increasingly, to the complementary uses of quantitative and ethnographic techniques. While the need was recognized early on for predicting quantitative changes (e.g. natality, morbidity and mortality rates), appreciation is growing for the need to better anticipate changes in the quality of local well-being, including such intangible forces as barriers to developing adequate epidemiological surveillance systems and delivery of health care services. An increasingly interpretive focus on 'impacts that count' – rather than simply those that can be counted easily – has drawn ethnographers into the field in recent years.

This is not to dismiss the importance of quantifiable indicators of health status or access to health care. On the contrary, populations subject to the effects of development proposals are often medically under-served, with higher localized prevalence of chronic and infectious diseases than what is reflected in regional or national trends, heightening the importance of establishment of baseline from which impacts are to be measured.

But in the bigger picture, what are environmental health 'impacts that count?' It is not merely the change in health status that is likely to result from economic development proposals of one sort or another. The distribution of these changes – who wins and who loses – matters greatly. The sources of possible changes in health status are multiple and cumulative, making attribution of impact to a single source largely inconclusive. That is, no one can say with reasonable certainty that an observed change in a particular person's health or in his or her ability to acquire adequate health care is due exclusively to a given environmental change. And if it is difficult to account for observed changes, it is even more difficult to predict changes accurately. Uncertain or inconclusive predictions are often dismissed, undermining local trust and confidence in the analyst's authority. The road back toward trust and confidence is built by collaboration between analyst and community, a style of engagement for which the cultural anthropologist is particularly well suited.

The practice of predicting environmental health impacts increasingly has turned to the use of qualitative data collection and analysis techniques, as local community opposition to proposed developments has persisted despite findings based on social indicator research that nothing is 'wrong', or that adverse changes are likely to be insignificant. Ethnography has been used to enrich our understanding of different viewpoints, and ethnographers have applied their expertise directly in making sure that previously unempowered communities are represented when decisions are made that affect their health and safety.

But unlike conventional anthropological research, where the ethnographer is usually alone in the field, in environmental health impact research, the ethnographer is almost always part of a multi-disciplinary team. He or she joins environmental, public health and medical specialists, frequently as the sole behavioural science specialist. Collaboration with other scientists adds a layer of complexity to the already challenging enterprise of collaborating with the potentially affected population.

The underlying premise of this chapter is that adequately predicting environmental health impacts depends upon a number of necessary preconditions. Because the impact assessment enterprise is predictive, it requires specific baseline data. Due to the same apparent need for change that prompts a development proposal, these baseline data often do not exist, or are poorly organized for the present analytical purposes. Because impact assessment work is interpretive, and because the specialists' values are a poor substitute for local insight, this work is by necessity a collaborative undertaking. 'Collaboration' in this instance means creating opportunities for direct local involvement in producing and managing baseline data and impact projections.

If the local capacity for this sort of involvement needs further development, the first responsibility of the impact assessment enterprise is to see to it that this capacity-building gets going. It is appropriate to complete a 'capacity-building needs assessment', and, as already noted, it is likely that anthropologists in particular will need to plan strategically on how to guide their colleagues from other scientific disciplines to collaborate with 'non-specialists'. It is also likely that 'capacity-building' will not be accomplished overnight, but instead will require a sustained investment of financial and technical assistance. As illustrated in Figure 8.1, only when this capacity building is underway does it make sense to talk about the mechanics of problem structuring, methods selection, data collection and analysis activities.

Hazard identification

- Information about public and private facilities

Risk characterization

- Ability to describe contamination likely to result from normal operations and emergencies
- Existing information and ability to describe locally relevant pathways

Problem structuring

Changes in risk factors

- Pathways
- Locally relevant behavioural risk factors

Changes in service delivery and differential access

Data collection and analysis

Hazard identification

- Archival materials
- Online databases
- Interviews to establish locally relevant geographic impact areas

Risk characterization

- Contaminant characterization (magnitude, duration, timing, mixtures)

Note: In a collaborative undertaking, the crucial problem-structuring step often must be preceded by correctly assessing local organizational development needs in those competency areas (hazard identification, risk characterization, and risk reduction) most central to assessing environmental health impacts. Effective problem structuring focuses our attention on potential changes in locally relevant risk factors, service delivery and perceptions of health risk.

Figure 8.1 Organizational Development Needs Assessment

Collaboration: Two Dimensions

A singular contribution that anthropologists can make to the assessment of environmental health impacts is to generalize from the past two decades of critical discourse on ethnographic authority to a more encompassing dialogue on scientific authority and what constitute acceptable scientific contributions to health policy debate.

In a sense, the anthropologist's involvement, often in the classic role of 'culture broker', is part of an unfolding transformation narrative. At the same time that affected populations recognized the need to learn the scientific talk of environmental toxicology, health physics and hydrology, specialists in these scientific disciplines have seen their models implode, their introspection highlighted as a poor substitute for elicitation of 'values' data, and the certainty of their world view about the place of local peoples in some larger social order – diversity as inscribed in bounded independent cultural groupings – undermined.

As anthropologists, we know the talk about 'ethnographic authority'. Over the early decades of the twentieth century, there emerged what Clifford called an 'international consensus: valid anthropological abstractions were to be based, wherever possible, on intensive cultural descriptions by qualified scholars' (1988:25). According to this model of practice, a lone ranger declares the 'truth' of a complex cultural experience – eg. Chagnon 1983, and Evans-Pritchard 1940. Although they are still less frequently presented in the published literature, we also know of alternate strategies of ethnographic representation, strategies that acknowledge and, indeed, embrace the collaboration of those whose insights and experiences form the subjects of cross-cultural inquiry.[2]

Anthropologists now take it on faith that this alternate strategy of inclusion, collaboration and acknowledgement renders intelligible a more complex intersubjective reality. This is relevant to impact assessment work, because such a strategy increases the chances that the right categories of impacts will be investigated in the first place. It should be patently apparent that if the wrong problem is articulated, then even the very best of intended changes will be misdirected, and bad policy will be the result. A strategy of inclusion, collaboration and acknowledgement of indigenous insight will help assure that the 'public interest' that policy purports to serve in fact embraces a broader scope of public perspectives, particularly those held by disadvantaged groups that historically have been excluded from having adequate airing for their perspectives.

Collaborative environmental health impact research involves affected community members in planning and implementing data collection and analysis, and emphasizes equity and respect among collaborators. Research strategies that do not emphasize community participation frequently fail to take into account local priorities and perspectives, are less likely to produce knowledge that is useful for action or planning, and run the risk of making inappropriate recommendations (Cornwall & Jewkes, 1995). Collaborative research, in contrast, recognizes the critical importance of including community members as key participants in all phases of the research process. In addition, this type of research focuses on 'knowledge for action' and on empowering communities, rather than on knowledge for the sake of knowledge or academic career enhancement.

Research projects that emphasize community collaboration have become more common in recent years and have gained attention within communities and in public health circles. Effective collaborative research partnerships have been guided by a set of principles jointly developed and agreed upon by all participants (including, for example, community representatives, government officials, and academic researchers) (Schulz, Israel, Selig & Bayes, 1998). Some or all of the following principles may serve as a guide for the collaborative process in the many environmental health impact assessment projects:

1 Affected community representatives will be involved in all major phases of the research process, including the design of the research questions and overall research approach, data collection and analysis, the interpretation of findings, report writing, and distribution of results.
2 The ultimate goal of the work is not the production of knowledge for its own sake, but knowledge that will directly benefit the communities involved in the project.
3 The process of collaborating on this project will enhance the knowledge and skills of both the community-based participants and the researchers involved.
4 The project will be conducted in ways that strengthen or enhance trust and the potential for future collaboration among the different people and organizations involved.
5 The project's findings will include the voices and interpretations of all collaborators. The findings will be documented and distributed using language that is clear and respectful to the communities involved, and in ways that will be useful for developing plans that might benefit the community.
6 The collaborative partnership will be based on values of mutual respect, open communication, and recognition of the knowledge, expertise, and resource capacities of all participants in the process.

7 If any participants experience barriers to collaborating to the extent desired, project staff will attempt to identify resources that may reduce these barriers (such as transportation resources, technical assistance, and so forth).

Organizational Development Needs Assessment

Although an impact assessment project often focuses on the likely effects of a single development proposal, the cumulative and chronic exposures to multiple health threats must not be overlooked. To fully grasp the encompassing context into which the proposed development is to be introduced, the multiple exposures need to be characterized from the local vantage point. This characterization, in turn, requires collaboration with the affected population, and to be prepared to collaborate effectively in the context of a single project often requires some fundamental organizational development. Upon first blush such organizational work may seem unnecessary, or beyond the scope of the individual project. However, the long-term benefit to the local community can be substantial, and the process of monitoring and mitigating impacts can benefit as well.

Local communities are absolutely essential partners in any collaborative venture involving environmental health activities. But they often need additional support for technical capacity building, development of institutional review boards, inter-organizational co-ordination, participation in development of epidemiology methods, upgrading of vital statistics functions, and innovative approaches to public health information/education for community members.

One critical area of need where collaboration with a public agency (NGO) and university-based researchers may be of particular value is in the development of methods for conducting epidemiological research in small areas and with small populations. Baseline morbidity and mortality trend data are rarely available for specific communities, so it is especially difficult to evaluate suspicious disease clusters. More emphasis needs to be placed on establishing relevant standard rates, methods for small area variation analysis, and even on simulations that include more lifestyle-relevant 'default' values.

In addition, impact assessment professionals need to look beyond the obvious aspects of capacity building and consider some long-term institutional approaches to assure that local environmental health interests can be promoted. First, it must be acknowledged that capacity building starts with researchers' formal academic training. National and regional public health agencies can play a key role in funding model curricula for students in training to become public health researchers – model curricula that teach these researchers to look not only at the molecular level of risk and toxicology, but at the macro-level of cultural variation. Public health researchers need to learn that it is inappropriate at key problem-formulation stages to substitute introspection and presumption based on their own value judgements for what should be developed in collaboration with affected communities. This is not something that is learned through a one-day in-service training. It needs to be a central feature of one's formative academic experiences.

Second, multi-year funding must be available for any sustained capacity-building effort to succeed. The typical local community's experience with funding for their participation is one of careering from one uncertain planning basis to another. To recruit and retain talented staff, acquire and maintain adequate equipment, and provide appropriate role models for aspiring young community members, the uncertainties in the transfer of financial and technical assistance to local governments for capacity-building purposes must be reduced.

Last, but hardly least, development agencies and impact assessment specialists need to create an internal co-ordination mechanism among their various organizations. An enormous administrative burden is now placed on communities to deal with assorted agencies and NGOs. Shouldering this burden is more than a bureaucratic nuisance; it is a diversion of time and resources from the very purposes the outside support is designed to provide.

The organizational development needs for a particular local community can be grouped into three categories:

1 Capacity to identify environmental hazards.
2 Capacity to characterize the health and safety risks associated with these potential hazards.
3 Capacity to design and implement risk reduction measures.

A formal evaluation is not necessary, but the list of questions presented in Figure 8.2 may serve as a semi-structured guide to gauging the local capacity to collaborate with impact assessment specialists. This list serves double duty, as it also identifies the main steps involved in the impact assessment work itself.

Problem Structuring

Environmental health impact assessment work is usually derived from plans to fix the stickiest problems, the ones for which no simple, ready

1. Hazard Identification

Describe *public* facilities (such as power plants and military sites) that may contaminate areas to which the community has geographic, historical, cultural and legal ties.

- What are our relevant local library collections? Nearby libraries with information about relevant facilities?
- What is the status of our on-line record retrieval abilities?
- Who (or what agency) is responsible for maintaining relevant information? For liaison with appropriate facility operators? What qualifications are required to carry out this responsibility? What co-ordination within our community is required to do this effectively? What barriers limit the effectiveness of knowing in detail what public facilities threaten our lands?
- What information is available that our community would find relevant? What capability exists to share information? What mechanisms are needed to make this information sharing effective?

Describe *private* facilities (such as industrial sites or mines) that may contaminate areas to which the community has geographic, historical, cultural and legal ties.

- What are our relevant local library collections? Nearby libraries with information about relevant facilities?
- What is the status of our on-line record retrieval abilities?
- Who (or what agency) is responsible for maintaining relevant information? For liaison with appropriate facility operators? What qualifications are required to carry out this responsibility? What co-ordination within the community is required to do this effectively? What barriers limit the effectiveness of knowing in detail what private facilities threaten our lands?
- What information is available that our community would find relevant? What capability exists to share information? What mechanisms are needed to make this information sharing effective?

2. Risk Characterization

Describe contamination likely to result from routine operation of the proposed development, and also from possible emergencies (in terms of magnitude, duration, timing, mixtures).

Figure 8.2 Characterizing a Local Community's Capacity-building Needs

- Has prior work been done for our lands and our people in particular? Do we have access to records concerning methods and outcomes for this work?
- What else do we need to learn that we don't know already? What staff and equipment do we need to learn this?
- What staff and equipment do we need to keep a record of ongoing estimates provided by others?
- What staff and equipment do we need to verify the ongoing estimates provided by others?
- What information is available that our community would find relevant? What capability exists to share information? What mechanisms are needed to make this information sharing effective?

Describe pathways to community members' exposures.

- How well do our records document potentially significant pathways of relevance to our local territory, traditions and lifestyles?
- How well do our records document where our members were living at times when they might have been exposed in the past?
- What should be the nature of local participation in developing information on toxicology and locally pertinent pathways? Who should be involved, and what staff qualifications/equipment are required?
- What information is available that our community would find relevant? What capability exists to share information? What mechanisms are needed to make this information sharing effective?

Define relevant health outcomes.

- How well do our records document the health status of our community members?
- How accessible are these records?
- What additional information is needed to define relevant health outcomes?
- Does our community need to consult with outside subject matter experts to accomplish this?
- What information is available that our community would find relevant? What capability exists to share information? What mechanisms are needed to make this information sharing effective?

Figure 8.2 Characterizing a Local Community's Capacity-building Needs *(continued)*

Assess risks.

- Has prior work been done to estimate risks associated with specific sources of contamination?
- Has prior work been done to estimate total exposures?
- Has prior work been done to estimate the susceptibility of our people to risks from specified sources?
- Has prior work been done to compare risks from different sources, including radiological risks and risks from micro-organisms?
- What should be the nature of local participation in performing risk assessments? Who should be involved, and what staff qualifications/equipment are required?
- What information is available that our community would find relevant? What capability exists to share information? What mechanisms are needed to make this information sharing effective?

3. Risk Reduction Measures

Public health information and education.

- What documented efforts have been undertaken to date? What audiences were targeted? What techniques were used? Has the effectiveness of these efforts been evaluated?
- What has been tried? How has it worked? What would help keep it working well/make it work better?
- What sources of assistance are available that our community would find relevant? What basic capability would need to be developed by our community before we could take advantage of such assistance?

Medical interventions.

- What documented efforts have been undertaken to date? What populations were targeted? What techniques were used? Has the effectiveness of these efforts been evaluated?
- What barriers to access and utilization must be overcome?
- How does our community co-ordinate with other public health officials and private care providers to overcome these barriers?

Figure 8.2 Characterizing a Local Community's Capacity-building Needs *(continued)*

Environmental surveillance.

- What is the status of our community's environmental surveillance/monitoring programme? What area does it cover? What staffing requirements does it have? What computers and field equipment does it use? Has the adequacy of this programme been evaluated?
- What are further monitoring/surveillance needs? How can these be prioritized? What staff and equipment are needed to accomplish this?
- What sources of assistance are available that our community would find relevant? What basic capability would need to be developed by our community before we could take advantage of such assistance?

Further research.

- What work on small area epidemiological methods has been completed? Has any of this work specifically focused on our community's membership? Has any work been done on biological indicators of locally relevant exposures?
- What are further research needs? How can these be prioritized? What staff and equipment are needed to accomplish this?
- What sources of assistance are available that our community would find relevant? What basic capability would need to be developed by our community before we could take advantage of such assistance?

Figure 8.2 Characterizing a Local Community's Capacity-building Needs *(continued)*

solution can be found, the ones where the stakes are high, the uncertainties great, and the impacts broadly felt for the longest time. It should be assumed that if one starts with the wrong formulation of the problem, one will inevitably end up with bad proposals for implementing change. 'Bad' in this instance means locally burdensome, and in the realm of problems entrusted to government solution, anthropologists often engage those peoples most likely to bear the local burden of national policies, and give them credit for their insight and expertise.

In the case of locally borne environmental health impacts, the central question is how to reduce the public's exposure to hazards. Finding acceptable answers involves value-laden, conflict-riddled choices over who will bear the burden locally in order to achieve a widespread benefit.

Nuclear and chemical weapons may have served the interests of national defence and global peace, but a legacy of contamination remains. Industrial activities may also serve the interest of the regional and national economies, but here too a legacy of contamination remains, a legacy that is especially threatening to groups whose identity derives from the place where they live.

In practical terms, the issue of national interests and local burdens is one of whose values should inform the choices. Who ought to sit at the table when the big decisions get made? Too often, choices are regarded as matters of 'fact' to be made only by specialists with the right knowledge or 'expertise.' Non-specialists are labelled 'inexpert', their judgements discounted as ill-informed, politically motivated, or both. Excluding them from decisions promotes a lack of trust in the specialists, a feeling that the hazards and remedies are beyond the control of those most affected.

The problem-structuring step, sometimes called 'scoping' in the formal context of Environmental Impact Statements (EISs), should focus our attention specifically on three sets of baseline/impact categories:

1 Changes in risk factors.
2 Changes in service delivery and differential access.
3 Changes in perceptions of risk.

Changes in Risk Factors Environmental health risk factors generally are placed into two categories: pathways of exposure, and behaviours leading to exposure. A 'pathway' is the process by which an individual is exposed to a contaminant that is released from a specific source. The pathway follows a contaminant from its release (contamination source) and dispersion into the air, water, or soil (environmental media and transport mechanisms) to its point of exposure (a location of potential or actual human contact) via a route of exposure (e.g. inhalation, ingestion, or absorption through the skin). A pathway also includes the so-called 'receptor population': the persons who are exposed or potentially exposed to the contaminants of concern at a point of exposure. A development proposal may introduce the possibility of airborne emissions that will be deposited in areas downwind from a source of release, or may stir up contaminants that had stabilized in the soil after their initial deposition. A proposed hydroelectricity project almost certainly would alter the flow of river water, perhaps disrupting a seasonal process of dilution and promoting a build-up of coliform bacteria that increase the risk of gastrointestinal disease among people for whom the river is a drinking water source.

A key facet of problem structuring, then, is to make sure that locally relevant pathways are included in the data collection and analysis plan. In anticipation of cleaning up the former British nuclear weapons testing site at Maralinga, South Australia, for example, Giles, Palmer & Brady (1988) found that the Aboriginal community most likely to use portions of the reclaimed area would probably pursue a semi-traditional subsistence and settlement pattern, rather than erecting permanent buildings in the Euro-Australian architectural style. This means that the greatest exposures to residual weapons-testing contamination would not necessarily come from ingestion, but rather from inhalation and dermal absorption.

Changes in Service Delivery and Differential Access Introducing or removing contaminants alter potential local health risks, but so do changes in the delivery of health care services. A temporary construction work force may increase the demand for health care services, and place a strain on existing facilities. Alternatively, new facilities and equipment or increased health care provider staff may be introduced to accommodate increases in demand caused by development-related population growth. If these facilities and their staff are available to the local population, improvements in preventive and treatment services may result. In addition, depending on the proposed development's location, changes in the accessibility of health care services may result. Transportation routes may be altered, satellite or mobile diagnostic and treatment facilities may become available, and a proposed development's construction and operation may result in changes in health care delivery cost or rules concerning who may be permitted access to treatment.

Changes in Risk Perceptions A final category of problems to consider in structuring the assessment of environmental health impacts involves changes in local perceptions of health risks. The public health risk controversy over chemicals in the environment is rooted in the notions of 'hazard' and 'stigma'. A distinction between these two notions is appropriate in impact analysis projects.

It has been amply demonstrated that popular concerns about possible personal hazards to health and personal safety are often inconsistent with scientific evidence, where it exists, about the likelihood that such hazards will occur. An associated concern is that even if possible hazards are never realized, the mere presence of the potential hazards' source can stigmatize the locale, affecting the market for certain locally produced goods and services, and perhaps limiting future economic development opportunities (Liebow, Branch & Orians, 1993). Thus, while the notion of ecological 'hazard' is associated with the risk of health impairment, 'stigma' is associated with the risk of financial or social impairment.

Ecological Hazards

Non-specialists are said to use an 'intuitive approach' to judging hazards, in contrast with an 'analytical approach' normally used by experts (e.g. Starr & Whipple, 1980). The 'intuitive' approach relies on vivid images of hazards and devastation, often drawn from dramatic news accounts, to focus on the controllability of hazards (can catastrophic consequences be averted?).[3] Using this intuitive approach, people are relatively accurate in ranking the seriousness of hazards, but relatively inaccurate in estimating a hazard's calculated magnitude (Slovic, 1987). Unlike their specialist counterparts, the general public usually takes a number of mental short-cuts when faced with complex decisions or decisions surrounded by a relatively great amount of uncertainty: for example, decisions about unusual events that may or may not take place at some indefinite point in the future (Tversky & Kahneman, 1973, 1974, 1981). In addition, people have been found to be swayed in their judgements by the way they are asked to form them (Fischhoff & MacGregor, 1983; Lopes & Ekberg, 1980).

It has also been amply demonstrated that the general public is often told that a product or factory is 'state of the art', only to see it malfunction (e.g. Perrow, 1984). Because of this, many of us have grown sceptical, and providing us with information about the safety of a proposed development will not, by itself, remove a generally held concern that the development is a source of possible health hazards. In addition, we generally need information that will help evaluate the proponent's credibility, trustworthiness and ability to manage the development. We want to know that we are being dealt with fairly, that the local benefits and environmental burdens of a proposed development are being distributed in equal measure (Douglas, 1985; Douglas & Wildavsky, 1982; Rayner & Cantor 1987; Wenz, 1988).

Credibility, trust and fairness as factors in judgements about hazards suggest that the potential source of hazards is not evaluated in a social vacuum. A process termed the 'social amplification of risk' may be at work, where the interaction between a potential ecological hazard and its social setting may increase the impacts of technology (Kasperson, Renn, Slovic, Brown, Emel, Goble, Kasperson & Ratide, 1988). Impacts of an industrial installation or chemical application – beyond those calculated by the risk assessment specialists – may occur as information about the possible hazard is exchanged. People receive such information either through word of mouth or through the mass media. Factors identified as contributing to the social amplification of ecological hazards include:

1 Selective, sensational, and sometimes inaccurate media reporting of risks and regulatory actions to control them.
2 The use of technical language.
3 Limits in the ability of non-specialists to understand technical information.
4 Intolerance for scientific uncertainties.
5 Failure to address the public's concerns (Keeney & von Winterfeldt, 1986).

Stigma

Researchers have argued that under certain circumstances an area might be cast in an unfavourable light, with the possibility of associated adverse economic effects, if it were to host a potential source of ecological hazards (Fischhoff, Lichtenstein, Slovic, Derby & Keeney, 1981; Fischhoff, Lichtenstein & Slovic, 1982; Slovic, 1987). The key to predicting whether a host area might be stigmatized rests with several characteristics of the potential hazard:

1 *Concealability*. Is the potential hazard hidden or obvious? To what extent is its visibility controllable?
2 *Course*. What pattern of change over time is usually shown by the condition? What is its ultimate outcome?
3 *Disruptiveness*. Does its presence block or hamper interaction and communication?
4 *Aesthetic qualities*. To what extent does the source make the possessor repellent, ugly or upsetting?
5 *Origin*. Under what circumstances did the source of potential hazards originate? Was anyone responsible for it, and what was he or she trying to do?
6 *Peril*. What kind of danger is posed by the hazard, and how imminent and serious is it?

Experiments suggest that people associate different types of industrial facilities with different levels of stigma on host regions (Slovic, 1987). Although this experimental approach has been taken to task as inadequately representing the general population (Beach, Christensen-Szalanski & Barnes, 1987), or because of its subtly disdainful distinctions between laypersons and experts (Bradbury, 1989; Liebow, 1993), its highly suggestive results should be tested further.

Another dimension of 'stigma' that bears mentioning, although it has not received a great deal of attention in the research literature, has to do with changes in political power that come along with large-scale industrial development in rural areas. Smaller, stable communities often rely on part-time officials and a certain informal way of avoiding or resolving conflicts. Cherished by some, this political style may become a liability in the face of outside growth and development pressures. There may not have been many occasions to build the local expertise required to create development controls and interpret environmental protection regulations, and this need for capacity-building may become a source of stigma in dealing with sophisticated outside development interests.

To review briefly, the crucial problem-structuring step should focus our attention on potential changes in risk factors, service delivery, and perceptions of health risks. Collaboration with locally affected population groups is necessary in further specifying the most meaningful of these changes. Methods for doing so are briefly touched upon in the next section.

Methods Selection

The key to prioritizing potentially significant environmental health impacts for further investigation is to employ a complementary set of qualitative and quantitative data collection methods. It is almost always the case with impact assessment research that the findings will be used to organize a knowledge base that may help resolve conflicts over environmental health and safety. The richness of an ethnographic data record certainly can contribute to conflict resolution. However, it is reasonable to expect some resistance to a 'qualitative' analysis on the grounds that it lacks precision, is incomplete, inaccurate, unrepresentative, or otherwise fails to capture adequately the knowledge, attitudes, and behaviour patterns that inform local community perspectives regarding a development proponent's plans. Indeed, in one recent instance (Liebow, Bradbury, Branch, Heerwagen, Konkel & Leyson, 1998), upon initially visiting both potentially affected communities and development proponents, we were almost always asked why we were not conducting a sample opinion survey, and what we hoped to gain from our work if its findings were not generalizable, in a statistical sense, to the larger population.

Resolving complex conflicts – and expecting them to remain resolved – cannot be accomplished by referendum, especially when at least some parties to the conflict are convinced that more is at stake than judging whose chemical residue predictions are more realistic. One should be concerned that if data collection efforts take the form of an opinion survey, the results would appear to grant approval to the development proponent's plans by the principle of 'plurality rules', yet resistance would escalate. With public approval apparent, the proponent might further discount or ignore altogether those opposing its plans, who for their part would make good on their threat to appeal directly to Congress/Parliament, the courts, and other regulatory authorities. Rather than helping to reach a productive and stable resolution to this conflict, a series of local attitude/opinion surveys easily could have the opposite effect.

As indicated earlier, the main analytical sequence focuses on hazard identification, risk characterization and risk reduction. In each stage of this sequence, methodological choices are available. Selecting from among the elements in one's 'tool kit' may depend heavily on local capacity for collaboration, time, and financial resources available to create the necessary knowledge base.

Hazard Identification

The purpose of this step is to describe facilities (both publicly and privately operated) that are already present as potential sources of contamination to areas over which the community has geographic, historical, cultural and other legally protected ties. Creating such a description is necessary to establish the baseline conditions into which a proposed developed is to be introduced.

Archival reviews, either from local and regional library collections or from on-line databases maintained by regulatory authorities, offer a good start in describing existing facility operations. However, it is also necessary to collect 'local knowledge' of the area through direct interviews about 'place' in order to establish the geographic extent of possible effects from the proposed development as judged by the affected communities. As Stoffle, Traugott, Stone, McIntyre, Jensen & Davidson have shown (1991), defining what is already present in the geographic area of most likely impacts is a critical, but not altogether straightforward, step in the initial hazard identification process. Affected populations are not necessarily organized according to the political and administrative units used for government data collection, and local social organization and mobility patterns can expand significantly the geographic domain over which a proposed development's health impacts are regarded as potentially significant.

Risk Characterization

The purpose of this step is to describe the projected introduction of environmental contaminants (in terms of magnitude, duration, timing and mixtures), the pathways that these contaminants might take to result in community members' exposures, the relevant health and safety outcomes associated with these contaminants, and the circumstances under which unhealthy exposure levels are likely to be experienced locally. Risk characterization usually requires the involvement of other specialists in a multi-disciplinary team the toxicologists, health physicists and ecologists.

It is useful for anthropologists to familiarize themselves with risk characterization procedures, and several prescriptive manuals are available to guide work at this stage of an impact assessment (for example, the United States Agency for Toxic Substances and Disease Registry, 1992). Left unspoken in these guides, however, is one of the more important contributions that ethnographic insights can make: according to what locally meaningful subgroup distinctions are contaminant pathways and exposure levels likely to vary? Government records rarely allow for designation of local identity and affiliation, relying instead on aggregate categories that overlook significant risk-related cultural and behavioural variability. The ethnographer needs to make sure that the risk characterization work on pathways, relevant health outcomes and exposure levels is framed by local sub-group distinctions. We might propose to ask, at the outset, such questions as:

1 Into what meaningful categories and sub-communities do local community members place themselves?
2 By what behaviours, meanings, attributes symbols do they maintain boundaries distinguishing between such categories and sub-communities?
3 How 'fixed' or rapidly changing are these categories and the means by which their boundaries are maintained?

Not only do the answers to these questions increase the chances of adequately capturing variability in behavioural risk factors, but they contribute the added value of increasing the face validity with which the specialists' risk characterization is presented to potentially affected populations.

Risk Reduction Measures

The purpose of this step is to determine what institutionalized capabilities exist to reduce or avoid altogether the risks to which affected communities would otherwise likely be exposed. These capabilities include institutions that can be mobilized to provide public health information and education, medical care and treatment, environmental and health surveillance, and, perhaps, additional research that will add to our collective knowledge about local health status and relevant risk factors.

One is compelled to acknowledge that the institutional landscape for risk reduction is highly territorialized, so the outsider's view of organizations and agencies that appear to be well-placed to reduce environmental health risks needs to be sensitized to the constraints with which these organizations frequently must operate. Adapting a useful model developed by Blaikie, Cannon, Davis & Wisner (1994), vulnerability to environmental health risks occurs in a progression from the proximate ('unsafe conditions') to intermediate ('dynamic pressures'), and finally to the least proximate (systemic 'root causes'). Root causes of vulnerability are to be found in limited access to power, structures and resources, and in ideologies that reinforce inequalities. Dynamic pressures are processes and activities that channel the root causes into particular forms of insecurity. Rapid population growth, urbanization, debt repayment schedules, deforestation, and declining soil productivity are all seen as macro-forces derived from underlying causes that lead to unsafe conditions for some population subgroups. These unsafe conditions may include environmental and economic fragility, a lack of preparedness, endemic diseases, and a lack of local institutions to fall back on when conditions of scarcity are exacerbated.

Effective risk reduction measures require institutional mobilization to address changes at all points along this progression, but institutions often lack the necessary scope of authority to do so. Authority to deal with unsafe conditions, for example, is often within the province of medical care providers and public health agencies. Dealing with dynamic pressures and systemic root causes of vulnerability, however, frequently is beyond the health institutions' territory, and requires collaboration between health institutions, government agencies and NGOs who do not necessarily regard environmental health risks as within their province. In the risk reduction arena then, the ethnographer's perspective must encompass a holistic look at institutions capable of being mobilized to intervene at the local level, including institutions whose terms of reference appear, on the surface at least, to be only indirectly tied to the immediate threat of unsafe environmental conditions.

Conclusion: Where does 'Culture' Fit in the Health Risk Equation?

Ethnographic methods can contribute substantively to changing the way we evaluate development-related environmental health and safety risks, and especially in recognizing the systemic institutional relations that must change in remedying past injustices visited upon disadvantaged and marginalized peoples. No one's interests are served, however, when an environmental health impact assessment has at its foundation an ill-conceived model of culture.

If one is to argue persuasively that cultural variability affects (or does not affect) variability in environmental health and safety risks – that is, people from different cultural backgrounds are (not) differentially vulnerable to risk because of their cultural backgrounds – then a specific spot must be cleared for a well-defined notion of culture. A well-defined notion of culture, in turn, will necessarily make explicit its assumptions concerning territorial, demographic and temporal reference frames, as well as assumptions about within-group variability with respect to enculturation.

Without the benefit of ethnographic research, environmental health assessment generally views 'culture' as constituting one set of variables in an equation whose outcome is a measurement of risk. For example, Harris & Harper (1997) assume that variability in the risk of health hazards depends on lifestyle variability. A 'native American' lifestyle leads to a distinctive vulnerability to contamination threats. They also assume however, that 'cultural' group affiliation is directly and uniformly associated with 'lifestyle': All 'native Americans' share a common and distinct 'lifestyle', and equations intended to quantify the exposure pathway for a given contaminant need to modify coefficients to account for this distinct lifestyle. Embedded in this view is an adversarial approach that aims to allocate responsibility to various possible causal factors, or 'affix blame' to individual actors (like polluters) within a territorial and economic system. Placing culture within an impact assessment framework directs analytical attention to producing estimates of dose and health risk under varying development scenarios, or to producing public health messages aimed at getting people to change the behaviours that expose them to health risks in the face of inevitable development. For the purposes of assessing environmental health impacts, it is perhaps more productive to promote an alternative view of 'culture'. From this alternative view, 'culture' is the encompassing context within which impact assessment problems are framed. Placing the impact assessment project within a cultural frame directs analytical attention to where it properly belongs, resolving conflicts over the distribution of burdens and benefits. With the focus on conflict resolution, emphasis is placed on problem-structuring techniques. The analyst's responsibility is to make sure all assumptions and uncertainties are clearly articulated, and the nature and degree of community collaboration recognized. Specialists' introspections are never an adequate substitute for observation, and specialists must relinquish sole authority for determining the legitimacy of problems allowed to surface.

References

Bahr, D.M., Gregorio, J., Lopez, D. and Alvarez, A. (1974), *Piman Shamanism and Staying Sickness (Ka:cim Mumkidag)*, Tucson, AZ: University of Arizona Press.

Beach, L.R., Christensen-Szalanski, J. and Barnes, V. (1987), 'Assessing Human Judgment: Has It Been Done, Can It Be Done, Should It Be Done?', in G. Wright and P. Ayton (eds), *Judgmental Forecasting*, New York: John Wiley and Sons, pp.49–62.

Blaikie, P., Cannon, T., Davis, I. and Wisner, B. (1994), *At Risk: Natural Hazards, People's Vulnerability, and Disasters*, London and New York: Routledge.

Bradbury, J. (1989), 'The Policy Implications of Differing Concepts of Risk', *Science, Technology, and Human Values*, 14(4):189–212.

Chagnon, N. (1983), *Yanomano: The Fierce People* (3rd ed.) New York: Holt, Rinehart, Winston.

Clifford, J. (1988), *The Predicament of Culture: Twentieth-Century Ethnography, Literature, and Art*, Cambridge, MA: Harvard University Press.

Cornwall A. and Jewkes R. (1995), 'What is Participatory Research?' *Social Science and Medicine*, 41:1667–76.

Douglas, M. (1985), *Risk Acceptability According to the Social Sciences*, Social Research Perspectives Occasional Reports on Current Topics No. 11, New York: Russell Sage Foundation.

Douglas, M., and Wildavsky, A. (1982), *Risk and Culture: An Essay on the Selection of Technological and Environmental Dangers*, Berkeley, CA: University of California Press.

Evans-Pritchard, E.E. (1940), *The Nuer, a description of the modes of livelihood and political institutions of a Nilotic people*, Oxford: Clarendon.

Fischhoff, B. and MacGregor, D. (1983), 'Judged lethality: how much people seem to know depends on how they are asked', *Risk Analysis*, 3:229–36.

Fischhoff, B., Lichtenstein, S., Slovic, P., Derby, S.L. and Keeney, R.L. (1981), *Acceptable Risk*, New York: Cambridge University Press.

Fischhoff, B., Lichtenstein, S. and Slovic, P. (1982), 'Why study risk perception?' *Risk Analysis*, 2(1):83–92.

Giles, M.S., Palmer, K. and Brady, M. (1988), 'Dose commitment estimates in an Aboriginal community: problem in rapidly changing social values', in *Radiation Protection In Nuclear Energy: Proceedings of an International Conference on Radiation Protection in Nuclear Energy*, vol. 1, pp.173–9, Vienna, Austria: International Atomic Energy Agency, Report No. IAEA–CN–51/51.

Harris, S.G. and Harper, B.L. (1997), 'A Native American Risk Scenario', *Risk Analysis*, 17(6):789–96.

Kasperson, R., Renn, O., Slovic, P., Brown, H., Emel, J., Goble, R., Kasperson, J. and Ratide, S. (1988), 'The social amplification of risk: a conceptual framework', *Risk Analysis*, 8(2):177–87.

Keeney, R.L. and von Winterfeldt, D. (1986), 'Improving risk communication', *Risk Analysis*, 6(4):417–24.

Liebow, E.B. (1993), 'Who is expert at interpreting environmental hazards? A commentary on the disabling effects of an "Expert/Layperson" dichotomy', *The Environmental Professional*, 15(3): 288–92.

Liebow, E.B., Branch, K.M. and Orians, C.E. (1993), 'Incinerating hazardous wastes: perceptions of risk and focus group interviews', *Sociological Spectrum*, 13(1):153–73.

Liebow, E.B., Bradbury, J.A., Branch, K.M., Heerwagen, J., Konkel, R.S. and Leyson, J. (1998), 'The landscape of reason: A scheme for representing arguments concerning environmental health, and safety effects of chemical weapons disposal in the United States', *High Plains Applied Anthropologist*, 18(2):115–37.

Lopes, L.L. and Ekberg, P.H. (1980), Test of an ordering hypothesis of risky decision making, *Acta Psychologica*, 45:161–67.

Perrow, C. (1984), *Normal Accidents: Living With High-Risk Technologies*, New York: Basic Books.

Rayner, S. and Cantor, R. (1987), 'How fair is safe enough? The cultural approach to societal technological choice', *Risk Analysis*, 7(1):3–9.

Schulz, A.J., Israel, B.A., Selig, S.M. and Bayer, I.S. (1998), 'Development and implementation of principles for community-based research in public health', in R. MacNair (ed.), *Research Strategies for Community Practice*, New York: Hayworth Press, pp.83–110.

Slovic, P. (1987), 'Perception of risk', *Science*, 236(4799):280–5.

Starr, C. and Whipple, C. (1980), 'The risk of risk decisions', *Science*, 208:1114–19.

Stoffle, R.W., Traugott, M.W., Stone, J.V., McIntyre, P.D., Jensen, F.V. and Davidson, C.C. (1991), 'Risk perception mapping: using ethnography to define the locally affected population for a low-level radioactive waste storage facility in Michigan', *American Anthropologist*, 93:611–35.

Tversky, A. and Kahneman, D. (1973), 'Availability: A Heuristic for Judging Frequency and Probability', *Cognitive Psychology*, 5:207–32.

Tversky, A. and Kahneman, D. (1974), 'Judgment under uncertainty: heuristics and biases', *Science*, 185:1124–31.

Tversky, A. and Kahneman, D. (1981), 'The framing of decisions and the psychology of choice', *Science*, 211:453–8.

United States Agency for Toxic Substances and Disease Registry (1992), *ATSDR Public Health Assessment Guidance Manual*, Ann Arbor, MI: Lewis Publishers.

Wenz, P.S. (1988), *Environmental Justice*, Albany, NY: State University of New York Press.

Notes

1 'Evaluation' research and 'impact assessment' research are, of course, related. A growing body of evaluation findings are available to place the expectation and attainment of desired health outcomes on a rational and reliable basis.

2 A formative standard against which models of collaborative writing are yet appropriately measured is found in the work of Bahr, Gregorio, Lopez & Alvarez (1974).

3 In contrast, the 'analytical' approach methodically relies on data from a number of less selective sources, taking into account the likelihood that a hazard will occur as well as the magnitude of its consequences.

–9–

Social Impact Assessment and Linear Projects

Richard Howitt and *Sue Jackson*

Social impact assessment research is inherently uncertain, time-consuming, resource intensive and difficult. Project advocates and development agencies that set terms of reference and deadlines for social impact studies are generally more familiar with the requirements of business deals or political compromise than demands of complex social research. In cross-cultural settings involving indigenous peoples, the need to take into account the interests of multiple stakeholders affects both the impact processes a project will generate and the way the assessment task can be approached. This chapter considers the particular case of linear projects and discusses methodological issues for meeting the challenges such projects raise. Drawing on the authors' 1998 assessment of the impacts on Aboriginal people of a proposed rail link between Alice Springs and Darwin in Australia's Northern Territory (Figure 9.1) (Howitt, Jackson & Bryson, 1998), the chapter outlines issues and approaches that facilitate better project planning, impact management, and regional development. Consistent with discussion elsewhere (Howitt, 1993), the approach outlined is participatory, empowering and interventionist. It proposes a consultative process which empowers marginalized stakeholders to understand changes likely to occur in response to a proposal, and frames a negotiation approach to address concerns of alignment, specific impacts, regional effects and general policy responses.

Linear Projects and Impact Assessment

Linear projects are those activities such as railway lines, power transmission lines, pipelines, roads, freeways and canals where project configuration involves a narrow strip of land over a considerable distance. Unlike site-specific projects such as mines and dams, linear projects always require project managers to deal with a diversity of environmental

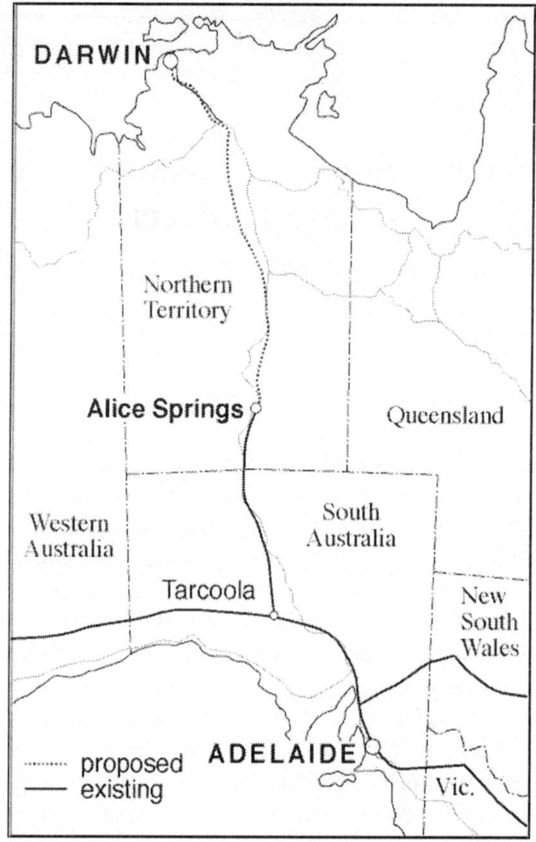

Figure 9.1 Map of Existing and Proposed Railways in Central Australia

conditions and stakeholder interests (Mejia & Kvam, 1997). Route planning, for example, must balance the imperatives of commercial financing with the wider environmental, social and cultural costs, to optimize positive development outcomes, minimize negative implications, and ensure a fair distribution of non-financial project costs and benefits. For mining projects, location options are constrained by the location, quality and quantity of a resource. For other single site projects, specific site criteria, market and labour force access and specific environmental and social conditions will influence decisions. For linear projects, however, locational choices and other aspects of configuration (alignment, scale, combinations of facilities, etc.) cannot be reduced to a limited set of criteria. In linear projects, relationships within and between many places, groups of people, stakeholder interests and project alternatives must be considered in informed decision making. Linear projects demand a sophisticated understanding of landscapes as simultaneously encompassing cultural and environmental complexity, because they not only traverse several distinct landscapes, but also create new links and relations between them.

In the wider social impact analysis (SIA) literature, several issues are identified as central to creating effective assessment frameworks. Many of these are relevant to assessment of linear projects. Finsterbusch (1995:231–5) identifies ethical foundations for SIA, in terms of :

1 Social impact assessment's utility in improving resource allocation and development decision.
2 Social impact assessment's ability to consider effects of specific actions on rights and liberties.
3 Social impact assessment's ability to systemize questions of justice in relation to policy decisions and their outcomes and impacts.
4 Social impact assessment's ability to reduce exploitative tendencies within decision-making systems.
5 Social impact assessment's efficacy in enhancing accountability and transparency in decision making and project design.
6 Social impact assessment's contribution to truly democratizing social decision making.
7 Social impact assessment's compatibility with ethnic pluralism (in Australia, multiculturalism).

He also warns of the need to balance the costs and benefits of SIA research: 'There is one ethical basis for claiming that certain SIAs should not be conducted – when the costs exceed the benefits of the SIA. This can occur when research costs are high and findings are highly uncertain' (p.236). For linear projects, this observation is particularly important, because the balance between the research costs, specific impacts, and community benefits in large-scale linear projects is less easy to assess and potentially much more marginal than in projects which are more geographically contained in terms of impacts. Along extended linear corridors, many stakeholders may be wary of undertaking an impact study which seems open-ended in terms of its costs and scope, even if it is widely agreed that some assessment of social impacts is needed as a guide to action. Ethically, the imperative is for impact assessment to include critical elements of current 'best practice' at a reasonable cost.

Many linear projects involve significant commitment of public funds to finance new infrastructure. Development of railways or highways, for example, establishes (or reflects) transportation priorities and policies; oil and gas pipeline or power transmission lines similarly establish the infrastructural parameters for future energy policies. Assessing the impacts of such projects, therefore, implies an evaluation of public policy settings, even though such policy settings may not be referred to in specific terms of reference.[1] This ensures that SIA of many linear projects will face a level of political interest and oversight that is uncommon in more routine, privately sponsored, site-specific development proposals.

It is not only governments that target linear projects for particular attention. Within the affected populations, too, linear projects often also face challenges in meeting compensatory expectations for negative impacts on affected communities because the level of benefits generated by public service projects is often limited and the share of profit or surplus available for distribution to affected parties is limited. Similarly, scope for generating flow-on benefits in any single affected community is often limited relative to the overall budget of the project, even though direct and indirect impacts on some communities might be quite large. Indeed, resettlement requirements of linear projects, along with changes in patterns of access and use of resources, detrimental effects on quality of life and increased levels of risk are distributed unevenly along the corridors of linear projects. Setting boundaries (social, spatial and temporal) around these effects and establishing equitable and ethical procedures for compensation and distribution of development benefits are problematic. In linear projects, the extension of the affected population across great distances that often encompasses considerable cultural, economic and environmental diversity means that consideration must be given to a greater range of factors than is necessary for more spatially contained projects. Such factors increase the importance of benchmarking in scoping, research, monitoring and management phases of impact assessment work on linear projects.

Yet, many of the international benchmarks are, at least implicitly, predicated upon relatively discrete, spatially contained project configurations rather than extended linear configurations. In the field of indigenous SIA, for example, there is a wide literature on the impacts of single site-mining operations on single-site indigenous communities (Connell & Howitt, 1991; Howitt, Connell & Hirsch, 1996; O'Faircheallaigh, 1991), and on resettlement issues around large dams (World Bank 1994), but very limited discussion on linear projects. This is ironic given the importance of the Canadian Berger Inquiry (Berger, 1977, 1988), which considered the implications of trans-Canadian pipelines and related projects, in setting standards for cross-cultural social and environmental assessment in the mid 1970s. In many ways, the methodological issues confronted by the Berger Inquiry remain central to social assessment of linear projects. In summary, then, the challenge in linear project assessment is development of equitable, cost-effective and robust methods for facilitating participation by affected communities from diverse cultural, economic and environmental circumstances in identifying, evaluating and responding to impacts, and framing ways of monitoring and managing impacts (including indirect impacts) into the future.

The approach developed in the recent social impact study for the Alice Springs to Darwin railway project illustrates many of these issues and offers insights into the challenges and how they might be addressed practically and ethically.

The Alice Springs to Darwin Railway Impact Assessment

In 1998 the Northern and Central Land Councils (Central Land Council) commissioned an assessment of the social and cultural impacts on Aboriginal people of the proposed rail link between Alice Springs and Darwin. Terms of reference for the study were agreed by the Land Councils and the Northern Territory Government in early 1998 as part of an agreement on how to deal with native title interests and Aboriginal land affected by the railway proposal.[2]

The Railway Project

The AustralAsia Rail project involves construction of 1,410 km of new standard gauge rail to link Alice Springs and Darwin in Northern Territory (Figure 9.2). Estimated cost of the project is A$1.2–A$1.5 billion. In 1998, the Commonwealth, South Australian and Northern Territory Governments committed A$300,000,000 of public funds to the project. Ownership of an existing line between Alice Springs and Tarcoola (South Australia) was to be transferred from the Commonwealth Government to the successful bidder for the project. The Northern Territory Government estimates the construction phase will generate about 2,000 jobs, with about 200 operational jobs. If it proceeds, the construction of rail line and related works will be amongst the largest transport infrastructure projects in Australia for many years.[3] Like many large-scale linear projects, the Alice Springs to Darwin Railway has a prolonged and highly politicized history. This has implications for social impact assessment of the project.

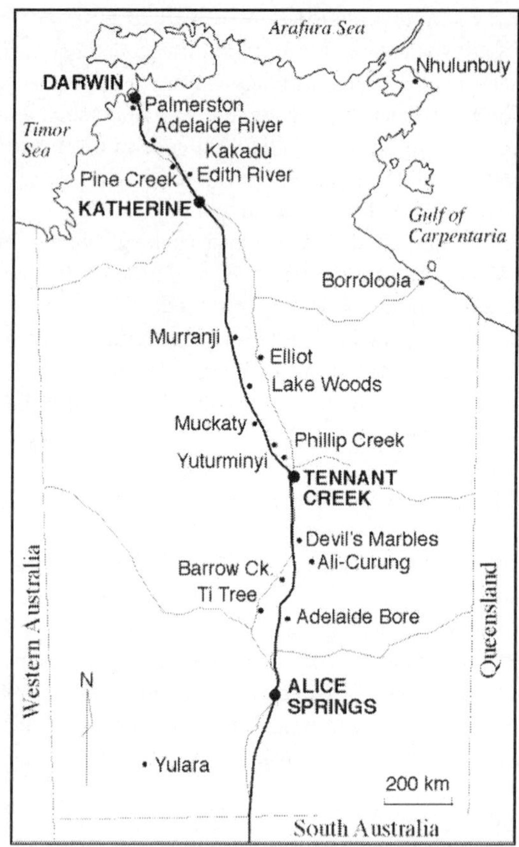

Figure 9.2 Map of Route of the Proposed Alice Springs to Darwin Railway Project

The idea of a rail link between Darwin and the southern states was first proposed in 1878 (Bromby, 1992:3). A narrow-gauge line between Port Augusta (South Australia) and Alice Springs was completed in 1928, and the line from Darwin reached as far south as Birdum (Northern Territory). In the late 1970s, a new standard-gauge line was built to link Alice Springs to the transcontinental railway at Tarcoola. Feasibility of continuing the standard-gauge link to Darwin reviewed by Australian National Railways (ANR) and the Commonwealth Government in 1979. A year later, the Commonwealth committed itself to completion of the line to Darwin. An Environmental Impact Statement (EIS) of that proposal was released for public comment in December 1982.

Following a change of government in 1983, the Commonwealth decided not to proceed with the railway. The EIS was finalized (Dames & Moore, 1984), and planning advanced to a point where construction could commence when funds were available. The proposal was revived as the AustralAsia Rail project in the mid-1990s, when South Australia, the Northern Territory and the Commonwealth of Australia signed a Memorandum of Understanding. Unlike the earlier ANR proposal, which had envisaged public ownership of a passenger and freight service, the new proposal was based on a private freight-only operation. The AustralAsia Rail project was linked into other major infrastructure and policy initiatives in the Northern Territory including new harbour works, expanded irrigated agriculture and offshore energy industry development. The new project was seen as part of a land bridge to Asian markets. A revised environmental management plan (Dames & Moore, 1997) was prepared to update environmental information about the proposal from the original ANR project. Expressions of interest for the build-own-operate-transfer project were called for in 1997.

The economics of the AustralAsia Rail project took account of the booming 'tiger' economies of East and South East Asia in the early 1990s, and offered efficient rail and sea-rail transfer services as a way of linking Australian and Asian industries and markets. Since the project was revitalized, however, many radical changes have occurred. Since 1996, changes in political and economic circumstances again shifted the ground around the project:

1 The South East Asian economic boom rapidly turned around into a widespread downturn and crisis, including dramatic political changes in Indonesia, East Timor, Malaysia and other areas central to the original vision for the railway.
2 Trading activities between Australia and Asia quickly became less secure and predictable than they had been.
3 Tourist numbers and patterns of travel changed, including dramatic changes to air travel services between Australia and Asia.
4 The Wik decision determined that native title rights could co-exist on pastoral leases on the railway route.[4]
5 Predictions about economic growth in north Australia became less certain.

The Railway and Aboriginal People

In dealing with the Alice Springs to Darwin railway proposals, Aboriginal people have consistently aimed to look after their 'country'.[5] In doing this, Aboriginal people and organizations have argued the railway should be dealt with by governments in terms of the existing multicultural landscape through which the railway will be built. The railway should not be planned as if it were being built through the empty spaces that earlier generations of planners and settlers imagined. In Aboriginal terms, the landscape is already 'full' and Aboriginal people have worked hard to help ANR and the Northern Territory to find a way to 'fit the railway in'.

Older Aboriginal people in the Top End recall the North Australia Railway, which operated from Darwin until 1976. It was a vital transport option for Aboriginal people. Sidings became a focus of Aboriginal settlement patterns (e.g. Maurice, 1990). The railway line itself became a marker on the landscape, and emerged as a boundary between land interests as the colonial frontier interrupted many aspects of traditional life for Aboriginal people in the Top End (e.g. Sutton Partners, 1984). In the 'land rights' era, the proposed development of the railway has been raised as a detriment issue during claims to land along the proposed route by the Northern Territory Government (e.g. Murranji, Muckaty and Philip Creek claims) as a basis for limiting these claims.

The ANR Proposal (1980–4) The route proposed by ANR in the early 1980s clearly affected Aboriginal interests. In the southern area of the CLC, development work damaged sacred sites. As a result, CLC was proactive in avoiding repetition of these problems in the ANR proposal. In turn, ANR was active and co-operative in undertaking careful site clearance work prior to detailed route survey work. This established goodwill with Aboriginal traditional owners of areas affected by the proposal. CLC expressed satisfaction about the site clearance procedures:

> In our way, Aboriginal way, it's been properly well done. They showed us everything that they wanted to do – which side they wanted to go – which ground they wanted to shift, and we showed them which important place, might be dangerous or sacred place to leave alone. If there's anything more they want to know they can come back again and talk to us, talk to our anthropologists. A good way to do it. (Wenten Rubuntja in McEvoy & Lyon, 1994:47)

The Draft EIS, however, was judged to have 'serious deficiencies in relation to its perception of Aboriginal interests' (Central Land Council, 1983:2). CLC had serious concerns about the EIS's understanding of relations between people and land in Aboriginal culture, aspects of its treatment of sacred sites and the implications of relevant legislation, the implications of the Land Rights Act, factual errors, and the social impacts the project would have on Aboriginal people. CLC proposed a separate social impact study, which would be designed in consultation with the affected Aboriginal people.[6]

The Private Railway Proposal (1995–8) In 1995, when the South Australian and Northern Territory governments signed the Memorandum of Understanding about the new AustralAsia Rail proposal, new sacred site legislation (Northern Territory *Aboriginal Sacred Sites Act 1989*) had been passed. This required new authority certificates and site clearance work. Site clearances, route surveys, and preliminary discussions with Land Councils were activated, and new consultations and discussions with Aboriginal people about the railway commenced.

Inevitably, the railway's long history and the extensive consultation with Aboriginal people in various phases of the project give rise to confusion in communities along the route. In some locations there have been major realignments of the route to avoid major scared areas such as the Devil's Marbles, south of Tennant Creek. The new project does not use any part of the old North Australia Railway corridor south of Katherine. And in the environmentally sensitive area near Lake Woods there has been a significant shift of the alignment to the west. There have also been a number of small shifts in the alignment, for example to avoid sacred trees. In some places, site protection concerns raised earlier (or early in the current process) were seen as being unresolved by some traditional land owners because they were not clear about which route was involved.

For the AustralAsia Rail proposal, the Northern Territory Government proposed delivering secure title to the land required to the successful private investor. While compulsory acquisition of land held under Northern Territory pastoral leases was possible, these areas were subject to native title claim in the wake of the Wik decision, which established the potential coexistence of native title and leasehold rights. The Northern Territory Government was not empowered to compulsorily acquire land held under the Land Rights Act. This created made it difficult for the government simply to acquire the land without addressing possible Aboriginal interests.

Aboriginal People's Negotiating Position in the 1995 Proposal In meetings about the railway extending over nearly twenty years, Aboriginal people have helped to shape the idea of the railway and to facilitate its development. Through site clearances, negotiations, myriad discussions, consultations and meetings, and careful explanation of circumstances to those who would listen, Aboriginal people have tried to weave the proposed railway into the complex and intensely valued existing cultural landscapes along the route. In consultations undertaken by the authors, many Aboriginal people made it clear they did not want to speak against the railway. Rather, people insisted, they wanted to speak for their country.

Aboriginal people have also argued that railway's development benefits for the Northern Territory and Australia should include sustainable and meaningful benefits for Aboriginal Territorians. The AustralAsia Rail proposal comes at the end of a century that witnessed massacres, dispossession, removals, dispersals and a systematic threat of genocide, as well as a slow and often grudging return of land and extension of recognition to Aboriginal people along the proposed route. It would be retrograde in policy terms for such a major investment project to either bypass or marginalize the indigenous peoples of the regions that will host it.

By the time the revised proposal was introduced in 1995, Aboriginal people had secured a much stronger role in development planning in the Northern Territory – although aspects of that role continued to be disputed by some development and political interests:

1 Experience under the Land Rights Act had greatly strengthened their skills as negotiators.
2 Successful land claims and applications for living areas on pastoral leases and the availability of Commonwealth funding had produced a decentralization of Aboriginal homeland centres, including several new areas along the railway route.
3 Institutional development within the Aboriginal sector (particularly of Land Councils and the community government sector) had produced considerable depth within the Aboriginal leadership of the affected communities.
4 Recognition of native title overturned the notion of *terra nullius* as a basis for land-management decisions.
5 Improvements in education, institutional innovation and economic development, including increased numbers of Aboriginal enterprises along the railway route had been achieved.

These circumstances meant that Aboriginal participation in discussions about the railway developed on a different basis to previous consultations. Participation was not limited to discussion of sacred sites, but extended to a range of issues related to compensation, environmental management, economic development and planning concerns. In many affected Aboriginal communities, the AustralAsia Rail proposal signalled a series of demanding and potentially stressful and even divisive meetings and inspections along the proposed route. While the new circumstances produced a stronger negotiating position for Aboriginal interests generally, some groups found their specific aspirations tied up in the new proposal.[7] These changes all produced expectations within the affected Aboriginal groups that consultation in the 1990s would be more extensive and responsive to Aboriginal concerns than it had been in the early 1980s. There were also expectations that genuine, meaningful and sustainable benefits would be received by affected Aboriginal groups if the land required for the railway was made available. In some areas, the flow of benefits from new projects provided foundations for these expectations. But in other cases, the failure to deliver promised benefits to affected Aboriginal people contributed to Aboriginal wariness about promises of the railway's benefits.

The Land Councils instituted research and community consultation processes, but the project's long history also produced cynicism about the likelihood of the project actually being built. Some work that might have facilitated a more effective social impact study was not commenced because of this. Despite earlier concerns about the need for social impact assessment (Central Land Council, 1983), and continuing discussions between Land Councils and the Northern Territory from 1995, it was not until January 1998, when the Northern Territory Government formally issued notices for compulsory acquisition, that detailed discussion of compensation with affected landowners and communities commenced.

The Railway Impact Study

Impact assessment is accepted as an integral part of project design and evaluation in Australia. Despite this, the railway proposal was not subjected to rigorous scrutiny of its potential impacts on social relations in the affected areas prior to necessary government approvals. ANR's earlier proposal included some consideration of social issues but, like many impact studies at the time, social assessment was not emphasized. AustralAsia Railway Corporation did not commission a new environmental impact statement, but an environmental management plan (Dames & Moore, 1997). This involved no new research on the nature or management of social implications of the project, despite substantial changes to the project and the social environment. On the basis of Commonwealth approval of the environmental management plan, the Northern Territory Government initiated a land acquisition process to secure title over the land required for the railway. It was this process rather than any pre-project evaluation that led to the negotiations between the Land Councils and the governments that ultimately led to the commissioning of the railway impact study (Howitt *et al.*, 1998). In other circumstances (e.g. O'Faircheallaigh, 1996a, 1998), Aboriginal organizations have commissioned community-controlled economic and social impact studies as part of their preparation for similar negotiations. Uncertainties surrounding the economic viability of this project, however, along with a lack of precedents in the Northern Territory and the logistical problems involved in assessing with such a large project, meant that this path was not pursued for the railway until a framework agreement between the Northern Territory and the Land Councils was already in place.

The railway impact study, then, was unusual in a number of ways. It was neither a formal document commissioned by the railway proponents as part of their official documentation for the project approval process, nor was it a community-controlled document commissioned as an input into negotiations. Rather, it was agreed to by the Northern Territory Government and the Land Councils as a way of providing advice on managing the likely impacts of a project that has already been approved by the governments involved, and already agreed to in principle by the Land Councils in a framework agreement approved by traditional owners. The research was funded by the Northern Territory Government and managed by the Central and Northern Land Councils as part of negotiations over leases for the corridor. Those negotiations continued during the research and resulted in leases being signed for the route in early September 1998.

Although it faced substantial practical constraints, the study pursued constructive consideration of the railway's impacts, and how they might be addressed. In reporting our research, we raised questions and reached conclusions that were relevant to each of the participants and stakeholders in the railway project. We framed specific recommendations not only to the Northern and Central Land Councils which managed the research, but also to affected communities, to governments and to the companies tendering to build, own and operate the railway. The principal mechanism available for weaving the proposed railway into the existing social and economic environment was the Northern Territory Government's requirement for the consortia tendering for the railway project to prepare regional development plans, including specific plans for involving Aboriginal people in the project. This provided the impact study with an opportunity to frame recommendations aimed at preparation of those plans. It must be noted, however, that the impact study process itself was not incorporated into the decision making of either the government or the consortia and its value for the Land Council's work was generally realized only after many important decisions had been finalized.

Good planning practice, and good governance, requires decision-makers to have a clear and sophisticated grasp of a development project and the cultural and biophysical landscapes of which a project will become a part. The Northern Territory is a multicultural society in which Aboriginal people are a substantial and politically, culturally and economically important minority. If planners and decision-makers limit their vision and understanding to those parts of the landscape and society which reflect what they already know – if they respond only to marks left on the landscape by their own culture or what their own science tells them of that landscape – they risk reproducing conflict, dispute and misunderstanding in their decisions. It is therefore imperative for environmental and social assessment of Northern Territory development projects to adopt a 'multicultural definition of environment': an approach which recognizes that different cultural groups define, use, value and construct meaning in the same environmental spaces in different way (Evaluating Committee *et al.*, 1992). In the case of major linear projects such as the proposed railway, it is imperative that social impact studies in the Northern Territory also adopt methods of researching and reporting that respond to the specific demands of the context. For example, the timeframe allowed for consultative research must accommodate the time involved in preparing materials which put information about key ideas and issues into language that is appropriate to the diverse target audiences. This will require use of translation and consideration of the implications of language and the assumptions about the world that are embedded in the language of 'research', 'impacts' and 'impact management'.

Similarly, resources sufficient to allow consultation with diverse groups within the affected communities will also be required – and this is where major linear projects face a particular problem. In the case of the railway study, it was necessary to involve people from 69 Aboriginal communities and the Aboriginal populations of Alice Springs, Ti Tree, Barrow Creek, Tennant Creek, Elliot, Katherine, Pine Creek, Adelaide River, Palmerston and Darwin. The benefits likely to be available for distribution to affected community groups from such a project may fall well short of the cost of such consultation. Framing a research method that identifies benefits, limits unrealistic expectations, and tackles the impact issues, therefore, is far from straightforward.

As with any major linear project, the railway impact study also faced the challenge of marshalling appropriate expertise. No single researcher or small research team could have a deeply intimate understanding of all the diverse communities and groups affected. Competing claims about the risk and disturbance threatened by the project, the need to test the basis of entitlement to participate in and benefit from the railway negotiations (e.g. claims based on traditional ownership of affected country and claims based on residential proximity) created risks of misunderstandings within and between affected groups. Division of the affected route between two major administrative structures with different organizational cultures, consultative approaches and policy priorities added to the complexity facing the impact study. The concern was that the impact assessment process itself would impact on social relations, contributing to longer-term rivalries and inequities along the route. Dealing with such issues transparently and coherently makes it possible for researchers, affected communities and other stakeholders alike to establish a shared understanding of the changes implicit in proposals under review. It is, however, not a simple task that can be achieved through formulaic checklists and technical solutions. The solution must involve continuing negotiation and explanation of the process.

It was clear from the outset that a wide range of issues had to be brought within the scope of the impact study, and be a topic for discussion in community meetings and interviews. Critical issues identified in preliminary discussion and research included noise, safety, sacred site protection, employment and training, access across the railway line (particularly its gender and resource implications), effects on boundaries between groups and on social relations, environmental issues, concerns about tourism and passenger services, effects on groundwater, and the location of quarries for ballast for the project. Questions of compensation and the basis for its calculation and mechanisms for its distribution were also fundamentally important. On some of these issues, consideration of the proposal had already had direct effects on social relations on the ground.

The railway impact assessment study offered a perspective on the proposed railway and its impacts that was based on recognition of Aboriginal people's ideas about 'country' and the existing multicultural environment already in place along the whole route. We endeavoured to address the tensions between Aboriginal priorities and the development imperatives of the governments and major investors involved in the proposed railway. In other words, we aimed to imagine the proposed railway simultaneously from the vantage point of the diverse Aboriginal stakeholders and the political and commercial stakeholders. In doing so, we developed an approach which facilitated all stakeholders engaging seriously with the complex processes of change that the railway would trigger.

The Railway Impact Study's Methodology

From the outset, it was acknowledged that a comprehensive and ideal social impact study of the railway could not be completed in the time and resource constraints imposed by circumstances on the impact study. The route was 1,410 km long and networks of traditional landowners and native title claimants stretched across the Northern Territory and throughout Australia. The cost of a comprehensive consultative process would be prohibitive, and the timeframe in which the report was required for procedural reasons made such consultation impossible to achieve. Preliminary discussions between the researchers and the Land Councils produced agreement on an approach that would provide an ethical and practical basis for understanding the impacts of the railway, and for framing recommendations about management of anticipated impacts. This was then incorporated with slight modifications into the terms of references negotiated between the Land Councils and the Northern Territory as part of their Framework Agreement about the railway.

The principles of the approach can be summarized quite simply. The study had to be credible (with the affected population, the Land Councils and the government), cost effective, and timely. It was agreed the study would undertake consultation along the entire length of the route, identifying all the affected communities and potential impacts, but the consultation would be limited. Detailed case study research at selected locations would be undertaken to illustrate the complexity of the impact issues, nature of likely impacts and range of impact management approaches available. Existing research on social, environmental and cultural matters in the various localities and communities affected by the proposed railway was incorporated into the impact study wherever possible, rather than seeking to produce detailed new research along the entire route. In particular, it was agreed that rather than establishing a multidisciplinary team of anthropologists, economists, environmental scientists, geographers and others, the impact study team would work closely with the Land Councils' existing multidisciplinary staff and consultants to draw on existing information, and would commission specific research and consultations where this was appropriate. Gender balance within the research team was required, but in the field, support from Land Council staff was often utilized to ensure that there was appropriate gender balance in specific consultative and research activities.

There was a difference in emphasis between the Land Councils and the Northern Territory Government. The latter wanted the impact study limited to a technical review of tangible physical impacts that were amenable to management through investment in physical works such as safety fencing, pedestrian and traffic management measures, minor realignments or other similar work. The government's priority was to avoid an open-ended commitment to unsubstantiated inferences about psychological impacts or indirect effects. In particular, the government was wary of a study that might allow Land Councils to escalate compensation demands on the project to a level that might threaten the viability of a project that many observers already considered marginal. In contrast, the Land Councils wanted a study that would identify the impact issues that would require management, recommendations on implementation processes and an understanding of how the project would impact upon native title, Aboriginal land management options and issues of cultural identity and practice. In part this difference reflected a deeper underlying difference in perceptions of the landscape through which the project was to be built and the development process itself. It was finally agreed that attention to the physical tangible impacts and the works required to address them would be the subject of a specific term of reference for the study. In reporting the research, detailed consultation with the government's engineering and project management staff involved extensive discussion and ultimately agreement on the need to understand both the physical tangible and the wider social, cultural and environmental impacts of the project.

In the major cities of Australia and Asia, it is easy for politicians and government planners to imagine that the proposed railway would be built across a remote and empty landscape. It is easy to imagine the 'large tracts of flat, almost featureless terrain which occupy most of the area between Tennant Creek and Katherine and part of the area south of Tennant Creek' (Dames & Moore, 1984:77) as an empty corridor linking these important places to each other, and creating a national benefit by doing so. On the ground between Alice Springs and Darwin among the Land Councils' constituents, however, a very different landscape emerges. It is a landscape full of named places. It is rich in social, economic and cultural activity. It is a complex, living cultural landscape with a long history. It is far from empty. The reality on the ground challenges the imaginary emptiness and space constructed in many representations of the railway and its impacts. In discussing the social impacts of the proposed railway with traditional Aboriginal owners, native title applicants and affected Aboriginal communities along the proposed route, we have been reminded that these landscapes have many meanings and values in addition to those related to the railway. The railway will cross country belonging to many Aboriginal peoples and will affect their experience and future aspirations.[8]

Consultation with affected Aboriginal people and communities was undertaken in a variety of settings in various combinations of study team members, Land Council staff and support workers from other organizations. Research and consultation protocols consistent with both university ethical guidelines and Land Council practice were put in place. Consultative meetings combined provision of information about the project to the communities, and acquisition of information about the communities, their concerns, needs and aspirations. Photographs of elements of the proposed railway (including material from the EIS and environmental management plan, photographs of the existing railway, and similar components such as rock quarries, etc.) were used to illustrate these discussions. Photo albums or laminated colour photocopies were passed around meetings, and questions answered as they arose. Existing anthropological and genealogical research was drawn on by the impact study team and the Land Councils to compile invitation lists to these meetings, and supplemented by further questioning of participants about others who should be involved. On several occasions, impact study team members attended and spoke to Land Council consultations with native title claimants and Aboriginal land holders about proposed leases for the railway. In discussing issues of access and road crossings, extensive use of maps was used, supplemented with aerial photographs and site inspections wherever possible. Where Land Council staff were undertaking field visits in association with other railway project work (site clearances, checking meeting lists, etc.), they were asked to pursue specific questions and issues that had arisen in the impact study team's work and report back to the impact study team.

Over the period May–September 1998, the impact study team provided information sessions and workshops with a range of Aboriginal organizations, including community councils, ATSIC regional councils,[9] community associations and service organizations. Meetings were arranged with residential communities such as town camps to address social impacts not related to specific land-owning interests. Staff in several organizations were also interviewed about specific impact issues, and in some cases workshops about the impact study and the railway were provided for organizations.[10] The two Land Councils provided the impact study team with field support, and access to a wide range of existing anthropological research and historical and other material relevant to the various communities affected by this proposal. Confidentiality provisions in the research contracts for the impact study required that some of this material remained confidential, being used to inform processes rather than incorporated in detail into the final report.

It was originally envisaged that the Land Councils would also facilitate the study team's access to Government authorities and the railway consortia to help define, clarify and evaluate construction and operational information relating to both positive and negative impacts of the railway. In practice, however, the Northern Territory Government limited access to the consortia not only for the study team, but also the Land Councils. This restricted information on key elements of the proposal. As a result, a number of matters were left unresolved at the time the final report of the study was circulated, particularly in relation to those issues discussed above related to operational configuration and location of specific facilities during construction and operation. It also meant that the crucial issue of the consortia's proposed regional development plans, and the thinking underpinning them, remained inaccessible to the impact study and the affected communities.

Specific research methods adopted during fieldwork and desktop research were consistent with other impact studies. No attempt was made to undertake any field-based quantitative survey of characteristics, attitudes and aspirations of the affected Aboriginal population. Existing Australian Bureau of Statistics, Census and departmental figures were drawn on for basic descriptive statistics for the affected population. Specific statistical profiles were commissioned from 1996 Census figures for each of the case study areas. Given the nature of the social networks considered in the research, attempting to represent impact issues through quantitative research would risk serious misrepresentation of circumstances. Rather, the research relied on a large number of open-ended interviews with individuals, group discussions on specific issues or areas with relevant small groups, and public meetings supplemented by specific consultation sessions where requested or needed. Site inspections in were undertaken in areas of particular concern, and interviews with officers of the Land Councils, other Aboriginal service organizations and government agencies were undertaken to increase understanding of the social setting to be affected by this project. Documentation relied principally on researchers' notebooks, with tape recordings being undertaken in some cases, particularly where the researcher was running workshop-style sessions that restricted note-taking opportunities.[11] In some sessions, particularly sensitive sessions such as those involving community relocations, notes or minutes were taken by Land Council officers or third parties and supplied to the impact study team. Literature and Internet searches were undertaken on a wide variety of topics and keywords. These literature searches failed to reveal directly comparable studies of the impacts of a major linear project on indigenous peoples anywhere in the world.

It was originally envisaged that a small number of 'case studies' would be sufficient to illustrate the complexity of impacts that would be experienced along the entire corridor. Case studies were completed on Alice Springs, the Anarpipe group, Katherine, and roads and access in the Tennant Creek area. As negotiations proceeded, however, the case study strategy was reviewed and it was clear that more detailed consideration of as many sections of the route as possible would be needed. As a result, study team members undertook additional community-level and regional meetings, including site visits, individual interviews, small group workshops and briefing and de-briefing regional staff in the Land Councils and other organizations. Ultimately, the final report of the study provided specific information on each section of the track, with those areas targeted as case study areas having more detailed information, but with quite specific information about impacts, mitigation and avoidance issues, and concerns provided for each area and community.

Brief progress reports were circulated widely amongst Aboriginal groups along the route in the form of a series of three plain English Information Sheets (May, July, September). The report itself went through several drafts. An almost complete draft was subject to peer review by two national experts on impact assessment and workshopped with participating communities in late September and early October 1998, along with circulation of a plain English executive summary of the whole report and extracts dealing with each area along the route. This proofing process face-to-face with affected communities allowed complex issues to be addressed. In some cases, it saw new information come to light. Final proofing of the report was undertaken with Land Council and Government officers. This permitted refinement of implementation plans so that proposals for impact mitigation and management, regional development and benefit distribution were realistic and achievable, and supported by those who would be required to implement them – or at least understood so that they could be debated intelligently in subsequent policy debates.

In designing a methodology to evaluate the AustralAsia Rail project, the Land Councils and their advisers had to establish that a credible study could be undertaken within the resources made available through negotiations with and the deadlines set by the Northern Territory Government. There was no legal requirement for an impact study as the Commonwealth had already signed off on the existing environmental impact statement (Dames & Moore, 1984) and environmental management plan (Dames & Moore, 1997) as meeting the legal requirements (Environment Australia, 1997). For the Northern Territory Government, acquisition of secure title over the proposed route was a pressing political imperative. For the Aboriginal land owners and native title interests, any agreement to provide secure tenure for this project voluntarily was dependent on adequate provision for protection and advancement of their interests. The social impact study was proposed and agreed to, therefore, not because of mutual recognition of its inherent value, but as a negotiated outcome in a difficult, complex and highly constrained negotiation between the Northern Territory and the Land Councils.

Issues and Solutions

The railway impact study made 62 recommendations about the management of the AustralAsia Rail project (Howitt *et al.*, 1998:180–2). These ranged from major initiatives such as the establishment of a new impact monitoring authority, to locally specific recommendations regarding railway crossings, site protection and noise mitigation. In framing recommendations, the study team was accountable both to the terms of reference framed by the Land Councils and the Northern Territory Government, and to the consultative process with the affected communities. Concerns raised within those consultations needed to be reflected in the report's final recommendations. To assist communities to access the relevant information, the report was organized geographically, with an introduction raising common issues along the entire route, and a separate discussion of each section of the route. In addition to its public report, the study team provided the Land Councils and the government with a confidential appendix on issues of railway suicide. Among the many issues dealt with in the study, concerns about safety, site protection, compensation, regional development and ongoing impact monitoring were critically important.

Safety, Access and Mobility

In some ways, safety issues fell squarely within the compass of the government's concern with physical tangible impacts of the project. The interplay of safety, access and economic issues in these matters, however, meant that they were rarely reducible to simple 'safety' matters. Adjacent to small bush communities such as Adelaide Bore, or town camps such as Trucking Yards and Morris Soak in Alice Springs, there was a need to consider not only engineering and design solutions to safety concerns (at some financial cost to the project), but also to frame recommendations about operating procedures to reduce risks (rail surveillance, running times, schedules, speeds, and physical clearance in some areas) and to propose educative programmes to increase public awareness of safety risks in culturally effective ways. Patterns of Aboriginal mobility, and land and resource use along the route were not well documented. The study considered 259 crossings of the proposed route, ranging from major highway crossings to irregular bush tracks in remote areas used by Aboriginal family groups to access country and resources. Rationalization of crossings and assessment of appropriate crossing types required consideration of traditional owners' access to sites and resources, and the interplay of people–people relationships and people–country relationships. Again, the task was not reducible to technical questions of physical tangible works to install crossings in appropriate places, but required a more dynamic social scientific analysis of the circumstances.

Compensation

Similarly, compensation for damage and loss of amenity was not reducible to a formulaic technical solution. In some areas, the proposed route involved displacement of communities or community facilities, or damage to significant sites. In other areas, the survey line for the proposed railway, which had been cleared on the ground in the late 1970s, had evolved as an important access route to remote Aboriginal settlements, and closure of routes would impose significant financial burdens on affected communities. Compensation for development impacts has been complexly evolving in the Northern Territory since the passage of the Land Rights Act in 1976. Under the Native Title Act few precedents are available to guide compensation for detrimental impacts. Lavarch and Riding (1998) tackle some of the conceptual difficulties involved in reaching compensation solutions. Altman (1998) also notes the severe practical limitations facing development of equitable compensation solutions. Government compensation proposals for securing 199-year leases over the railway corridor translated into derisory annual rental equivalents on a per-kilometre basis. Yet the government felt strongly that higher payments would jeopardize the project's overall viability. The project's ambiguous status as partly 'public infrastructure' and partly 'private, for profit' exacerbated the tension over compensation levels. Within the communities, the question of compensation raised potentially divisive issues of entitlements, debates about the best combination of cash and other benefits, and the best configuration of individual and collective allocation of benefits. There are strongly held opinions about the suitability of cash payments as compensation in some places, and in the context of a large pool of unmet development needs (housing, services, community development and so on), there is vigorous debate about balancing immediate consumption aspirations for compensation with inter-generational justice concerning community development. Similarly, gender equity in access to and application of compensation entitlement is a source of continuing debate in the affected communities. There is no simple solution to the dilemmas. Aboriginal people clearly experience much distress and heartache both in accepting the disruption and damage that gives rise to the need for compensation, and in tackling the debates about its use. Local rather than global solutions are required if compensation payments are to avoid exacerbating negative project impacts.

Regional Development and Cumulative Impacts

Concerns about safety and compensation reflect a wider concern about regional development impacts of large-scale linear projects. From its inception, the AustralAsia Rail project aimed to produce cumulative impacts. It is being proposed because of perceived benefits to be derived from enhanced development opportunities based on improved transportation infrastructure. It was meant to change economic conditions to facilitate expanded economic activity such as mining, tourism, agriculture and so on. In this case, the concern was that existing colonial development patterns, which had marginalized Aboriginal people through inappropriate planning and entrenched structural racism, would be reinforced rather than overcome by inappropriate policy settings and operational procedures. For the study team, the challenge was to unsettle the taken-for-granted policy parameters without threatening the dialogue that was needed to implement the study's recommendations about regional development planning. The wider societal shift in Australia towards Aboriginal reconciliation (e.g. Howitt, 1998) has achieved a significant opening of policy processes to such considerations, but it remains a difficult task of documentation and diplomacy to shift entrenched values and procedures. At both the micro scale of specific communities – where some negative effects (e.g. noise, access, stress) will accumulate on top of existing processes – and at wider scales – where the direct impacts of the railway will interact with flow-on effects of other activity – documentation and management of cumulative effects environmentally and socially is needed. There is also a need to consider how the railway itself may trigger additional projects, which in turn produce additional impacts for a range of Aboriginal interests

Cumulative impact assessment is increasingly acknowledged as an issue that is poorly addressed in most impact studies. There have been few examples of application of cumulative impact assessment in Australia, and international practice is still at a developmental level. The consistent shortcomings of project-by-project assessments in the region in terms of social impacts are reflected in the one major regional scale cumulative study in Australia that has been identified: the Upper Hunter Valley Cumulative Impact Study (New South Wales Department of Urban Affairs and Planning, 1997). Cooper and Canter (1997) provide a review of substantive issues in cumulative impact assessment based on a survey of the United States professional impact assessors (Clark, 1994). In most of this work the emphasis is on cumulative impacts on biophysical environmental elements, and it is clear from this review that most practitioners see cumulative impact assessment as an arena in which quantitative methodologies are used for addressing additive environmental effects. Qualitative approaches for addressing synergistic or interactive social and economic effects are less specifically developed at this point. This report seeks to tackle this issue in relation to the railway, but identifies this as an area requiring further professional and academic attention.

Ultimately, the railway impact study recommended establishment of a new impact monitoring authority with sufficient resources, including community participation, to allow it to address these concerns in an ongoing way and to meet appropriate international practice standards. Establishment of such a committee would not ensure effective responses to project impacts. Australia has witnessed previous attempts to establish ongoing oversight of inquiry recommendations, negotiated settlement arrangements and governmental commitments. Some, for example the Office of the Supervising Scientist in Kakadu, have been relatively successful within the biophysical realm. There is, however, a very poor record in dealing with social and cultural matters once projects are established. In the case of the Ranger uranium mine, for example, a recent audit by the Northern Land Council revealed extensive non-implementation of recommendations from the Ranger Inquiry and the Australian Institute of Aboriginal Studies (AIAS) Social Impact of Uranium Mining Project (Howitt, 1997). In the same area, publication of the recent Kakadu

Region Social Impact Study (Dodson *et al.*, 1997; Levitus and Aboriginal Project Committee, 1997) has produced no secure government commitments to implement its recommendations. In other Australian cases, recommendations derived from community consultation have been ignored, bypassed, redirected or overruled once projects have received approval. Effective monitoring to achieve agreed development goals relies on resources, vigilance and commitment. It also involves empowerment of local people to respond to issues as they arise. In the case of the AustralAsia Rail project, the problem was that many of the identified impacts seemed likely to fall between statutory responsibilities of existing authorities, suggesting that a new agency with specific responsibilities was necessary. To be effective, however, this Committee must be resourced to monitor and respond to impacts and initiate research and other responses, and empowered to deal directly with the railway company.

Human Rights and SIA

Finsterbusch's discussion of the foundations of social impact assessment emphasizes a concern for justice, accountability and exploitation in the context of plural democratic societies. The challenges of linking pro-development policies and processes to enhancement of minority rights is one of the critical issues facing the development of mature democratic institutions in the Northern Territory. The incorporation of human rights issues into social impact assessment has been an issue of discussion within the International Association for Impact Assessment, particularly in the context of large-scale resource projects in the Third World. The railway's interaction with issues of indigenous land and resource rights, cultural heritage protection, religious freedom and issues of individual and collective identity all place the issue of human rights squarely on the agenda for this study. The International Association for Impact Assessment (IAIA) as a professional body has addressed questions of ethical practice in impact assessment, and its discussion of this issue recognized the importance of social justice implications of development as an arena in which SIA has an interest. It was also acknowledged, however, that the discourse of 'human rights' is rooted in other arenas of practice. There is an emerging consensus that a commitment to integrating evaluation of human-rights implications of projects during impact assessment would have positive consequences (in terms of respect for human rights and social justice) in project design, and that integration of consideration of human rights rather than simply addition of another 'topic' to a list of topics to be covered in an SIA is preferred. In the railway impact study, issues of indigenous rights are integrated in consideration of impacts throughout.

Benchmarking Assessment of Linear Projects

One of the challenges faced by the railway impact study was identifying best practice procedures and benchmarks against which to review proposed impact management strategies. In particular, the need to relocate one community on Aboriginal Land north of Alice Springs (Mpweringe-Arnapipe Land Trust), and possible relocations elsewhere along the route, required careful attention to international standards on resettlement. The history of Aboriginal marginalization within the Northern Territory also demanded consideration of international standards on recognition and protection of indigenous rights. Within Australia there are no performance requirements prescribed in legislation, and the nature of the agreement that produced the study was outside specific statutory requirements in any case. As elsewhere (Boothroyd, Knight, Eberle, Kawaguchi & Gagnon, 1995), there is little *post facto* evaluation of the accuracy of predictions and effectiveness of proposed impact management strategies for major EIS reports in Australia. This situation emphasizes the importance of the setting of guidelines and terms of reference for these studies.

The World Bank and the Organization for Economic and Community Development The railway study team referred to World Bank (World Bank, 1990, 1991) and Organization for Economic and Community Development (OECD, 1992) guidelines for evaluation of development projects as examples of international benchmarks for assessing development impacts for projects requiring resettlement and affecting indigenous peoples. These guidelines describe policies and procedures to avoid or minimize adverse project impacts. Had the Alice Springs to Darwin Railway Project been funded by the World Bank project, it would have triggered both operational directives: 4.20 – Indigenous Peoples, and 4.30 – Involuntary Resettlement (OECD, 1992).

Operational Directive 4.20 – Indigenous Peoples (World Bank, 1991) is premised on 'full respect for [indigenous peoples'] dignity, human rights and cultural uniqueness'. It aims to ensure that projects funded by the World Bank do not cause indigenous peoples to 'suffer adverse effects during the development process', and that they 'receive cultural compatible social and economic benefits' (World Bank, 1991:4.20.6). Specifically, the directive precludes funding consideration of projects until impact mitigation plans have been drawn up. It requires preparation of an Indigenous Peoples Development Plan and spells out the contents required for such a plan.

Operational Directive 4.30 – Involuntary Resettlement (World Bank, 1990) recognizes that for those affected by displacement and involuntary resettlement, development projects give rise to:

> severe economic, social and environmental problems: production systems are dismantled; productive assets and income sources are lost; people are relocated to environments where their productive skills may be less applicable and the competition for resources greater; community structures and social networks are weakened; kin groups are dispersed; and cultural identity, traditional authority and the potential for mutual help are diminished. Involuntary resettlement may cause long-term hardship, impoverishment, and environmental damage unless appropriate measures are carefully planned and carried out. (World Bank, 1990:4.30.2)

Although the scale of the railway's resettlement requirements are relatively modest, the underlying principles are consistent, and the need for a strategy which ensures that people are not impoverished or disadvantaged by involuntary resettlement remains. The guidelines explicitly anticipate preparation of a resettlement plan with high levels of participation from the affected population(s). The guidelines also emphasize maintaining community viability and identity, protecting environmental quality at the relocation site(s), and ensuring monitoring and *post-facto* evaluation. These issues are directly relevant to the railway proposal, although the Northern Territory Government required no explicit procedures to be adopted in dealing with resettlements.

In 1992, the OECD endorsed a series of guidelines on environmental impact assessment, environmental surveys and strategies, involuntary displacement and resettlement and global environmental problems. In the case of the guidelines on involuntary displacement and resettlement (OECD, 1992), the OECD: 'calls on project designers and implementors to ensure that the population displaced by a project receives benefits from the changes and that is re-established on a sound productive basis' (OECD, 1992:2). The OECD acknowledged that projects that are not required to explicitly deal with displacement and resettlement often managed to underestimate the complexity and impact of displacement. The OECD Guidelines, like those of the World Bank, require project design, management and monitoring to maximize benefits and minimize negative impacts on affected populations:

1 Involuntary population displacement should be avoided or minimized whenever feasible by exploring all viable alternative project designs.
2 All involuntary resettlement should be conceived and executed as development programmes, providing sufficient resources and opportunities for resettlers to share in project benefits.
3 Participation by environmental agencies and community participation in planning and implementing resettlement is essential and should include women.
4 Indigenous groups who may have informal customary rights to the land or other resources taken for the project must be provided with adequate land, infrastructure and other compensation – the absence of legal title to land by such groups should not be a bar to compensation.
5 Planning for relocation should explicitly consider the preferences and specific needs and constraints of women affected.
6 Implementation of resettlement should be effectively supervised. (Summarised from OECD, 1992:6–7)

In the preparation for resettlement, the OECD Guidelines required preparation of a detailed resettlement plan 'including timetable and budget', and that the plan be 'designed around a development package for improving, or at least restoring, the economic base of those relocated' (OECD, 1992:7). They note that cash compensation alone is generally inadequate and often even counter-productive. Cost estimates are required to include 'full costs of resettlement' as part of the overall project costs.

Although such guidelines provide an international benchmark of practice, they also have limitations. Kardam (1993:1774) points out the World Bank is 'accountable to a small range of mostly homogenous actors, the major donor nations'. The World Bank has also been widely criticized for its responsiveness to developmentalist agendas which prioritize economic growth over human development (e.g. Shiva, 1992), and even at the cost of human development in the Third World (e.g. Foster, 1993). Responding to social impact issues was not a major priority for the World Bank during the 1970s. Indeed, Kardam's review (1993:1777) suggests that:

> Sociological issues do not naturally fit into the goals and procedures of the World Bank. Neither have the major donors [who influence the Bank's policies] pressured the Bank to incorporate sociological issues into their operations. Increased profitability as a financial institution and increased economic growth . . . put constraints on consideration of non-quantifiable issues that do not directly promote efficiency and that cannot be transformed into cost benefit ratios.

Francis & Jacobs (1999) document the internal processes within the Bank that produced pressures to institutionalize social analysis in the Bank's predominantly economic orientation. In the late 1970s, social scientists within the Bank began to advocate change, including expansion of the operational definition of 'development' to include issues of social cohesion, social equity, maintenance of indigenous cultures and cultural diversity, and other sociological rather than economic indicators, and development of operational guidelines on matters such as environmental assessment, indigenous rights and gender (Goodland, 1982; Kardam, 1993:177). These processes ultimately produced the Operational Directives referred to above and exercised considerable influence on professional standards in anthropology and impact assessment.

Others have been much more blunt about their view of the World Bank's record on human development. For example, Davis (1996, 30) argues that:

> Since its formation 52 years ago, the World Bank has built up a disastrous record. It has financed dozens of massive hydropower projects, like the infamous Sardar Sarovar dam complex in India, and the Pak Mun dam in Thailand; it has supported road-building projects through the heart of the Amazon, leading to massive deforestation; and it has helped support toxic mining operations in India, Guyana, and elsewhere. And throughout its history, the Bank has shown a blatant disregard for the rights of the people and communities most affected by its projects.[12]

In many ways, such guidelines can be considered as conservative and supportive of the general developmentalist project, disciplining it to minimal standards rather than challenging its fundamental goals. From the perspective of Aboriginal people, organizations such as the World Bank and OECD give priority to government objectives and wide-scale economic indicators rather than indigenous cultural values, or local community concerns and aspirations.

In developed countries such as Australia, there is no obvious trigger for application of such international performance standards. The conventional path in Australia is to adopt project-specific guidelines. In an advanced and wealthy democracy such as Australia, it would seem reasonable to anticipate that governments and project managers would achieve higher performance standards in the protection of minority rights and environmental and social standards than those applied in poorer nations. In the Northern Territory, however, there has been little explicit consideration of any benchmarks and performance standards on minority rights, resettlement and indigenous participation in regional development.

Lessons for Social Impact Assessment of Linear Projects

Howitt (1993) argued that impact assessment research that is participatory, empowering and interventionist can address the marginalization and disempowerment that often accompanies the development of projects linking local communities to larger scale arenas through trade, tourism, governance and other mechanisms (Gagnon, Hirsch & Howitt, 1993). In the wider literature on impact assessment, it is increasingly acknowledged that impact studies can provide means of equipping all stakeholders to manage change more effectively, equitably and sustainably (Burdge and Vanclay, 1996; Dale, Chapman & McDonald, 1997; Lane, 1997; Howitt, 1998; Lane, Ross & Dale, 1997; O'Faircheallaigh, 1998), but governments' and other stakeholders' understanding of what this means in terms of supporting the impact assessment process, integrating it into decision making and responding to it remains uneven. In places like the Northern Territory, it remains a process which is poorly integrated into project development and regional planning. Stakeholders often recognize its value after opportunities to initiate more timely work have passed and deadlines created in financial, engineering and political timeframes have been given precedence.

In situations where governments take for granted the value of development projects, the organizational culture of decision-making agencies (including many community organizations) often sees social impact assessment research as threatening or disruptive to orderly decision making. Where project planning is dealt with as a technical task, and negative social (or environmental, or localized economic) effects are seen as an inevitable cost of progress, the idea of changing a project to accommodate minority interests is difficult to accept. In recent political debate in Australia, there has been a shift away from the defence of minority rights as the hallmark of a mature democracy. It has become commonplace to hear criticism of minority rights as intruding unfairly on the right of the leadership of the majority (the 'dominant culture') to do whatever it wishes or thinks it can get away with. Indeed, there have been increasingly serious political proposals to restrict or diminish minority 'rights' by a majority vote in parliaments.

The unresponsiveness of developmentalist societies to SIA cannot be characterized simply. It reflects precisely the difference in values and perspectives that cross-cultural impact studies have to come to terms with. It reflects the competing goals of different stakeholder groups. It reflects a long history of domination by one sort of decision making in areas affecting, for example, Aboriginal groups. In terms of specific hesitations about incorporating social impact assessment into development planning and negotiation of deals between developers, governments and indigenous groups in the Northern Territory, it may also reflect a feeling that many people in these agencies are already working long hours in circumstances that are already difficult. In the absence of a clear understanding of (or local precedents for) the sorts of differences that a social impact study might make, the value of 'diverting' resources to such work is not obvious.

This situation places impact assessment generally in a dilemma: on the one hand, an impact study with inadequate resources will be limited in its effectiveness; on the other hand, the limited number of effective studies that demonstrate the value of SIA means stakeholder organizations remain sceptical about providing adequate resources. O'Faircheallaigh has taken up this issue in terms of integrating economic and social impact assessment research into community-based decision making and preparation for negotiations about development proposals with private sector interests and governments (Gagnon *et al.*, 1993; O'Faircheallaigh, 1996b). Dale *et al.* (1997) reviewed Queensland's experience in integrating impact assessment into public decision making (Dale & Lane, 1995; Lane, 1997). Beckwith (1994) considers the experience of Western Australia. In each case, the research suggests that efforts to control impact assessment for political ends, rather than integrating impact assessment, monitoring and mitigation into development decision making has reduced the effectiveness of impact assessment research.

The scale, policy context and complexity of many major linear projects creates a number of difficulties for any effort to assess, monitor and manage their cultural and social implications in situations characterized by ethnic pluralism. Project evaluation and management principles of major international development agencies such as the World Bank and the OECD provide a benchmark for local decision-makers and stakeholders, as do 'best practice' guidelines from other projects. Fundamental principles to be observed include:

1 The need for community participation in planning and decision making.
2 The need to create opportunities for popular participation as early as possible in the development planning process.
3 Early consideration of and response to likely social and environmental impacts of the project.
4 Taking action to ensure a flow of meaningful and sustainable development benefits to those people and communities that face disruption, displacement and disturbance from a project.

Where such principles are not reflected in either the legislative framework or planning and project management practice, as is the case in the Northern Territory (Jackson, 1997), dealing with impacts of linear projects is often limited to *post facto* problem solving. Such solutions often rely on the protest and advocacy of stakeholder groups disadvantaged by the project, and contribute to conflict and division rather than equitable and sustainable development outcomes.

In the case of the Alice Springs to Darwin railway project, inclusion of these principles in the statutory framework implicated in evaluation of the proposal might have reduced or even avoided some of the negative impacts that have already occurred in the pre-project planning and negotiation phases. The task of developing and implementing monitoring and mitigation plans would also have been much simpler.

Acknowledgements

The authors would like to acknowledge the work of Ian Bryson in the research for the railway impact study discussed in this chapter. We would also like to acknowledge the range of people who have supported, debated, argued and disputed this work, particularly our principle contacts in the Northern and Central Land Councils: Cath Elderton and Andy Kenyon. In Central Land Council, we would also like to thank Julia Munster, Sofia Borges, Philip Watkins, Susan Donaldson, Chris Athanasiou, David Avery, Brian Stirling, Sarah Larson, Graeme Smith and Gina Smith. In Northern Land Council, we would like to thank Ben Scambery, John Cook, Jeff Stead, Siv Parker, Ted Lowe, Dotty Ross, Ron Levy, John Roberts, Eddie Ross, Carol Barbour, Ken Lum, Patrick Briston, Sebbo, and Belinda Oliver. Within the Northern Territory Government we would like to acknowledge the support of Brendan Lawson. We would also like to thank David Alexander, Joanne Fox, Anthony Gatti, Robert Graham, Ceinwen Grose, Annie Keely, David Nash, James Nugent, Ciaran O'Faircheallaigh and Peter Sutton. We would also like to thanks our families who tolerated our absences for the project, and Andria Durney, Toney Hallahan and Frank Siciliano who provided research assistance at various points.

References

Altman, J.C. (1998), *Compensation for Native Title Land Rights: Lessons for an Effective and Fair Regime* (Land, Rights, Law: Issues in Native Title, Issues Papers, 20), Canberra: Australian Institute of Aboriginal and Torres Strait Islander Studies.

Australian Institute of Aboriginal Studies (1984), *Aborigines and Uranium: Consolidated Report on the Social Impact of Uranium Mining on the Aborigines of the Northern Territory*, Canberra: Australian Institute of Aboriginal Studies.

Beckwith, J.A. (1994), 'Social Impact Assessment in Western Australia at a crossroads', *Impact Assessment*, 12(2):199–213.

Berger, T.R. (1977), *Northern Frontier Northern Homeland: the report of the Mackenzie Valley Pipeline Inquiry* (2 volumes), Toronto: James Lorimer & Co.

Berger, T.R. (1988), *Northern Frontier Northern Homeland: The Report of the Mackenzie Valley Pipeline Inquiry*, revised edition, Vancouver: Douglas & McIntyre.

Berger, T.R. (1994), 'The independent review of the Sardar Sarovar projects 1991–1992', *Impact Assessment*, 12(1):3–18.

Boothroyd, P., Knight, N., Eberle, M., Kawaguchi, J. and Gagnon, C. (1995), 'The need for retrospective impact assessment: the mega-projects example', *Impact Assessment*, 13(3):253–71.

Bromby, R. (1992), *Rails to the Top End: the Adelaide–Darwin Trans-continental Railway*, Alice Springs: Outback Books.

Burdge, R.J. and Vanclay, F. (1996), 'Social Impact Assessment: a contribution to the state-of-the-art series', *Impact Assessment*, 14(1): 59–86.

Central Land Council (1983), *Alice Springs to Darwin Railway: comment on Draft Environmental Impact Statement* December 1982, Submission by Central Land Council on behalf of Aboriginal traditional owners, April 1983, Alice Springs: Central Land Council.

Clark, R. (1994), 'Cumulative Impact Assessment: a tool for sustainable development', *Impact Assessment*, 12(3):319–31.

Connell, J. and Howitt, R. (eds) (1991), *Mining and Indigenous Peoples in Australasia*, Sydney: Sydney: University Press.

Coombs, H.C., McCann, H., Ross, H. and Williams, N.M. (eds) (1989), *Land of Promises: Aborigines and development in the East Kimberley*, Canberra Centre for Environmental Studies, Australian National University and Aboriginal Studies Press.

Cooper, T.A. and Canter, L.W. (1997), 'Substantive issues in cumulative impact assessment: a state-of-practice survey', *Impact Assessment*, 15(1):15–31.

Dale, A. and Lane, M. (1995), 'Queensland's Social Impact Assessment Unit: its origins and prospects', *Queensland Planner*, 35(3):5–10.

Dale, A., Chapman, P. and McDonald, M.(1997), 'Social impact assessment in Queensland: why practice lags behind legislative opportunity', *Impact Assessment*, 15(2):159–79.

Dames and Moore (1984), *Alice Springs–Darwin Railway: Final Environmental Impact Statement*, Report prepared for the Commonwealth Department of Transport and Construction, Canberra, May 1984.

Dames and Moore (1997), *Alice Springs to Darwin Railway: Environmental Management Plan*, Report prepared for the Northern Territory Department of Transport and Works, April 1997.

Davis, A. (1996), 'It's time for the World Bank to close its doors', *Development Today* (22 October 1996).

Dodson, P., Altman, J., Yunupingu, G., Cooper, V., Hicks, J., Jones, N., Johnston, A., Jones, M., Jackson, A., Roeger, S., Scott, D. and Carbon, B. (1997), *Kakadu Region Social Impact Study: Report of the Study Advisory Group*, Canberra: Supervising Scientist.

Environment Australia (1997), *Alice Springs to Darwin Railway: Environmental Notes*, Canberra: Environment Australia.

Evaluating Committee; Kativik Environmental Quality Commission; Federal Review Committee North of the 55th Parallel; Federal Environmental Assessment Review Panel (1992), *Guidelines: Environmental Impact Statement for the proposed Great Whale River Hydroelectric project*, Montreal: Great Whale Public Review Support Office.

Finsterbusch, K. (1995), 'In praise of SIA – a personal review of the field of social impact assessment: feasibility, justification, history, methods, issues', *Impact Assessment*, 13(3):229–52.

Foster, J.B. (1993), 'Let them eat pollution: Capitalism and the world environment', *Monthly Review*, 44:10–20.

Francis, P. and Jacobs, S. (1999), 'Institutionalizing social analysis at the World Bank', *EIA Review*, 19:341–57.

Gagnon, C., Hirsch, P. and Howitt, R. (1993), 'Can SIA empower communities?' *EIA Review*, 13:229–53.

Goodland, R. (1982), *Tribal peoples and economic development: human ecologic consideration*, Washington: World Bank.

Howitt, R. (1993), 'Social Impact Assessment as "applied peoples' geography"', *Australian Geographical Studies*, 31(2):127–40.

Howitt, R. (1997), *Aboriginal social impact issues in the Kakadu region*, Sydney: School of Earth Sciences, Macquarie University.

Howitt, R. (1998), 'Recognition, reconciliation and respect: steps towards decolonisation?', *Australian Aboriginal Studies*, 1998–1:28–34.

Howitt, R., Connell, J. and Hirsch, P. (eds) (1996), *Resources, Nations and Indigenous Peoples: case studies from Australasia, Melanesia and Southeast Asia*, Melbourne: Oxford University Press.

Howitt, R., Jackson, S. and Bryson, I. (1998), *A railway through our country: final report of the Railway Impact Assessment Study – social and cultural impacts of the Alice Springs to Darwin Railway project on Aboriginal people*, Darwin, Alice Springs and Sydney: Northern and Central Land Councils and Macquarie Research Ltd.

Jackson, S. (1997), 'A disturbing story: the fiction of rationality in land use planning in Aboriginal Australia', *Australian Planner*, 34(4):221–6.

Kardam, N. (1993), 'Development approaches and the role of policy advocacy: the case of the World Bank', *World Development*, 21(11): 1773–86.

Lane, M. (1997), 'Social Impact Assessment: strategies for improving practice', *Australian Planner*, 34(2):100–2.

Lane, M.B., Ross, H. and Dale, A.P. (1997), 'Social Impact Research: integrating the social, political and planning paradigms', *Human Organization*, 56(3):302–10.

Lavarch, M. and Riding, A. (1998), *A New Way of Compensating: maintenance of culture through agreement* (Land, Rights, Laws: Issues in Native Title, 21), Canberra: Native Title Research Unit, Australian Institute of Aboriginal and Torres Strait Islander Studies.

Levitus, R. and Aboriginal Project Committee (1997), *Kakadu Region Social Impact Study: Report of the Aboriginal Project Committee*, Canberra: Supervising Scientist.

McEvoy, P. and Lyon, P. (eds), (1994), *The Land Is Always Alive: the story of the Central Land Council*, Alice Springs: Central Land Council.

Maurice, J. (1990), *Mataranka Area Land Claim: Report by the Aboriginal Land Commissioner to the Minister for Aboriginal Affairs*, Canberra: Australian Government Publishing Service.

Mejia, M.C. and Kvam, R. (1997), 'Involuntary Resettlement in Linear Projects', Draft outline of issues and topics prepared for inclusion in *World Bank Resettlement Sourcebook*, August 1997.

New South Wales Department of Urban Affairs and Planning (1997), *Upper Hunter Cumulative Impact Study and Action Strategy*, Sydney: New South Wales Department of Urban Affairs and Planning.

Organization for Economic and Community Development Assistance Committee (1992), *Guidelines for Aid Agencies on Involuntary Displacement and Resettlement in Development Projects*, Guidelines on Aid and Environment No 3, Paris: OECD.

O'Faircheallaigh, C. (1991), 'Resource exploitation and indigenous people: towards a general analytical framework', in P. Jull and S. Roberts (eds), *The Challenge of Northern Regions*, Darwin: North Australia Research Unit, pp.228–71.

O'Faircheallaigh, C. (1996a), 'Negotiating with resource companies: issues and constraints for Aboriginal communities', in R. Howitt, J. Connell and P. Hirsch (eds), *Resources, Nations and Indigenous Peoples: case studies from Australasia, Melanesia and Southeast Asia*, Melbourne: Oxford University Press, pp.184–201.

O'Faircheallaigh, C. (1996b), *Making Social Impact Assessment Count: A Negotiation-based Approach for Indigenous People*, (Aboriginal Politics and Public Sector Management Research Papers, 3), Brisbane: Centre for Australian Public Sector Management, Griffith University.

O'Faircheallaigh, C. (1998), *Process, Politics and Regional Agreements* (Native Titles Research Unit, Regional Agreements Paper, 5), Canberra: Australian Institute of Aboriginal and Torres Strait Islander Studies.

Rose, D.B. (1996), *Nourishing Terrains: Australian Aboriginal Views of Landscape and Wilderness*, Canberra: Australian Heritage Commission.

Shiva, V. (1992), 'The Greening of the Global Reach; conflicts in global ecology', *Third World Resurgence*, 14(15):58–60.

Sutton Partners (1984), *Desire for Murranji Custodians for Railway Alignment to be West of the Current Planned Route*, Report to Aboriginal Sacred Sites Authority, January 1984.

World Bank (1990), *Involuntary Resettlement, Operational Directive OD 4.30*, Washington, DC: World Bank.

World Bank (1991), *Indigenous Peoples. Operational Directive OD 4.20*, Washington, DC: World Bank.

World Bank, Environment Department (1994), *Resettlement and Development: The Bankwide Review of Projects involving Involuntary Resettlement, 1986–1993*, Washington, DC: World Bank.

Notes

1 It is worth noting the extent to which the energy modelling underpinning provincial policy settings in Quebec were a focus for attention

in the Great Whale Hydro project (Evaluating Committee *et al.*, 1992: 20–1).

2 The route crossed land held as Aboriginal Land under the *Aboriginal Land Rights (Northern Territory) Act 1976* (LRA) and land claimed under the *Native Title Act 1993* (NTA). Under Section 29 of the NTA, native title claimants had a right to negotiate about proposed development of land under claim. The Land Councils acted as representative bodies for these claimant groups. Under the LRA, Aboriginal traditional owners had a limited veto over the development. The Commonwealth had the power to compulsorily acquire land for the project as essential public infrastructure project, but the reconfiguration of the project as a privately owned, profit-orientated project, as well as political issues related to the politics of native title processes created substantial difficulties for land acquisition processes. In the Katherine area, the route traversed freehold land owned by the Jawoyn Nation.

3 See Northern Territory Government's project information at http://www.nt.gov.au/rail/information/default.html The current status of the proposed railway remains uncertain. A preferred tenderer for the project was selected by the Northern Territory Government in early 1999, but investment decisions remain to be finalized as a result of questions about taxation, government investment and market conditions.

4 During the research for the railway impact assessment, amendments to the Commonwealth *Native Title Act* introduced additional changes and complexity to the native title situation.

5 In Aboriginal English, and increasingly in discourses addressing relations between all Australians and the environment, the term 'country' is used not only as a common noun but also as a proper noun:

> People talk about country in the same way they would talk about a person: they speak to country, sing to country, visit country, worry about country, feel sorry for country, and long for country. People say that country knows, hears, smells, takes notice, takes care, is sorry, is happy. Country is not a generalised or undifferentiated type of place . . . Rather, country is a living entity with a yesterday, today and tomorrow, with a consciousness, and a will toward life. Because of this richness, country is home, and peace; nourishment for body, mind, and spirit; heart's ease. (Rose, 1996:7).

6 The Central Land Council's 1983 proposal came in the wake of path-breaking cross-cultural SIA work in the East Kimberley Impact Assessment Project in Western Australia (Coombs, McCann, Ross & Williams, 1989) and subsequent work of the Australian Institute of

Aboriginal Studies in the Social Impact of Uranium Mining Project in the Kakadu region of the Northern Territory (AIAS, 1984; also Dodson *et al*., 1997; Levitus *et al*., 1997). The proposed guidelines (Central Land Council, 1983) were sophisticated and consistent with best practice principles available at the time. The loss of Commonwealth support in the wake of the 1983 election meant that this proposal was not followed up, but it was unfortunate that they were not used to frame guidelines for the Australasia Rail project.

7 For example, the Land Claim over Muckaty Station north of Tennant Creek was subject to an intervention by the Northern Territory, which sought excision of the railway corridor from the land to be granted. A proposed outstation at Yuturminyi on Phillip Creek pastoral lease was delayed because the railway corridor cut the proposed excision in two. The Mpweringke-Anarpipe communities north of Alice Springs faced reduction of their already narrow Aboriginal Land Trust (ALT) and relocation of one of their communities. Custodians of the Devil's Marbles again worried that this major site was under threat from the new route. At the Edith River crossing, north of Katherine, Jawoyn interests faced loss of economic opportunities because the route affected a site that Jawoyn Association planned to develop as a roadhouse and camping area.

8 Aboriginal languages groups along the route of the proposed railway line include: Larrakia, Kungarakany, Warai, Wagaman, Jawoyn, Wardaman, Dagoman, Yangman, Djingili, Mudbura, Warlmanpa, Warlpiri, Warumungu, Alyawarr, Kaytetye, Anmatyerr, and Arrernte. Representing the complexity of the Aboriginal interests affected by the railway proposal is no simple task. It is not a matter of simply listing languages, enumerating communities, counting individuals or listing 'countries'. The intention here is simply to indicate the great diversity of groups implicated.

9 ATSIC is the Aboriginal and Torres Strait Islander Commission, the Commonwealth Government's peak indigenous affairs advisory and service delivery body.

10 For example, the study team dealt with Tangentyere Council, Alice Springs; Central Australian Aboriginal Congress, Alice Springs; Anmatyere Council; Anyinginyi Congress, Tennant Creek; Julalikari Council, Tennant Creek; Julalikari Buramana, Tennant Creek; Thangkenharenge Resource Centre, Barrow Creek; Jawoyn Association, Katherine; Wardiman Association, Katherine; Wurli Wurlinjang, Katherine; Aboriginal Development Foundation, Darwin; Larrakia Nation, and regional offices of ATSIC.

11 Tape recordings were limited because of the limited resources available for transcriptions and the limited time available. Delays in tape transcriptions and circulation of material within the research team was undesirable because of the intense field programme demanded by the limited fieldwork opportunities.

12 For a powerful critique of the Sadar Sarovar project, undertaken for the World Bank, see Berger (1994).

Part IV
Monitoring

–10–

Social Impact Assessment Monitoring and Household Surveys

Glen Banks

Introduction

The establishment of an ongoing programme to monitor the social and economic effects of a development project should be an integral part of the impact assessment process, in the same way that environmental monitoring programmes are established to monitor the effects of development projects on the physical environment. Ortolano and Shepherd (1995:22) advance two arguments for environmental monitoring which are equally as applicable to social monitoring: firstly providing opportunities to ameliorate adverse impacts, and secondly to enhance future impact assessment by measuring the actual as opposed to predicted impacts of a project.

In terms of the first of these, even with state-of-the-art social impact assessment (SIA) techniques, unanticipated impacts occur regularly over the life of a project. The rapid pace of social and economic change in all areas of the world, and the multifaceted and unpredictable nature of this change, means SIA can be redundant before the project or development they were carried out for is even complete. Social monitoring provides an opportunity to identify effects over the life of the project or development, and implement new strategies or adjust existing ones so as to mitigate adverse impacts and enhance opportunities for communities. With the increasing concern for sustainable communities and livelihoods, social monitoring programmes provide the potential to adjust programmes and introduce new elements to provide for real sustainable community development. The second proposition put by Ortolano and Shepherd argues that the experience obtained from one project in terms of the actual impacts can then be utilized to develop more sophisticated impact assessments for future similar projects.

Taylor, Hobson and Goodrich (1995:89) similarly argue that monitoring is central to the management of social changes arising over the life of a project or programme, and also forms a research basis for social impact prediction models. Mitigation of the impacts of a development should continue throughout the period of change, and indeed they argue that a social monitoring programme should be initiated as early as possible in the social assessment process: that is, possibly even before a formal impact assessment has been carried out.

In addition there is increasing recognition by corporate actors and other resource developers (states, for example), that a lack of attention to local issues, concerns and changes can pose a significant risk to large scale projects. The most frequently cited example in the Asia-Pacific is the Bougainville Copper Limited (BCL) mine on the island of Bougainville, Papua New Guinea. Here, in 1989, long-standing community frustration boiled over into violence, forcing the closure of the massive copper and gold mine (Connell, 1991; Filer, 1990). It has not reopened, costing the operators, Rio Tinto, hundreds of millions of dollars. In these circumstances, the absence of a systematic social monitoring programme can pose a serious corporate risk.

The principle of social monitoring has been adopted within the regulatory framework in several countries. In most of the mining agreements in Papua New Guinea, for example, there is a requirement that something labelled social monitoring be done, with few other details in terms of what is required. This is contrast to the extensive, detailed and sophisticated requirements for environmental monitoring programmes at the same mine operations. Partly because of this lack of detailed guidelines or best practice codes, the practice of social monitoring has lagged considerably behind the principle (see Banks, 1999a; Taylor *et al.*, 1995).

This chapter begins by outlining the features of an effective social monitoring programme. Household surveys – instruments that often form the core of social monitoring programmes but are also used extensively in baseline studies, rapid rural assessments and social impact assessments – are then discussed in detail. The utility and nature of secondary data sources form the third section. Finally, two brief case studies taken from experience at the Porgera gold mine in Papua New Guinea and the PT Freeport Indonesia copper and gold mine in Irian Jaya, Indonesia illustrate and reinforce a number of key lessons and conclusions.

The Social Monitoring Programme

The principle on which social monitoring is based is that assessment of the impacts and effects of a mining development should be ongoing throughout the life of a project. This also allows for the enhancement of positive effects and opportunities and the active mitigation of negative impacts to occur throughout the project cycle.

For such social monitoring efforts to be effective, three major issues need to be addressed: the nature of the monitoring programme, the institutional framework within which social monitoring needs to occur, and the nature and extent of community participation in the social monitoring programme.

Sketch of the Monitoring Program

An effective social monitoring programme needs to provide the most complete description of changes in the social environment as is possible. To do this requires a combination of regularly recorded quantitative data, qualitative material and specialized projects. While the emphasis on each of these elements will vary from setting to setting, it is hard to envisage a situation in which only one or two of these elements could provide sufficient data for a social monitoring programme. Household surveys, discussed in detail in the following section, can provide a range of qualitative and quantitative data to provide a reliable view of change from the community perspective.

One of the ways to monitor change within a community is through the use of quantitative measures: a series of indicators of social or economic change (population, infant mortality, education levels or income levels, for example). While the collection and use of such data are often an anathema to anthropologists and other social scientists, authors and practitioners such as Burdge (1994) consistently record the ways in which decision-makers and planners are more easily able to understand, and hence more likely to act on, quantitative measures of change. The appeal of such indicators is that they are simple to understand and able to be absorbed quickly by management and policy makers. A danger of such measures is that the indicators come to be seen as the sum total of the changes that are occurring in the community. In addition it should be obvious that indicators can provide a quick, sketch description of changes, but cannot by themselves start to explain the changes that are occurring.

With the recognition of the limits of numerical descriptions of complex social environments within the social sciences has come a profound scepticism of the use of such descriptors. It is now widely recognized that such indicators cannot adequately measure critical aspects of community change such as cohesion, spirituality or inter-generational respect. To address such issues as part of a social monitoring programme requires the use of qualitative techniques including interviews, focus groups and textual analysis, tools with which many social scientists feel more comfortable. The adaptation of household survey techniques to include open-ended questions on attitudes, concerns, aspirations and the like is another similar technique discussed below.

In addition to the collection of regular qualitative and quantitative data, there is generally a need for specialist studies on an as-required basis. In many cases the regular data collection (through household surveys) provides information pointing to anomalies or trends in the community which by themselves are not well understood. As a result, within the social monitoring programme there should be provision for a separate stream of special projects that can be carried out as required. An example of the integration of regular social monitoring data with specialized projects is given below in the Porgera gold mine case study.

One of the key issues in any social monitoring programme is the role of community participation in the process. While this is discussed in more depth below, it should be noted here that the form that any social monitoring programme takes, and the types of material collected, should be decisions in which community members play a central role. Not only does this make community commitment to the programme more likely, but it also will generally lead to better-targeted monitoring, with a focus on those issues or changes of greatest relevance to the programme.

Like SIA there is also argument about the extent to which social monitoring should confine itself to issues for which agencies or community interests can actually act: for example, to what extent can a migration of non-local, non-employees to a resource development area be reversed? The issue here is often one of including relevant agencies and institutions in the program. Hence, in the example given above, although the social monitoring may be focused on the local area around the resource development, it may be appropriate to include on the social monitoring committee representatives from broader, provincial or district institutions who can be involved in reducing unwanted migration to the site by increasing services or opportunities in the home areas of the migrants.

As a stand-alone exercise, the benefits of social monitoring are largely academic: that is, it provides a record of the changes that a community is going through, either directly or indirectly as a result of the particular resource or development project. While such information may assist in shaping or informing new approaches to similar projects, or perhaps even larger theories of rural change or development, it provides little benefit to the affected community. For this to occur, the social monitoring programme must be embedded in or at least integrated with community or local area planning processes.

The Institutional Context

The management and control of the social monitoring programme is a central issue that should be established as soon as is possible. While it may appear of peripheral concern to the individual researcher or consultant brought in to examine some aspect of social change, in the early stages of a programme the researcher or consultant should expend a large proportion of their time facilitating the establishment of the framework within which the social monitoring programme can be situated.

The monitoring of social and economic change requires co-ordination and integration into local area planning frameworks (Taylor *et al.*, 1995:92). One possible way to approach this is through the establishment of a social monitoring committee, comprising representatives from the various local, national and possibly even international stakeholders. Such a committee should essentially control the form and the direction that social monitoring takes, and should in particular concern itself with a number of critical concerns for monitoring to be effective.

First, and critically, there needs to be a link between social monitoring and local area planning. To be effective and true to the purpose noted in the introduction, the results of social monitoring must be able to be used to mitigate negative social impacts identified, and to try and obtain the maximum community benefit from opportunities that arise. As noted earlier, if monitoring is carried out without a link into processes which can influence the social environment, then it is largely only of academic value. In remote or under-developed areas, the committee may well become the surrogate local area planning body. This establishes the relevance of the programme and provides a foundation for the long-term commitment by all parties to the process.

Second, as the Papua New Guinea experience suggests, if there is no effective co-ordination of the social monitoring programme then any work carried out as part of the programme will be intermittent, and poorly integrated with the work of other agencies or individuals. The maximum or long-term benefits of one-off pieces of work are unlikely to be realized in this situation, regardless of the quality of the individual piece of work done. Clearly in this situation even a reasonably comprehensive review of social and economic change over the life of the mine is unlikely to occur.

Third, and related to this, if there is no overall framework within which the programme operates, it is hard to establish and meet general and locally defined goals of the programme. It is difficult, for example, to assess the extent to which the project or development has had the effects predicted in any SIA process. In the context of rapid change, people's expectations and aspirations are constantly changing and remain always sensitive to perceived effects of major resource development. As a result the types of issues and concerns that a social monitoring programme addresses will be dynamic, and hence a framework is required that provides the programme with flexibility, within the constraint of the agreement of the various stakeholders.

A fourth imperative for an institutional framework is funding. The social monitoring of a large-scale resource or development project should ideally be funded and driven by government as regulator. This, on paper at least, provides the programme with a high degree of independence. The reality in many countries is that the resources are not provided to appropriate departments to allow them to carry out such a function. There is also a common argument that the project operator should fund social monitoring of large-scale projects. While this 'user pays' philosophy has some validity, the danger is that corporate actors may not be as motivated or committed to social monitoring as other parties, particularly during periods of poor financial returns. In virtually every case where a social monitoring programme has been established, it has been funded solely by the project operator. There is also an argument that all the stakeholders (community, government, corporate players, etc.) should contribute to the funding of social monitoring as this will provide them with a greater level of commitment to the process. Again this is a valid argument: in practice it has never occurred.

Regardless of the source of funding, the committee that controls the nature, direction and extent of the social monitoring programme should include representatives from all the stakeholders, including any relevant external stakeholders, such as churches, non-governmental organizations (NGOs) or other independent parties.

Finally, a central concern in terms of the management of the programme is the issue of community involvement in, and agreement on, the control, rationale, direction and nature of the monitoring programme. This is discussed further in the following section, but a key point in the management of the programme is that, from the outset, community interests must have an central role in the design of the programme and the institutional framework within which it operates.

It is certainly in the interests of the key stakeholders in any large-scale development that the management of the social monitoring programme operates effectively. Effective management should be guauged not by compliance with regulatory regimes, but rather by whether the programme brings results: are social and economic conditions in the community improved as a result of the programme? Forums where concerns are continually presented and no action taken are unlikely to be supported or sustainable. This places a burden on the various stakeholders to ensure that commitments arising from the monitoring programme are acted on. It also places an onus on the individual researcher or consultant to facilitate the integration of their work into an effective management framework for social monitoring.

Community Involvement and Participation

Social monitoring is about recording and explaining economic and social change within communities and, on the basis of this information, facilitating improvements in conditions for affected communities. In the past work along these lines could (and did) proceed with minimal community involvement, particularly in developing countries. The recognition that development planning regularly failed because of this lack of community involvement was slow in coming, but it is now widely accepted that if communities are actively involved in shaping and directing their own futures, the outcomes are much more likely to be positive and progressive.

Today in academia and industry there are other imperatives. Most universities and many industry associations to which consultants are affiliated have ethical guidelines or codes that govern interactions with their research subjects. Although these vary substantially in content, a common theme is that studies of individuals or communities can only proceed with the permission of those same people. Hence a social monitoring project of a particular community must, minimally, obtain the agreement of the community being studied. This community consent is also necessary, obviously, to gain the co-operation of the community for household surveys, for example.

In practice, there are two competing imperatives that researchers or consultants are continually confronting. The first are time and budgetary constraints on social monitoring work. Corporate and government budgets for social monitoring are rarely large, and project deadlines ensure that time is generally another scarce resource. As a result, the scope for community involvement can be markedly reduced. This is particularly the case where the individual or team is brought in to carry out a limited part of a larger project. Researchers and consultants in such situations need to be wary of the extent to which the project imperatives are placing them in positions that conflict with the ethics of their professional bodies.

Balancing, and indeed in some situations overriding, this first imperative is a greater community interest in many countries in taking control of projects and programmes that impinge on their lives. While the minimal requirement for much work remains community consent to the research or monitoring, communities are increasingly concerned to influence the type of monitoring being carried out, the management of the overall programme, the issues being targeted, the design of the programme, the dissemination of results, and other such critical issues.

Clearly such matters may slow the progress of social monitoring programmes (and hence attract concern from corporate or state bodies, particularly if they are the funding agency) but they unequivocally make the programme much more relevant to the community and thus provide a much greater level of community support for the monitoring programme. In turn this is likely to provide a far more effective form of monitoring.

This far more participatory approach to social monitoring is in line with trends among other social assessments (SIA and participatory appraisal techniques, for example) and helps remove the overtones of control and surveillance that accompanied earlier philosophy behind attempts at social monitoring. Social monitoring as a means to improve the situation of affected communities is better served by this relinquishing of control as it provides for greater community self-determination and responsibility (see Taylor *et al.*, 1995).

Having said this, there is still a need for accurate and timely information on social and economic change in the community. The ‘middle ground’ suggested by Taylor *et al.* (1995) between technocratic empirical studies and participatory action-orientated research is an appropriate place to situate many social monitoring programmes. In such a position there is still a place and a need for household surveys to provide information on community change at its most basic level, although central issues such as the control and direction of the programme maybe very different. An integration of participatory and standard techniques is likely to provide a more comprehensive programme, and make the integration of the monitoring with local area planning easier (Jiggins, 1995).

Household Surveys

Household surveys are a key instrument for a number of assessment and evaluation techniques including rapid rural appraisal, community baseline studies, SIA and social monitoring (see Brown, Marczewski, Miller, Roberts & Scott, 1978 for other uses). While household surveys have gone out of vogue in recent years, to be replaced by more participatory methodologies such as participatory rural appraisal (PRA), they remain a most effective means of collecting a wide range of material on community conditions, concerns and aspirations. The advantage of household surveys is that they can provide both quantitative and qualitative data on a wide range of household and community issues as well as, if carried out appropriately, collecting much of the same material as more unstructured techniques (such as participant observation or workshops, for example). If carried out on a regular and systematic basis, household surveys can provide the basis for a social monitoring programme that is both community-centred and rigorous. They are also very effective at highlighting areas or issues where further research, discussion, negotiation or actions are necessary.

A good household survey instrument addresses issues of concern to local environments and asks questions in a way (and a language) that is well understood by the community involved. As a result the specific details of the process outlined below are unlikely to apply in every context. All household surveys, though, require three broad and to some extent overlapping stages: background, question formulation and implementation.

Survey Design

Prior to designing a structured household questionnaire (also known as an interview schedule) the researcher needs to review all available background information. This includes as wide a range of information as possible. Historical sources such as community histories, anthropological papers, books and theses, and government and previous administration reports on the community should all be collected. Government sources in particular can be useful. Pre-independence Administration Patrol Reports in Papua New Guinea, for example, provided much of the historical information on population and agriculture used as baseline material in the Porgera social monitoring programme. The tracing, collection and compilation of these sources can be time consuming and involve many days of frustrating non-progress, but the results of a thorough search can be rewarding.

In an ideal world a social monitoring programme will emerge seamlessly from the SIA phase of the project or development. In practice this has not occurred, but, regardless, the data and documentation associated with the SIA (assuming there was one) will itself usually prove crucial to the framing of any household survey. Similarly there may be other material in project feasibility studies or environmental impact assessments that can provide further data to inform the compilation of an effective household survey instrument.

Previous surveys are often the most valuable source of comparative data, as well as providing ideas for the specific issues and questions that make up the household survey. National census forms can be of varying utility as a basis for questionnaire design. In the Porgera case, the original household survey form was a heavily modified variation of the Papua New Guinea national census form. At Freeport, however, the Indonesian census form, and a recent survey based on it, were found to be largely irrelevant as a basis for the household survey utilized during the Universitas Cenderawasih-Australian National University (UNCEN-ANU) Baseline Studies (UABS) project. In that instance the form was more closely related to similar studies carried out in similar settings in Papua New Guinea.

Historical and contemporary maps – and other forms of spatially referenced data such as aerial photography, satellite imagery and output from geographic information systems (GIS) – are an invaluable source of past community change (settlement movement and growth, for example) and contemporary settlement patterns, location of infrastructure and transport routes.

A census – either a standard census or the output of an earlier social mapping project – is an invaluable tool at the survey design stage of the process. It provides background demographic data on the population (age distributions and sex ratios), as well as usually giving information on the location of the population within the area. A recent and accurate census is a necessity if the household survey is intended to produce data on which statistical tests are to be performed. Unfortunately such data are rarely available.

A very important source of information on the current setting and the nature of the issues that the community faces are local informants, in the broadest possible sense. This would include representatives from the local community, NGOs working in the community, local government officials, corporate community affairs staff, and others who may know the area well: long-term residents or a 'resident' anthropologist, for example. These informants are able to provide information on community attitudes, concerns and issues which is invaluable for the framing of broad themes and even specific questions within the questionnaire.

Once all this data has been absorbed and digested, work can begin on the framing of the questionnaire for the household survey. It is at this stage that decisions need to be finalized in relation to the specific objective and aims of the household survey as these will directly effect the nature and types of questions that are incorporated into the survey instrument. Such decisions should generally been made earlier, as the decision to include a household survey as part of a social monitoring programme will generally be made for a particular purpose. With all the background data at hand, the specific aims and objectives of the survey can be spelt out. It is also very important to make clear at this stage what the limitations of the proposed survey are: in the Freeport case study discussed on pp.327–30 it was made clear that the survey was not specifically collecting information on village projects funded by the company.

At this point several other decisions need to be determined. One of the most critical is the household unit that is going to be the focus of the study. To make this decision the researcher needs information on household composition, and residence and kinship patterns. There are situations where more than one family resides in a dwelling, and others where a single family is spread between two (or more) dwellings (see the Freeport case study on p.329 for differences within one study area). If the interest is in the household unit as an economic unit, the decision needs to be made as to what constitutes an 'economic unit': a working definition of this could be 'a group of individuals that functions as an economic unit on a day to day basis'. Using such a definition it is possible to have more than one economic unit per household, but also to have a single economic unit spread over more than one dwelling. There are no absolute rules on this issue, except that once a decision has been made it is applied consistently throughout the study.

The study area can also pose definitional problems. Resource developments may be bounded by lease areas, but these are invariably poor boundaries in terms of social and economic interactions. Similarly administrative boundaries have an unusual propensity to divide ethnic, language or kinship groups. Again the rules, as they are, are flexible, but the researcher should ensure that all communities significantly affected by the development or project are included. Obviously the key term here is 'significantly': and decisions over this will tend to be as much to do with politics and practicalities as with any 'rational' decision. The other principle is that once agreed and decided on, the study area should only be altered in exceptional circumstances.

If the survey is to try and make estimates of household income and/or expenditure patterns, the survey will need to be focussed on an appropriate time period. With cash crops, for example, how many times a year are they harvested and sold? How regular is the nature of employment, and how often are employees paid (usually fortnightly or monthly)? Such information will impact directly on the specific sorts of questions that can be asked of respondents.

Sampling A critical aspect of the project design is the sampling regime to be applied. Given the level of detail usually required, the size of most communities and the standard time and resource constraints that apply to such work, it is exceptionally rare to be able to include all the households in the community in the survey. A sample of the population must then be selected. The type of sample chosen generally falls into two categories: probability sampling and non-probability methods.

Probability sampling seeks to obtain data in a systematic way that is then subjected to statistical testing. The basic principle that underlies sample selection for probability samples is that the probability of any potential individual or household in the 'target population' being included in the sample is known before the survey begins. Thus, in a homogenous population, each individual or household stands an equal chance of being included (Dixon & Leach, 1984:13). Using a strict probability sampling regime improves the ability to be able to generalize from the sample surveyed to the whole population, and reduces the chances of bias in the sample.

The most simple and reliable (and hence least likely to go wrong in field settings) way of selecting a sample is through random sampling. In a simple example, if a third of the households in an area were to be interviewed for the survey, from a census every third household head would be selected to be interviewed.

One of the potential practical problems with a randomized sample is that they are likely to be spread randomly across the study area, making the survey coverage time-consuming. One way around this is through clustering, whereby the sample is chosen from a small number of randomly selected sub-areas, although this not recommended where there are significant spatial variations within the study area (Dixon & Leach, 1984:18). With probability sampling regimes, different groups in the target population (for instance, different ethnic or tribal groups) should be included in proportion to their size within the larger population. Stratification of the sample (into sub-samples drawn from each of the different impact areas or from different ecological zones, for example) relies on having good estimates of the breakdown of the target population by each of the factors the researcher wishes to stratify by (Dixon & Leach, 1984:18).

The probability-based sampling methods are the most rigorous and, if adhered to, provide data which can be tested statistically, significantly adding to its value, in the eyes of engineers and other scientists at least. The weakness of the approach is that it relies on having accurate and current information on the make-up of the target population that is going to be sampled. In many contexts this is simply not available.

In these circumstances, the absence of an accurate description of the target population, either because of the simple lack of a recent census, or because of its mobility and fluidity, means non-probability sampling methods must be used. Non-probability methods are less rigorous and onerous in terms of sample selection, and it means the outcomes are categorized as 'general impressions, rather than figures open to rigorous statistical testing' (Dixon & Leach, 1984:26). Given the limited data available in many parts of the world from which to construct a sampling frame, this is often unavoidable.

There is a range of non-probability sampling techniques available, all of which provide ways of selecting individuals or households from within a defined study area. These include:

1 Walking transects (from a randomly chosen point in a randomly chosen direction) and interviewing at every house, or in every field or garden, intersected by the transect.
2 If the area makes the use of a straight line walk impossible, a random walk could be constructed by introducing rules about decision making at crossroads or rules about maximum distances or times walked in a certain direction.
3 Interviewing every *n*th adult male (or female, depending on what had been devised beforehand) encountered in a walk along a road or path, or through a village.

All of the above techniques continue to rely on an element of randomness, but unless this is tied back to information about the existing population it should not be confused with rigour. Depending on the circumstances, a sample may need to consist of whoever is available in certain locations: what Dixon and Leach (1984:26) refer to as quota sampling. In the Freeport case study discussed on p.00, the indigenous population is very dynamic and mobile. Any attempt to construct before the event a sampling frame would have run into a very high absence rate, particularly among household heads. In these circumstances, an attempt was made to ensure that the sample was evenly distributed among each of the villages, but within each village the survey team carried out interviews with any (and in some cases, all) respondents found to be at home in the village during the day of the visit. This may have introduced an element of bias into the samples, by only interviewing those at home during the time of the visit (which implies that they are not representative of the majority who were not at home during the day), but given time and resource constraints it was the only course available.

A working rule of thumb with quota surveys is that with large villages (over 100 households), at least 25 per cent of the households should be included in the survey, while for smaller villages a minium of twenty households should be included, and for very small villages (less than forty households), the survey should aim to take in 50 per cent of the households. This 'rule' has evolved from experience and is based partly on practicalities (a team of five interviewers will struggle to complete more than thirty comprehensive household surveys in a day), and partly on a minimum sample size required to provide an impression of trends and comparisons. It should be stressed again that the data from such samples is indicative only, and only probability samples can provide statistics on which to base firm comparisons between areas and through time.

A final method note on sampling concerns the use of a longitudinal household survey. Such a survey, once a sample has been selected, attempts to survey the same households over an extended period of time. Longitudinal surveys, if carried out properly, can provide stunning insights into household and community change through time, and permits a deeper rapport to develop between the survey households and the interviewers. They can be especially useful if using a non-probability sample as they can provide insights into change at the household level through time which some weight can be attached to. In such instances, there is a real need to select a sample which is as representative of the whole population as is possible. If a probability sampling frame is being used, the survey is able to produce statistically significant data on change through time regardless of whether or not a longitudinal survey is used, so long as the sampling methods remain the same.

In sum, the results of a household survey are only as good as the sampling regime used. It is particularly important that the methods used to select the sample are clearly spelled out in the reporting of the survey results, and that the limitations of the data are clearly acknowledged.

Question Types: What to Ask Information on six broad areas can commonly be obtained through household survey work. Which of these are used will depend on the objective and aims of the survey. Similarly the order of the questions will largely depend on the context and the aims of the exercise: experience has shown though, that a progression from most neutral topics (often but not always demographic and housing issues) through to the most sensitive (often economic and attitudinal ones).

While each of the broad areas overlap to an extent, they are dealt with below separately.

1 Household demographics.
2 Housing.
3 Household economics.
4 Subsistence resources.
5 Social measures.
6 Concerns and aspirations.

Demographics These questions seek to determine the household residents and the relationship between them. Depending on the level of accuracy and detail in previous census work, these questions as part of a household survey can either provide a check on census information, or fill in additional information.

Basic demographic data such as sex, age, place of birth, relationship to household head and occupation are standard as part of this set of questions. Such data also allows the researcher to compare their sample demographics with other sources such as census work to get a sense of the representativeness of their sample: in some cases, depending on the sampling regime and the accuracy of the work, this can be tested using probability statistics.

Although there are various ways of obtaining information on occupancy, a favoured question used in census work is 'Last night, who slept in this house?' The disadvantage of such an approach should be obvious: people who are usually resident in the household but for one reason or another happened to be absent the previous night are excluded. The advantage of this question is its clear and unambiguous nature: there is no messy definitional and subjective question of whether a person is 'usually' resident. And, assuming the sample size is large enough, people absent for one night are likely to be balanced by others who are only resident for one night in another household in the sample.

Housing and Assets Housing and household assets can provide a relatively useful surrogate for economic standing and social conditions in many parts of the world. Questions about these items are particularly effective because, so long as the interview occurs in or near the respondent's home, the answers are easily verified.

Basic questions on housing should cover the types of material used in the house construction (walls, roof, floor), the number of rooms, and the facilities available (depending on the setting, electricity, internal running water, internal kitchen, and internal bathroom/toilet may be absent, rare or common). Extra features should also be noted: what shape or style the house is may be significant. When combined with the demographic data instances of overcrowding can then be identified, based on a range of predetermined criteria.

Household assets are another relatively straightforward matter. The types of assets asked about should cover a range from the most likely (spades, shoes or water containers) to the most expensive or exotic (outboard motors, motor vehicles or satellite dishes). Such a list should be devised to cover the types of items that are found in the study area, based on the background research previously carried out.

Household Economics In some cultural settings questions about finances are considered inappropriate, even rude. In such cases alternatives measures of affluence (such as housing, as noted above) and secondary data sources will need to be used, if coverage of the economic situation or economic change is an aim of the survey work.

This said, in many societies individuals are less slighted by appropriately sensitive questioning on such matters than might be anticipated. One of the more effective is a weekly household income and expenditure survey. Respondent is asked first to list sources of income for household members in the last period of interest (two weeks or a month, depending on the context, see above). They are then to estimate the value of each of these sources. If this is too difficult it may be possible to get the respondent to rank the various sources in terms of their value. The same is then done for household expenditures over the same period. If there are significant discrepancies between the two totals, further questioning may be appropriate. With both the income and expenditure, a list of the main sources of income and major expenditure categories (housing, food – market and store, savings, etc.) likely in the area can be used as prompts.

While such a survey is excellent for establishing the daily patterns of households of economics, it is likely to miss larger irregular forms of income in the local area: seasonal sales of crops, royalty payments and the like. With communities involved in any form of commercial or cash crop agriculture, the question needs to be directed at determining annual income, to take account of seasonal variations. The interview schedule should provide room to record details such as when the payments were received, and how regular and consistent the income from this source is.

The cash economy has penetrated in to most parts of the developing world. This is not to say, however, that traditional economies and forms of exchange have been supplanted by the cash economy. More accurately in many parts of the world, traditional economies have integrated cash into pre-existing systems. The use of cash as part of bride-price ceremonies in Papua New Guinea is an example of this practice (Banks, 1999a). For this reason, collection of information about contributions by households to forms of traditional exchange can be central to understanding how household and community economies work. In most areas, such exchanges tend to be remembered as significant events, and hence questions regarding such contributions over the past year can be answered relatively easily. Traditional exchange, however, takes on myriad forms in different parts of the world, and particular questions should be framed in the light of background research and study.

One final remark on questions regarding household economics is that illegal sources of income will have to treated with a great deal of caution. These may be a significant source of income in some areas: however, in some cases respondents will be reluctant to talk about these, while in others the information may be freely offered but the researcher will have to consider carefully the implications of reporting such information. The nature and depth of the relationship between researcher and the community (and individuals within the community), and the relationship between the state and the community generally, will obviously influence decisions on such matters.

Subsistence Resources In addition to involvement in the cash economy, and the ongoing cultural and economic significance of traditional forms of exchange, many households in the developing world continue to rely heavily on subsistence food production. One commonly reported consequence of large-scale developments in these areas is a shift away from subsistence production. This potentially has important nutritional implications, as well as affecting pressure on these resources and having consequences for sustainable development in the community. As a result, the availability, use and importance of subsistence resources is an important element to include in most social monitoring programmes.

One simple way to collect data on this through time is through the use of a 'food consumed' question with respondents being asked simply what foods they have eaten in the past twenty-four hours. While this does not provide data on the amount of food, its nutritional value or overall diet, it is a simple tool for looking at the transition from subsistence to store-bought foods. When combined with data on the amounts that households are using to purchase foods, it can provide strong evidence of any shift away from subsistence resources.

The relevant subsistence resources to include in a household survey will depend on the local environment and should be the outcome of the background work prior to drafting the household survey instrument. In different circumstances these may include: freshwater fish, ocean fish, other marine resources, gardens, wild forest resources, cultivated 'wild' trees (such as sago stands or pandanus trees in Melanesia) and birds and animals.

As part of the household survey, questioning about subsistence gardens is generally productive, although for the full benefit of this exercise it is preferable to visit each of the household gardens with the respondent. While this can be time consuming, especially where gardens may be spread through a range of ecological zones, the location (using a global positioning system), measurement and enumerating of the various plants and crops in the garden can provide detailed and useful data, against which subsequent changes can be measured.

Social Measures There are aspects of social change which cannot be adequately addressed by a social scientist through the use of a household survey. One of the most important is conclusive evidence of changes in the health of the sample population. In virtually every case, only fully trained medical scientists are able to effectively assess such factors as nutrition, malnutrition, infant and maternal health, and diagnostic medicine. For the non-medically trained to become involved in this area is both unethical and dangerous.

That said, there are numerous relevant social indicators that can be collected through the use of a household survey instrument. These include accessibility to health facilities (distance or time to nearest functional medical services), water supply used (including river or stream, spring, well, rainwater tank, reticulated water supply, etc.) as well as, if appropriate, distance or time to water source, and toilet facilities.

Within the education field, a household survey could include questions on the highest level of schooling achieved by each household member, as well as notes on which family members were currently attending school, and the costs of this education (school fees, uniforms, etc). This last question is important not just in terms of household economics, but also in terms of access to education for households within the community.

Concerns and Aspirations While many of the above issues can be addressed through structured questions, these are of little use in terms of gaining an insight into household and community concerns, aspirations and expectations. The background research, interviews and conversations carried out prior to the survey should highlight current issues of concern within the community, and one section of the questionnaire (often the final section) should allow the respondent to present their views on what their major concerns are, their expectations and needs in terms of development, and/or other issues about which the monitoring committee would like to gauge community sentiment. Prompts, based on the background research, can assist in drawing out views on topics in which the social monitoring committee has a particular interest.

Implementation: Carrying out the Survey

Once the questions have been devised, a number of other issues need to be addressed before the household survey can be initiated. Teams of interviewers need to be assembled and trained and a pilot survey conducted. During the interviews there are other protocols which must be observed, such as the introduction of the survey to households, the issue of which household member should be interviewed, and the question posed by deceit and truth in survey answers. Finally, once the interviews are over, the data analysis is carried out, and the results of the survey presented to the various stakeholders.

Assembling a Team It will almost invariably be the case that a single individual will not be able to cover all of the interviews required to get a sufficiently large sample. In most situations, then, there will be a team of interviewers using the same survey instrument. This team may have personnel from a range of sources: government, corporate interests, community members, university students, or other outsiders. In many instances the make-up of the team will be determined by a mix of the wishes of the team leader, the politics of the social monitoring committee, and the availability of individuals to work with the team.

The involvement of individuals from each of these categories presents certain advantages and disadvantages, largely because their position will affect the relationship with the respondent. A resource company interviewer, for example, should generally have more background on individual relationships within the community having worked in the area, but may be less likely to receive negative feedback on company activities due to reluctance on the part of the respondent to offend. Or, alternatively, a local interviewer, while possessing far more background on the social and kinship relationships within the community, and hence perhaps having a better rapport with the respondent, may find the respondent less inclined to talk about household economics with someone else in the community. And finally outsiders, such as university students, may be seen as being less partisan by community members, and hence they may be able to collect better information on attitudes, opinions, concerns, and aspirations of people in the community than someone regarded as having a greater stake in the answers provided. The trade-off of course is that outsiders will not have the same background on the community, its social dynamics and factors such as resources and traditions.

Regardless of how the team is selected and the background of its members, all members should ideally be involved in the drafting of the questionnaire. This may require several sessions at which the wording of specific questions is discussed and refined. In the interests of ensuring that the meaning and quality of data are standardized between interviewers, it is imperative that all members of the team understand the intent of each of the questions, and the protocol for interviewing (discussed below).

Pilot Survey Once a questionnaire has been developed, and all the team members who will be administering the survey clearly understand the intent of the questions and the type of information to be recorded, the questionnaire should be tested on a small group of the target population. The completed forms may not be included in the final sample, and so do not count towards the total sample numbers to be collected. Practicalities often dictate that this is a limited exercise, but the team should try and make the pilot sample as diverse as possible from within the target population. If probability sampling is being used, the sample should be selected in the same manner as the full sample, although obviously on a much smaller scale.

Pilot surveys offer two critical benefits: they allow the questions to be refined, expanded and altered to make them more intelligible to the respondents and to fit better into the local social setting and environment; in addition, a pilot survey provides a useful introduction to the application of the survey for the team members. This practice usually means that interviewers are more confident about the questionnaire and their own role by the time the full survey begins.

For these reasons it is imperative that the team spend some time reviewing the pilot questionnaires to ensure that the data they are collecting are comparable, and to allow them to work through problems encountered during this phase. It is also worth remembering that: 'No matter how thorough the design and piloting, faults will remain, for there is no interview schedule that is not capable of improvement by a researcher prepared to learn continuously' (Dixon & Leach, 1984:35). While the questionnaire can, if required, be further refined during the full survey, this makes data analysis problematic, and should be avoided unless absolutely necessary. Similarly, differences between surveys through time, while often inevitable due to changing circumstances and environments, have the disadvantage of making comparisons and analysis of change more difficult. In the interests of standardization and comparisons, then, keep changes to a survey instrument over the course of a survey, and between surveys, to a minimum.

Who to Talk to? Once the team is in the field, issues will be encountered for which a team policy should be in place before hand. Regardless of the sampling method used, the team will be confronted with situations where a decision must be made as to which member or members of the household should be the respondent. A census form may list a male as a head of household, for example, but upon arrival it may become clear that this individual is elderly and plays little role in the household finances, for example. Similarly males may be less likely to have a clear understanding of the household expenditures than their wife or wives. As a working rule, it is better to conduct the interview with more than one adult household member present, unless this is likely to cause offence or conflict (a male may be less likely to speak of his gambling or alcohol expenditures in the presence of his family, for example). Ideally, and wherever possible, the head of the household and their spouse should be interviewed together.

The location of the interview can also be significant. In ideal circumstances the team member should meet or accompany the respondents to the main household dwelling. This makes the interview more private, and allows for the verification of the household housing and asset questions. In some situations it may be necessary to conduct the interviews in other locations. At all times the privacy of the respondent must be respected: in some circumstances (such as where it is necessary to interview in public places) this can be difficult, and the respondent should be given the option of discontinuing the interview or talking elsewhere. In situations where a group of people are listening in on, or even contributing to, an interview the responses given are likely to be different from those that would be given in a more private setting.

Once the respondent(s) for the interview have been approached, and a location for the interview agreed, the first requirement is to provide the respondent with as much information as possible about the survey: the rationale for it, the uses to which the data will (and will not) be put, the sorts of issues addressed, and as much background on the interviewer as is appropriate (who they work for, where they come from, etc.). Once this information has been provided, the respondent should then be asked whether they wish to participate in the interview: the assumption that permission obtained from community representatives automatically allows individual interviews to proceed is clearly not justifiable. Neither, for obvious reasons, is coercion. It must also be stressed that if at any time the respondent wishes to suspend or conclude the interview, that is their prerogative.

A final note here is that the tracking down of particular individuals for interviews (usually as a requirement of a probability sampling regime) can at times be frustrating: they are not available when the interviewer calls, they have moved out of the area, they are temporarily absent, etc. In such circumstances the sample should be expanded so as to allow the minimum number of respondents still to be met: this can mean, for example, that the original sample selected is 25–30 per cent larger than needed to allow for those who are not available, or who refuse, to be interviewed.

Interpreting and Presenting the Results Once all the interviews required by the survey sample have been completed, data entry and analysis can proceed. The details of how this is carried out will obviously depend on the specifics of the data collected. A large amount of analysis can be carried out using a spreadsheet: this makes the calculation of ranges and averages, and the drafting of figures and graphs, relatively straightforward. For more sophisticated analysis, and particularly where the households are to form a core of a longitudinal study, a relational database is more appropriate.

As discussed earlier, unless the survey employs a strict probability sampling regime, with a pre-prepared sample frame and adequate sample size (a minimum of thirty households in each target area), then it is not possible to carry out statistical tests on the data collected. In most cases, where these conditions do not hold, the data can only provide impressions and broad level comparisons between places and through time. Examples of the sorts of analysis which can be carried out on data from non-probability samples are contained in Filer (1999b), which presents the results of household surveys used around the Porgera gold mine as part of the Porgera social monitoring programme.

Presentation of the results of the household survey should be tied into the presentation format used for the wider social monitoring programme. One of the critical elements is to ensure that there is feedback to the community on the results of the surveys. In the case of the Freeport UABS project, community organizations were given an oral presentation as well as copies of the final reports translated into Indonesian, the *linga franc* of the area. If carried out as part of a research or consultancy project, the various stakeholders on the monitoring committee should be provided with the results of the household survey incorporated into social monitoring reports, that integrate the results with data from other sources, as discussed below.

Memory and Deceit With all of the questions in the survey, the interviewer is reliant on both the memory and the integrity of the respondent for reliable data. There are ways to assist both of these. A respondent is less likely to deliberately provide misleading information if the background to, and relevance of, the study is clearly spelt out, they feel they have some stake in providing accurate information, they have a good rapport with the interviewer, and they have seen the results of previous surveys lead to positive changes in their community. While rapport largely comes down to the interpersonal skills of the interviewer, the way in which the survey is developed, and its context, will strongly influence whether respondents feel they have a stake in accurate outcomes. This is another reason to ensure that the community is closely involved in the design of the survey instrument. This also underlies the fact that such surveys must be integrated into responsive local area planning: if communities are regularly surveyed and see few benefits as a result, research fatigue and disinterest are likely to set in.

Problems can also exist, as they do in all interview settings, with the respondent providing answers they believe the interviewer wants. Similarly, in politically charged environments, there is a danger that the information provided may well reflect political positions rather than the actual situation. In both these cases, if the problems persist in the face of clear explanations of the intent and purpose of the survey, then the use of the survey instrument may need to be reassessed. This point again underlines the importance of the interviewer having a thorough understanding of the local environment so that such biases become apparent.

Where deliberate deception is absent, the respondent may still provide inaccurate information because their recollection of events or time periods is unclear. The fallibility of human memory can be a major constraint on household surveys. The impact of this on the quality of the information obtained can be lessened in a number of ways. First, the principles of memory decay dictate that 'significant or less-frequent events are remembered longer than trivial ones, and that the memory decay over the initial period is very rapid, and becomes increasingly less so as time elapses' (Dixon & Leach, 1984:44). The survey should, therefore, minimize the extent to which respondents are expected to recall over very long periods. In a simple example, asking about weekly or fortnightly income and expenditure is likely to elicit greater detail than focusing on periods of a month, or longer. Second, as was suggested above, there is a need to ensure that the reference periods used for the questions fit both the local use of time periods (wet season/dry season, for example), and the rhythms of the local economy, be they subsistence or the cash economy.

Finally, it is important to keep in mind that the data provided by respondents, if it concerns relatively trivial household matters (the amount spent on foods in a week, for example), will only ever provide data of an indicative or comparative nature. To recognize the limits of such work, try to recall exactly what items (and their cost) you have spent in the last fortnight/week!

Other Data Sources

The results of a well-designed and implemented household survey will provide an incredibly rich source of data about lifestyles and livelihoods, but, for all the reasons outlined above, there are very real limits on the utility of this data. To maximize the quality of the material in a social monitoring programme, and hence to improve the relevance and direction of community planning, data from household surveys should be supplemented with material from as many other sources as possible. This allows conclusions from the household survey to be triangulated with data from other sources, as well as expanding the scope of the information that is utilized for local-area planning and decision making.

Primary Sources

There are a range of other surveys and primary data sources that can be incorporated into a social monitoring programme. The usefulness and application of these will depend largely on the specific environment, and issues that are of greatest concern to the community. Likewise, the regularity of these other surveys will vary depending on the significance of the issues, and the speed at which changes are anticipated. These other forms of surveys may include business, market, agricultural, and health and/or nutrition surveys.

Business Surveys A survey of businesses in the local area can reveal information about a range of diverse issues including changing consumer consumption patterns, the size of, and flows of money within, the local economy, the degree of local ownership, the extent of local business management skills, and the aspirations of locals in relation to business. It is usually possible to include all formal businesses in this kind of survey, and it is also feasible to include some or all of the informal businesses (roadside sellers, temporary food stalls, etc). As with the household surveys, care needs to be taken to ensure that the survey picks up variations in the local economy, be they weekly, fortnightly, monthly or seasonal. Banks (1999b) is an example of a comprehensive business survey that, along with household survey data, permitted the modelling of flows of money into, within and out of the local economy around a major mining development.

Market Surveys A survey of sellers at local market places can provide data on consumption patterns of local residents, as well as information about the volume and the value of goods and produce being brought in to the area. A simple market survey would seek to cover either all sellers at any particular site, or a randomly selected sample of the sellers, depending on the size of the market and the available resources. The origin of the sellers may be significant, as well as the type of goods or produce being sold, the frequency with which they attend the market, and an estimate of their average daily takings. Again care must be taken with variations through time, in this case possibly daily.

Agricultural Surveys If changes in agricultural practices, either subsistence or commercial, are expected to have been rapid, or if there is community concern expressed at the effects of developments on the agricultural sector, then regular surveys of the agricultural production cycle may be appropriate. These could include detailed and, depending on time and resource constraints, comprehensive garden surveys, surveys of productivity from particular gardens, and/or local or regional surveys of total production. Whenever possible an agronomist or local agricultural extension official should head up the survey team, and should take responsibility for the design of the survey instrument.

Health and/or Nutrition Surveys As with the other cases above, if health is expected to be altered (for either better or worse) by the project or development, then regular monitoring of the health of individuals should be included as part of the social monitoring programme. This will provide an early warning to the community and other stakeholders to any trends (particularly detrimental ones) in the health status of the community. In the case of health or nutrition, the team should preferably comprise medical professionals, and although they should consult with the community and the other members of the social monitoring team, the medical team should have primary responsibility for the design of a regular health or nutrition monitoring programme.

Secondary Sources

While primary sources are certainly able to provide better targeted and often more independent sources of information on community change, it is rare to find a social monitoring programme with the resources (time and financial) for extensive and regular primary surveys. For this reason, most social monitoring programmes should be constructed around actual or potential secondary data sources. In most settings there are a number of data sets that are continuously recorded, usually compiled and sometimes presented to various institutions on a regular basis. In many cases the data available from these secondary sources can be extensive.

Examples of these data sources can include local government official reports (often done on a sectoral basis with separate reports on agriculture, education, health, business development, police, etc.), corporate internal reports on interactions with the affected communities (minutes of meetings, payments of local wages or compensation, community development programme assessments), and community records (minutes of local council or association meetings, applications for funding, formal complaints lodged with government, developer or aid agency, etc). Other stakeholders (including provincial or national government departments, churches and other interested NGOs) may also have regular reporting systems in place which provide data on aspects of community change.

Most of these secondary sources should have been identified and utilized in the social impact assessment phase or the background to a household survey. For regular social monitoring, it is imperative to tap into as many of these as is possible. Local council officials, for example, will generally provide annual reports on their activities that can often provide detailed material on social trends such as health and education. Company records should be able to provide details of development initiatives, community interactions, and estimates of the monetary flows from the company into the community (wages and salaries, compensation, royalties and the like). These latter figures also allow estimates derived from household surveys to be triangulated against other data sources. Similarly, if they are available, local banks may be able to provide (at a gross rather than individual level) an indication of the changes in savings and investment levels in the community. Corporate or government stakeholders may also have available regular remotely sensed data, such as aerial photography or satellite imagery. Either of these is useful for measuring agricultural land clearance and pressure. Schools and hospitals or medical centres will generally be able to supply information on the overall status and trends for their student or patient bodies, respectively. Local businesses, particularly wholesalers, can be an important source of information on changes in the local economy.

In many developing countries there are often serious data quality problems with official reporting systems. Instead of simply excluding data as a result of this, it is more productive to use the integration of these data into the programme as an opportunity to improve the quality of this reporting. The improvement of these existing reporting systems is certainly much more cost-effective than the establishment of duplicate systems. Modifications in many instances will be relatively minor: the routine data collected by state officials may need to be expanded to better fit in with the local environment and community concerns, for example. These adaptations of local systems also make local area officials, who are often under-resourced and feel isolated from wider systems, a key part of what should be an integrated approach to local area planning and development, and may well improve the relationship between these officials and the local community. This will also contribute to a legacy of improved and more relevant institutions in the longer term.

In these situations, the major task of social monitoring is to pull these diverse data sets together to allow all the stakeholders an overview of the changes that are occurring in the community. One common way of doing this is through the use of social or economic indicators: indeed, for many corporate and institutional actors, indicators are now seen as a relatively cost-effective way of keeping check on social and economic changes in the community. There are several lists of social monitoring indicators that have been developed: Taylor *et al.* (1995:91) has a useful and comprehensive set, largely derived from the experience of developed countries. These generally cover aspects such the nature of the project workforce, demographic and economic changes, infrastructure development and institutional development, and community change.

Indicators of this type are certainly useful at assessing gross changes in a few key areas, such as health and education. For these purposes, many (though not all) of the issues can be monitored by the use of indices such as infant mortality, admission patterns, and student participation and retention rates, for example. In the context of what has been discussed above, though, the regular updating of a set of social monitoring indicators does not constitute social monitoring. The scope of community concerns, aspirations and the nature of the relationships between the various stakeholders, to name but a few issues, cannot be adequately assessed by a set of quantitative indicators or variables. And neither does the collection of such data ensure that the results are used to guide broader community and planning.

Case Studies

In this section two brief case studies of social monitoring programmes are presented. Both were developed around large-scale mine sites in Melanesia: specifically the PT Freeport Indonesia mine in Irian Jaya, Indonesia, and the Porgera Gold mine in Papua New Guinea. Neither of these programmes was without problems, and indeed both are to some extent in abeyance at present. Both do illustrate some of the principles highlighted above, though, and several lessons can be drawn from each.

The Porgera Social Monitoring Programme

The first field day of the Porgera Social Monitoring Programme (PSMP) in November 1992 began badly. No sooner had we (the author and six staff and students from the University of Papua New Guinea) rolled up to a market area in one of the relocation areas close to the mine and begun our interviews than a drunk son of one of the community leaders came down and demanded we stop. The community, he said, had not been told we were coming, and he wanted time to get the people together so 'they could agree on the answers'. 'Come back on Saturday,' he said. It was not an auspicious start, but it illustrated several points very clearly: first, speaking to community representatives (which we had done) is often not enough in terms of informing the wider community about a social monitoring programme or household surveys. Related to this, the agreement of community representatives to such a survey does not necessarily mean the agreement of all households in the community. Finally, it illustrates the need to have some flexibility in the timetable for any household survey: fieldwork rarely progresses in accordance with a plan.

The PSMP had its origins in a condition of the Environmental Approvals for the Porgera mine, issued by the Papua New Guinea government in 1989 (see Burton, 1999 and Filer, 1999a, for a full discussion of the history of the PSMP). A requirement of the government was that the mine establish an environmental monitoring programme, largely focused on the downstream environmental effects of the mine. Two paragraphs in the thirty-page environmental monitoring and management programme document referred to a requirement that 'socio-economic surveillance' be carried out to monitor the effects of the mine development on the local Ipili people.

In response to this, a census project was initiated in 1990 (Burton, 1992), and in 1992 two separate projects began, one focusing on the economic changes induced by the mine, and the other a review of social impacts. All of these studies were initiated by the company, with minimal community or state involvement in their design or approval, and no linkages into local area decision making. In this sense the company saw them largely as a means to meet compliance requirements.

During this first phase a series of household surveys were carried out. They sought to provide largely household-level economic data. The survey used a simple quota sampling method, using population figures derived from the census. Various areas were targeted based on their proximity to the mine operation itself to provide a sense of the differences in household economics between the different areas of the valley. In total 120 households were surveyed, an estimated 10 per cent of the valley population. The surveys took between thirty minutes and three hours to complete, depending on the interest and responses of the respondent. Additional surveys focused on income and expenditure, foods consumed in the previous twenty-four hours, and garden areas.

In 1993 an attempt was made to establish social monitoring in a more systematic way, with the convening of a PSMP Committee, convened by the Department of Environment and Conservation (DEC) and made up of representatives from the major stakeholders in the area, including local landowner representatives. At this time it was proposed that the PSMP comprise two major streams: the annual compilation and reporting of a wide range of social and economic variables from corporate and government sources, including a range of qualitative material; and a series of special projects established to investigate the issues of particular importance or concern. Due to a range of factors, but primarily because of the lack of resources available to DEC, this proposal was not implemented at the time and instead a series of one-off projects were completed by late 1994 after which the programme effectively lapsed for two years.

In 1996, the Porgera Joint Venture (PJV) and DEC, independently, initiated moves to re-establish the Porgera Social Monitoring Programme. After some confusion, the two approaches were melded into a single programme, under the direction of a reformed PSMP Committee. This reformed committee had wider local representation (the Porgera Women's Association, and the Porgera Development Authority), and these local representatives took the lead in shaping the sorts of issues that should be addressed by the programme. They also articulated clearly what they considered to be the most appropriate process by which the Committee should function.

The structure and process initiated involved the production of Annual Reports that brought together information on all aspects of social and economic change in the Porgera area over the previous twelve months. This drew on existing sources such as school, medical centre and police records, as well as information on company activities, which related to the community, such compensation payments and business contracts to the local community. In the 1996 Annual Report (Banks & Bonnell, 1997a) there was very little primary data presented: virtually the whole document drew on secondary sources.

Linked to this Annual Report was a draft Action Plan (Banks & Bonnell, 1997b), which highlighted issues requiring attention by one or more parties to the PSMP Committee. Suggested actions were spelt out as draft recommendations. The Annual Report and the draft Action Plan were presented to a meeting of the PSMP Committee and, following discussions, each of the recommendations were either agreed to by the parties targeted by the recommendation, or alternative means of addressing the issues were developed. In line with the recommendations of the PSMP Committee, the draft Action Plan then became the Agreed Action Plan (Banks & Bonnell, 1997c), and quarterly meetings were initiated at which the various parties reported on progress towards their agreed actions.

The process worked relatively well for a short period, but a range of factors conspired to make the process redundant. The lack of effective co-ordination of the programme by DEC, largely due to a lack of resources, continued to plague development of the process. Perhaps the most significant factor was that the process had been developed in a local planning vacuum: there was not an overall vision of what the community (or the company) wanted to see happen at Porgera in the future. Recommendations had been targeted at individual issues without a broader context. This lack of an overall direction for development at Porgera was in fact one of the targets of the Action Plan, with a recommendation that local government, with widespread community involvement and national government financial support, develop a long-term economic and social development plan for Porgera.

In 1997 the PJV, the financier of all previous social monitoring at Porgera, switched their efforts away from social monitoring towards assisting in the development of this more integrated approach to planning, with social monitoring a central part of this process. One result of this is that there has not been any social monitoring carried out since 1997 and, despite some moves towards a broader focused planning process (the planning of how to develop a plan), no integrated planning document or process was in place by late 1999. It is also worth noting that no primary data collection has been carried out as part of a social monitoring programme since 1994.

Despite these setbacks and delays, social monitoring at Porgera has contributed to a broader understanding of the changes that the Porgera mine has brought to the Ipili community. The information and ideas generated by the programme have shaped company, community and government approaches to community planning and development. Just as significantly, the publication of the programme's findings – and particularly the results of the surveys (household and business) – in Filer (1999b) contributes to a broader understanding of the processes of change associated with large resource developments in developing countries. This in turn should inform future SIA work around such projects, returning us to the earlier chapters in this volume.

The UNCEN-ANU Baseline Studies Programme at Freeport

The social monitoring programme initiated at the PT Freeport Indonesia mine in Irian Jaya, Indonesia, had a very different background and format. Established in the late 1960s, the mine has had a controversial record of dealings with the two communities indigenous to its contract of work (COW) area: the Amungme and Kamoro (for a general introduction to the history of the mine, see Mealey, 1996, and for its record on community affairs from critics, see Project Underground, 1998). No SIA work was carried out prior to the construction of the mine. An appalling history of military and corporate relations with the local community, including widespread claims, many verified, of human rights abuses in the area, meant an extremely poor relationship existed between the company and the highland Amungme and lowland Kamoro communities.

In this context, the author and a colleague were invited in 1994 to establish some form of social monitoring, to assist the company in improving its relationship with the communities and to help the company better direct it development assistance to the communities. After discussions, spread over two years, with company and community representatives and many other interested parties a project was developed which emphasized community control over the process. The project team was drawn from staff and students at the provincial Universitas Cenderawasih (UNCEN) in Jayapura, as well as local community nominees, occasionally a company employee, the author and Chris Ballard from the Australian National University (ANU) and various other researchers working in the area. The project was formally known as the UNCEN-ANU Baseline Studies (UABS) project.

It was made clear to the company, who were funding the work, that community participation in, and indeed control over, the project was non-negotiable. The community representatives were consulted over the project design, at least one of them accompanied the team in the field at all times, they were briefed at the end of each period of fieldwork, and received a report from us for their consent prior to any work being discussed with, or handed over to the company. They also had a veto over any aspect of the work, a right that they exercised on occasions.

The result of this process was that the programme enjoyed widespread community support and recognition from other observers, although at times corporate support for the process was less than enthusiastic. That said, to the credit of the company staff, funding of the project continued, and there was recognition of the value of the process and the results from at least some quarters within the company.

A deliberate decision was made during the project design phase to not link the project in with several of the other community development initiatives and research programmes in the area. This was due to the political and controversial aspects of these processes, none of which had widespread community support. While this meant the UABS project had a very good relationship with the local community, a major weakness of the process was the lack of integration of the UABS process into any of the existing community planning initiatives, government or corporate. Instead, the project did provide the basis for a new series of negotiations between the communities and PT Freeport, as well as the government, which sought to redefine the nature of the existing relationship between the parties.

The UABS project consisted of three major components: a background study, a social mapping phase and a socio-economic household survey. The intention was to provide the communities themselves, and the various parties involved in dealings with them, with accurate information on the history, population, land and resources, and socio-economic status of the different communities. The social mapping phase revolved around a genealogical census (see Goldman this volume, p.00).

Using the results of the census, a household survey was designed which sought to cover the three Amungme highland valleys and the seven lowland villages where the bulk of the Kamoro community were resident. Despite having a relatively accurate census of the communities available from the social mapping phase, the dispersed and mobile nature of the populations meant that, as with the Porgera case described above, the use of a fully randomized sample was not possible. Instead a quota sample of 20 per cent of the households in each valley or village was used as the minimum sample size, and in each area this was met or exceeded.

The forms of social organization, the nature of resource use, and the level of inter- and intra-household exchanges were markedly different for the Amungme and the Kamoro, and hence the survey instrument had to be altered for each. In the case of the Amungme, for example, the economic unit was taken to include extended families residing in either single houses or small clusters of houses. Exchange of cash and goods within these extended families was significant, as were exchanges between households within and between valleys. These exchanges were usually directed by kinship relations, mirroring the nature of pre-contact exchanges in the region. Among the Kamoro, however, both intra- and inter-household exchanges were much less significant, and the economic unit equated to a single (predominantly nuclear) family, with one family in each house.

The Kamoro surveys also highlighted how easy it is to miss some significant economic flows in communities, particular when switching from one cultural context to another. Using the survey instrument, which had been developed for the highland Amungme, one emphasis was on noting the large, irregular contributions to brideprice and compensation exchanges, with prompts and further questions relating to each of these types of exchanges. These showed up as consistently low among Kamoro, in line with what was known about the community from the background work. In the case of the Kamoro, however, it only became apparent during the course of the survey that smaller, more regular *kaokapaiti* or 'woman-shame' payments to a man's in-laws were common within the communities, particularly where the man was a wage earner.

Because it is not currently continuing, and because it was not effectively integrated with local area planning, the UABS programme is not a model for a social monitoring programme, but it did provide communities in the area with the first complete assessment of their own populations and socio-economic profiles. This information was of value to the communities in itself, and the dialogue that they were able to establish with outside agencies – provincial and international universities, among others – was likewise seen as being of worth. Perhaps most significantly, though, the Freeport communities valued the UABS work because of the degree of input and control they had over the process.

Conclusion

The above brief history of the PSMP and UABS projects highlights several points which underlie much of what has been discussed in terms of both social monitoring and household surveys.

In terms of social monitoring, the lessons from both Porgera and Freeport centre on two main themes. First, for effective social monitoring there must be a strong element of community involvement and control over the social monitoring programme. Community 'ownership' of the programme helps ensure greater relevance, which in turn assists with issues of participation and accuracy of the data collected. Second, social monitoring needs to be integrated into planning processes focused on the community. These may be community, government and/or corporate planning structures and processes. This integration helps ensure that the results of social monitoring programmes are used to provide better directed community development, with the end result that the communities gain benefits (preferably tangible) from the social monitoring process. Integration into existing planning structures also helps ensure the continuity of the programmes, rather than making them a series of one-off exercises, which is the dominant pattern to date. The objective should be, then, to get community-centred and controlled social monitoring incorporated into effective planning for the community. The bottom line is that, if this does not occur, the programme is not serving the long-term interests of the community, and the spectre of the ethical concerns discussed above returns.

In terms of household surveys, these can be employed in variety of contexts and can provide a rich source of information on existing social and economic conditions for community members. In this sense they should be a central component of any social monitoring programme. To be effective the survey instrument should be developed and implemented with strong community involvement, which helps to ensure that they are more appropriate to the particular context in which they are to be applied. A mix of qualitative and qualitative questions should be included as these tend to complement each other, and ensures that the situation of the community as well as the range of community sentiments on issues are well represented and made available to decision making and planning institutions.

Large-scale developments and projects usually lead to massive and rapid changes among neighbouring communities. An effective social monitoring programme, with regular household surveys as a core component, which is integrated into local area planning processes can allow the maximum benefits to accrue to the community from the project and provide for effective mitigation of the negative social and economic effects of the development on the community.

Acknowledgements

Much of this chapter is based on experience obtained while working on the Porgera Social Monitoring Programme and the UNCEN-ANU Baseline Studies project funded by the Porgera Joint Venture and PT Freeport Indonesia, respectively. Work on these projects was only possible due to the enormous contribution made by teams from University of Papua New Guinea (Benedict Imbun, Londe Powell Imbun, Nick Kakapae, Mogola Kamiali, Jiro Kandoiya, Michael Leamon, Norit Luio, John Samboek, Martin Sabrini and Gary Sali) and Universitas Cenderawasih in Jayapura (Naffi Sanggenafa, Agus Dumatubun, Agus Yarona, Fredrik Sokoy, Nella Fakdawer and Nella Kilangin). In addition, the Porgera Social Monitoring Programme has included Susanne Bonnell, John Burton and Colin Filer. At Freeport the UABS team social monitoring team also consisted of Junus Omabak, Methodius Mamapuku, Steve Rahangiar, Karolus Tsunme, Chris Ballard, Carolyn Cook and Todd Harple.

References

Banks, G. (1999a), 'Keeping an eye on the beasts: Social Monitoring of large-scale mines in Melanesia', *Resource Management in Asia-Pacific*, Working Paper No. 21, Canberra: Research School of Pacific and Asian Studies, The Australian National University.

Banks, G. (1999b), 'Business as usual', in C. Filer (ed.), *The Dilemmas of Development: The Social and Economic Impact of the Porgera Gold Mine 1989–1994*, Canberra and Port Moresby: Asia-Pacific Press, The Australian National University (Pacific Policy Paper 34) and The National Research Institute (Special Publication 24), 148–83.

Banks, G. and Bonnell, S. (1997a), *Porgera Social Monitoring Program, Annual Report 1996*, unpublished report prepared for Porgera Joint Venture, May.

Banks, G. and Bonnell, S. (1997b), *Porgera Social Monitoring Program, Draft Action Plan 1997*, unpublished report prepared for Porgera Joint Venture, May.

Banks, G. and Bonnell, S. (1997c), *Porgera Social Monitoring Program, Action Plan 1997*, unpublished report prepared for Porgera Joint Venture, September.

Brown, J., Marczewski, W., Miller, D., Roberts, D. and Scott W. (1978), *Multi-purpose household surveys in developing countries*, Paris: Organisation for Economic Co-operation and Development.

Burdge, R. (1994), *A Community Guide to Social Impact Assessment*, Middleton, WI: Social Ecology Press.

Burton, J. (1992), 'The Porgera Census Project', *Research in Melanesia*, 16:129–56.

Burton, J. (1999), 'Evidence of the "new competencies?"' in C. Filer (ed.), *The Dilemmas of Development: The Social and Economic Impact of the Porgera Gold Mine, 1989–1994*, Canberra and Port Moresby: Asia-Pacific Press, The Australian National University (Pacific Policy Paper 34) and The National Research Institute (Special Publication 24), pp.281–302.

Connell, J. (1991), 'Compensation and Conflict: The Bougainville Copper Mine, Papua New Guinea', in J. Connell and Howitt, J. (eds), *Mining and Indigenous Peoples in Australasia*, Sydney: Sydney University Press in association with Oxford University Press, pp.55–76.

Dixon, C. and Leach, B. (1984), *Survey Research in Underdeveloped Countries*, Norwich, England: Geo Books (Concepts and Techniques in Modern Geography No. 39).

Filer, C. (1990), 'The Bougainville rebellion, the mining industry and the process of social disintegration in Papua New Guinea', *Canberra Anthropology*, 13(1):1–39.

Filer, C. (1999a), Introduction, in C. Filer (ed.), *The Dilemmas of Development: The Social and Economic Impact of the Porgera Gold Mine, 1989–1994*, Canberra and Port Moresby: Asia-Pacific Press, The Australian National University (Pacific Policy Paper 34) and The National Research Institute (Special Publication 24), pp.1–18.

Filer, C. (ed.) (1999b), *The Dilemmas of Development: The Social and Economic Impact of the Porgera Gold Mine, 1989–1994*, Canberra and Port Moresby: Asia-Pacific Press, The Australian National University (Pacific Policy Paper 34) and The National Research Institute (Special Publication 24).

Jiggins, J. (1995), 'Development impact assessment: Impact assessment of aid projects in nonwestern countries', in F. Vanclay and D. Bronstein (eds), *Environmental and Social Impact Assessment*, New York: J. Wiley, pp.265–82.

Mealey, G. (1996), *Grasberg: Mining the Richest and Most Remote Deposit of Copper and Gold in the World, in the Mountains of Irian Jaya, Indonesia*, New Orleans, LA: Freeport-McMoRan.

Ortolano, L. and Shepher, A. (1995), 'Environmental Impact Assessment', in F. Vanclay and D. Bronstein (eds), *Environmental and Social Impact Assessment*, New York: J. Wiley, pp.3–30.

Project Underground (1998), *Risky Business: the Grasberg gold mine. An Independent Annual Report on PT Freeport Indonesia*. Berkeley, CA: Project Underground.

Taylor, N., Hobson B. and Goodrich, C. (1995), *Social Assessment: Theory, Process and Techniques* (2nd edition), Christchurch, New Zealand: Taylor Baines.

Appendix 10.1

UNISEARCH PNG
PORGERA SOCIO-ECONOMIC MONITORING PROJECT
Kaiya River Baseline Study Questionnaire

INTERVIEWER: ______________________________

DATE: ____________________ **YEAR**: ________________

INTERVIEW NUMBER: ____________________

NAME OF PERSON (both names): ______________________________

CLAN: ______________________________

SUB-CLAN: ______________________________

FAMILY: ______________________________

(1) HOUSEHOLD MEMBERS:

Starting with the person you are interviewing, collect the following information for all the people who stayed in the house last night: go through wives, then children, then other people.

	1		2		3		4		5		6	
	M	F	M	F	M	F	M	F	M	F	M	F
Name *(give both names)*												
Sex *(circle one)*	M	F	M	F	M	F	M	F	M	F	M	F
Age *(in complete years, baby=0)*												
Relationship to household head *(tick one box for each person)*												
Head of household												
Wife/husband												
Child												
Brother/sister												
Parent												
Other relative												
Other												
Born in Porgera?	Y	N	Y	N	Y	N	Y	N	Y	N	Y	N
If no, where were they born? *(give district/ province)*												
How many years living in this house? (*less than 1=0, visitor=0)*												
Highest school grade completed? (*from 0 to 12)*												
Current occupation (*at school, employment – name employer, gardener, etc.)*												

	7		8		9		10		11		12	
	M	F	M	F	M	F	M	F	M	F	M	F
Name *(give both names)*												
Sex *(circle one)*	M	F	M	F	M	F	M	F	M	F	M	F
Age *(in complete years, baby=0)*												
Relationship to household head *(tick one box for each person)*												
Head of household												
Wife/husband												
Child												
Brother/sister												
Parent												
Other relative												
Other												
Born in Porgera?	Y	N	Y	N	Y	N	Y	N	Y	N	Y	N
If no, where were they born? *(give district/ province)*												
How many years living in this house? (*less than 1=0, visitor=0)*												
Highest school grade completed? (*from 0 to 12)*												
Current occupation (*at school, employment – name employer, gardener, etc.)*												

How many other wives and children does this person have who were not staying with them in this house last night?

Wives	Children

(2) HOUSE TYPE

How many houses does this household have? [ ]

(complete one page for each house: make it clear that we are not interested in garden houses or haus kuk, just those in which the family or other wives live in most of the time).

House number [ ]

(tick or give numbers as required – tick more than one box if necessary)

Roof	Pandanus		**Walls**	Danus – one layer	
	Pitpit			Pandanus – multiple	
	Sail			Pitpit blind	
	Tin			Timber	
	Kunai thatch			Tin	
	Other			Other	
Roof pitch	Steep		Shape:	Rectangle	
	Shallow			Square	
No. of rooms			**Floor**	Sugarcane cuttings	
				Timber	
				Other	

Usual food preparation & cooking area:

Inside [ ] Outside [ ] House kuk [ ]

Shower/washing facilities

Inside [ ] Outside [ ]

Toilet	Inside		Outside		None	
Type	Pit		VIP		Flush	

Source of drinking water *(give percentage figure over whole year for each type used)*

Taps in house		Rainwater tank	
Community standpipe or tank		Stream or creek	

Cooking fuel *(give percentage figure over whole year for each type used)*

Electricity		Kerosene (paraffin)	
Gas cylinders		Firewood	

(3) DOES THIS FAMILY POSSESS ANY OF THE FOLLOWING ITEMS?

Interviewers should name each item in the list and then circle 'YES' or 'NO' according to the response.

Watch	YES	NO	Electric stove	YES	NO
Radio	YES	NO	Television	YES	NO
Tape recorder	YES	NO	Video	YES	NO
Sewing machine	YES	NO	Generator	YES	NO
Washing machine	YES	NO	Car or truck	YES	NO
Refrigerator	YES	NO			

How many of the following items does this family have? *(Write number; if none, write '0')*

Pressure lamps		Aluminium pots	
Axes		Brush knives	
Spades or shovels		Buckets	
Pairs of shoes or boots		44-gallon drums	
Mattresses		Blankets	

(4) DOES ANYONE IN THE FAMILY CURRENTLY:

(circle YES or NO for each question and fill in details)

(a) WORK FOR PJV? YES NO

If yes, who? Give number ________________

What position/department? ________________

(b) WORK FOR ANYONE ELSE? YES NO

If yes, who? ________________

Which company or organization? ________________

OWN A BUSINESS? YES NO

If yes, give number ________________

What kind of business? (Tradestore, PMV, etc.) ________________

(c) BELONG TO A BUSINESS GROUP? YES NO

If yes, who? ________________

Name of business group ________________

(d) RECEIVE ROYALTIES? YES NO

If yes, how much did they receive in the last 12 months? Kina [ ]

(e) RECEIVE OCCUPATION FEES, OR LEASE PAYMENTS? YES NO

If yes, how much did they receive in the last 12 months? Kina [ ]

(f) SELL CROPS or OTHER GOODS in the last 12 months? YES NO
(at a market, to a company, etc.)

If yes, who? ____________________

What kind? ____________________

Where do they sell them? ____________________

How often do they sell the goods? *(Circle one only)*

Daily [ ] Weekly [ ] Monthly [ ] Less often [ ]

How much money do they usually make each day they are selling? Kina [ ]

(g) GO ALLUVIAL MINING? YES NO

If yes, how much money have they made in the last 12 months? Kina [ ]

If yes, how much did they receive in the last 12 months? Kina [ ]

(5) HAS THIS FAMILY EVER RECEIVED COMPENSATION MONEY FROM PJV? YES NO

If yes, when, what for, and how much? When (year)?	(Get details of three most recent payments) What for (loss of garden etc)?	How much?
____________	____________	____________
____________	____________	____________
____________	____________	____________

(6) DO MEMBERS OF THIS FAMILY HAVE ANY INVESTMENTS?
(IBD, Placer shares, passbooks, etc.)

TYPE OF INVESTMENT (IBD, passbook, company shares – give name)	AMOUNT (Kina) (give balances or share value)
____________	____________
____________	____________
____________	____________
____________	____________

(7) HOW MUCH DOES THIS FAMILY SPEND ON:

	Kina *Monthly*	*Per year*
(a) School expenses	________	________
(b) Other regular payments *(specify)*	________	________

(8) THIS YEAR HAS THE FAMILY MADE ANY CONTRIBUTIOS TO BRIDEPRICE OR COMPENSATION PAYMENTS, ETC.? YES NO

If yes, for what occasion, how much, and what type of payment (pigs, cash, etc.)?

What were the payments for? (note reason)	How much were the payments? (note type – cash, pigs, etc.)
________	________
________	________
________	________

(9) IN THE LAST YEAR, HOW MANY TIMES HAVE YOU GONE TO:
(If none, write 0)

(a) Wabag or Mt Hagen?	Why? (Visit wantoks, business, holiday, shopping, etc.) ________	[ ]
(b) Port Moresby?	Why? (Visit wantoks, business, holiday, shopping, etc.) ________	[ ]
(c) Overseas?	Why? (Visit wantoks, buisness, holiday, shopping, etc.) ________	[ ]

(10) IN THE LAST TWO WEEKS, HOW MUCH MONEY HAS THIS FAMILY RECEIVED FROM:
(check each category, give amount, write '0' if none)

	Kina
• Wages from PJV	
• Wages from any other source (specify who)	
• Sale of fish, crops or other goods	
• Other people outside the family	
• Profits from business (make sure it is not the total income of the business)	
• Any other income (i.e. compensation, bank withdrawals, etc.) (specify)	
TOTAL INCOME (add figures)	

(11) IN THE LAST TWO WEEKS, HOW MUCH MONEY HAS THIS FAMILY SPENT ON:
(check each category, give amount, write '0' if none)

	Kina
• Gifts to other people (outside the family)	
• Buying food, etc. at a market	
• Buying food, etc. at a tradestore	
• Buying other goods at a store or market (specify goods)	
• Transport (fares, petrol, etc.)	
• Savings/investments	
• Alcohol	
• Other spending (compensation, etc.) (specify)	
• Still have with them (cash)	
TOTAL EXPENDITURE AND RETAINED (add figures)	

> Interviewers should now check that total expenditure approximately equals total income from previous pages and, if not, try and establish why not.

We would now like to ask you about the types of food you have eaten in the last twenty-four hours and where they came from.

(12) IN THE LAST TWENTY-FOUR HOURS, WHAT FOODS HAVE YOU EATEN?

Go through the list of foods below. (Ask what they had for dinner, etc., and where it came from)

	Source (circle one source only)			
Tinned fish	Tradestore	Market	Other	
Rice	Tradestore	Market	Other	
Biscuits	Tradestore	Market	Other	
Taro	Tradestore	Own garden	Market	Other
Kaukau	Tradestore	Own garden	Market	Other
Taro	Tradestore	Own garden	Market	Other
Kaukau	Tradestore	Own garden	Market	Other
Potato	Tradestore	Own garden	Market	Other
Carrot	Tradestore	Own garden	Market	Other
Bread	Tradestore	Own garden	Market	Other
Pork	Tradestore	Own garden	Market	Other
Other meats	Tradestore	Own garden	Market	Other
Greens	Tradestore	Own garden	Market	Other
Buai	Tradestore	Own garden	Market	Other

Taro	Tradestore	Own garden	Market	Other
Other (specify) ________	Tradestore	Own garden	Market	Other
Other (specify) ________	Tradestore	Own garden	Market	Other
Other (specify) ________	Tradestore	Own garden	Market	Other
Other (specify) ________	Tradestore	Own garden	Market	Other

(13) DOES THE FAMILY HAVE ANY GARDENS? YES NO

If yes, how many separate gardens? (include house gardens) [ ]

How far from the house are they? (in minutes)

Garden 1	[ ]	Garden 4	[ ]
Garden 2	[ ]	Garden 5	[ ]
Garden 3	[ ]	Garden 6	[ ]

(14) HOW MANY PIGS DOES THIS FAMILY HAVE? [ ]

(now visit those gardens in the Kewai area, using the garden survey forms)

COMMENTS: (Ask the person about problems or worries they have, how regular their income is, what new businesses they would like to see in the area, feelings about people moving in to the area, and any other comments, especially relating to money.)

____
____
____
____
____
____
____

Interviewers should now thank the person.

GARDEN SURVEY

Household number [ ] Garden number [ ]

Draw rough map of garden, showing location of houses, cultivated areas and unused portions.

Distance from the house (in paces, minutes, etc.): ____________

Length of sides: ____________

____

____

How long has it been planted (years) ____________ (number)

Count: Kaukau mounds: ____________

Taro plants: ____________

Sugar cane plants: ____________

Others: (name) ____________ ____________

(name) ____________ ____________

(name) ____________ ____________

(name) ____________ ____________

(name) ____________ ____________

Description:

(setting, by bush, stream, what kind of fences, etc.) Slope angle: Altitude:

Index